SIMPLE SERMONS
FROM THE
BOOK OF ACTS

BOOKS BY THE SAME AUTHOR . . .

Simple Sermons on the Great Christian Doctrines
Seven Simple Sermons on the Second Coming
Simple Sermons From the Book of Acts, Volume I
Simple Sermons From the Book of Acts, Volume II
Simple Sermons on the Saviour's Last Words
Simple Sermons on Salvation and Service
Simple Sermons for Saints and Sinners
Simple Sermons on the Ten Commandments
Simple Sermons on Simple Themes
Simple Sermons for Special Days and Occasions
Simple Sermons From the Gospel of John, Volume I
Simple Sermons From the Gospel of John, Volume II
Simple Sermons on the Seven Churches of Revelation
Simple Sermons for Today's World
Simple Talks for Christian Workers
Simple Sermons About Jesus Christ
Simple Sermons on the Christian Life
Simple Sermons for Funeral Services
Simple Sermons From the Gospel of Matthew
Simple Sermons for Time and Eternity
Simple Sermons for Times Like These
Simple Sermons for Sunday Morning
Simple Sermons for Twentieth Century Christians
Simple Sermons for Sunday Evening

SIMPLE SERMONS
FROM THE
BOOK OF ACTS

Complete in One Volume

VOLUME I

By
W. HERSCHEL FORD, B.A., D.D.

Introduction by
ROBERT G. LEE, D.D., LL.D., LITT. D.

ZONDERVAN PUBLISHING HOUSE
GRAND RAPIDS, MICHIGAN

Simple Sermons from the Book of Acts
Copyright 1950 by
Zondervan Publishing House
Grand Rapids, Michigan

First printing 1950
Second printing 1955
Third printing 1957
Fourth printing 1961
Fifth printing 1963
Sixth printing 1965
Seventh printing . . . 1967

Printed in the United States of America

DEDICATION

This book is affectionately dedicated to
my sons,
WALTER AND ROBERT
two of the finest boys God ever gave
to any man.

INTRODUCTION

In his book *Simple Sermons from the Book of Acts,* Dr. W. Herschel Ford, with delightful divisions of the Word of truth and with unusually effective alliteration, has shown mastery in the art of simple and plain preaching. Preaching plainly, yet reaching peaks of lofty language at times, he holds true to his belief that an expository sermon should contain interpretation, application to the heart and life, and inspiration.

In these plain sermons, in which profound truth is expressed in simple language easily understood, the author has placed warm sympathetic hands on practical life. Sensible, sound, solid, Scriptural, these messages give evidence of great concern that Christians should live up to the fullness of their possibilities. Moreover, there is evidence, on the part of the author, of a spiritual passion for the lost, and of great love for and loyalty to the Christ who came to seek and to save that which was lost.

In the delivery of these sermons by this consecrated, soul-winning, scholarly and successful pastor, many souls have been brought to think on their ways and to turn from death to life. Moreover, many Christians have, after hearing these sermons, gone forth to greater living. Profitable, in many ways, will it be to all who read and teach and use this book in the study, teaching, and preaching of the Book of Acts.

Yours earnestly,
ROBERT G. LEE
Former Pastor, Bellevue Baptist Church,
Memphis, Tennessee
Past President of the Southern Baptist
Convention

FOREWORD

These simple sermons were preached first to large Sunday morning congregations while I was pastor of the First Baptist Church of El Paso, Texas. An entire chapter of the Book of Acts is given to each sermon. I enjoyed preaching these sermons more than any series I have ever used. The response from the congregation was most gratifying.

This volume contains messages from the first fourteen chapters. Volume II contains messages from the remaining fourteen chapters of Acts. Although much of a sermon's power is lost when transferred to the printed page, I do hope that these messages may help and bless and inspire many hearts, and bring glory to our blessed Lord.

I would like to express my heart-felt thanks to Mr. and Mrs. Hosmer W. Hill, two of the finest and most faithful members of the Church, who made possible the publication of this book — to my faithful secretary, Miss Eva L. Gass, who spent many, many tedious hours helping me to prepare the manuscript — and to that prince and peer of all preachers, Dr. Robert G. Lee, for writing the introduction.

W. Herschel Ford

6235 *Oram Street*
Apt. 204
Dallas, Texas 75214

CONTENTS

CHAPTER ONE

"SPIRITUAL SUBORDINATION"

Acts 1

I believe that an expository sermon should contain three things. First, it should contain interpretation—if the verse is not clear the preacher should seek to explain it. Second, it should contain application—the truth in the Scripture should be applied to the heart and life. What is the use of knowing the Bible if we do not apply it to our lives? Third, it should contain inspiration. We should seek to inspire the listener to apply these truths to his own heart and live closer to Christ.

With these things in view let us begin our study of the Book of Acts by getting the setting for the first chapter: Jesus has been crucified, He has risen from the dead, He has been here for forty days, and it is now time for Him to go back to heaven. We see Him meeting His disciples for the last time before the ascension. Luke, the beloved physician, a Gentile, wrote the Book of Acts, and he himself took part in many of the events.

I am giving this message the title, *"Spiritual Subordination."* If you watch these disciples you will know why . . . in all the things that they did their wills were absolutely surrendered to Christ. They lived and acted only under His direction. They had no will of their own—they were subordinate to Christ's will.

I. THE PRESENCE. Verse 3

"He shewed himself alive . . . by many infallible proofs

13

. . ." (Acts 1:3). Jesus lived as a man but He was the Son of God. He died as a man. He was buried in the usual way, but no tomb could hold Him. He burst the bonds of death and the grave and came back to live forever. He showed Himself on the first day to Mary Magdalene, to the women returning from the tomb, to Simon Peter, to the two disciples on the road to Emmaus and to all the Apostles, except Thomas. Later He showed Himself to all the Apostles—and Thomas was there. Then He met them by the seaside and ate with them. Then we are told that He appeared to more than five hundred.

Yes, He is a living Saviour. Mohammed died and is dead—Confucius died and is dead—Buddha died and is dead—Martin Luther died and is dead—John Knox died and is dead—George Washington died and is dead—Abraham Lincoln died and is dead. But when we go to the tomb of Jesus we hear the glorious message, "He is not here: for he is risen, as he said" (Matthew 28:6). Someone has asked, "Those who crucified and hated Him saw Him arise again—what did they think?" They did not see Him—He appeared only to His own. It is even so today. He shows Himself to His own people.

He showed Himself to Saul on the Road to Damascus and sent him out to be a flaming evangelist. He showed Himself to a man who worked in a shoe store and Dwight L. Moody went out to shake the world for Christ. He showed Himself to Billy Sunday and that dynamic little man preached the Gospel to great crowds in tabernacles all over the land and saw millions of people hit the saw-dust trail and surrender their hearts to Jesus Christ. Hhe showed Himself to a South Carolina farm boy during a revival meeting. That boy's heart was stirred and warmed and in a corner of the old rail fence he gave himself away to Jesus. Now Robert G. Lee, the golden-voiced preacher of the Southland, speaks daily in behalf of Jesus and thousands of people marvel as they listen to him tell the old, old story. Thank God, Christ has shown Himself to you and to me, too! He shows us our sins, then He shows us His own glorious self and invites us to come unto Him and be saved.

He shows Himself in time of sorrow. When I was four years of age, my mother died and I think that Jesus said, "I will take care of that poor, little motherless boy and make a preacher of him." There have been many other sorrows since, but I can testify that He has been with me all the way.

He shows Himself in time of need. When I felt the call to the ministry I wanted to get some college and seminary training but I was married and had a family and no money. I went to a man and asked him if he would lend me the money for my college expenses, and he said, "Yes, I will gladly do it." I went to another man and asked him if he would lend me the money for my seminary expenses, and the reply was the same. I felt that God was supplying my need. In time, with His help, I paid the money back with interest.

The second Sunday I was in college, I was called to a church where I preached through all of my college days. The same thing happened when I went to the seminary. A few weeks before my graduation, a pulpit committee came several hundred miles to see me and I was eventually called to their church. Yes, God will take care of you if you will try to do His will. "His grace is sufficient for every need." "My God shall supply all your need according to his riches in glory by Christ Jesus" (Philippians 4:19). So in this chapter, first, we see Jesus appearing to the apostles.

II. The Promise. Verses 6-8

Jesus told the Apostles to wait for the promise of the Father. They saw visions of an earthly kingdom and high honors. "Wilt thou at this time restore again the kingdom to

Israel?", Acts 1:6) they asked Him. What did they mean by this? Their country was under the Roman yoke and they looked back to the time of David and Solomon and Israel's glory, so they were simply saying, "Are you going to set us free? Are you going to make our country great again?" Listen to His answer, "It is not for you to know the times or the seasons, which the Father hath put in his own power" (Acts 1:7). It is still God's business. When will Jesus come back? . . . when will He set up His Kingdom? We do not know the day nor the hour—this is left in God's hands. But we do know this—He is coming back—it may be tomorrow or it may be a hundred years from now, but we must be busy and as we look forward to His coming, we must push forward in His work.

What else did Jesus say? He said in effect, "I will not tell you when I am coming back, but I will tell you what to do in the meantime. Ye shall receive power, after that the Holy Spirit is come upon you." They were common, ordinary, mediocre men, but they had had a mighty experience—they had seen One rise up from the dead. He had told them to go and tell the story to all nations, but He knew they were not capable of doing this within themselves, and so He promised them extra power. He tells us to go and serve Him, but He knows we are weak, so He promises us the same power. Now what were they to do with this power? Today men use power for different purposes. They use it to get wealth, to get more power, or to crush other people. The power Christ gives is the power to witness and serve. He simply said, "You are to use this power in witnessing for Me, both in Jerusalem and in Judaea and in Samaria, and to the uttermost part of the earth." Verse eight is the key verse of the entire Book of Acts. In the second chapter we see the Apostles receiving this power—in the remaining chapters of the book we see them witnessing unto Him.

Freely did they receive, and freely did they give in the Name of Christ.

III. THE PARTING. Verses 9-11

When He had finished speaking, while they were looking upon Him, suddenly a cloud engulfed Him and they saw Him move upward in the clouds. Up, up, up He went straight to heaven. What a reception He must have received! What great rejoicing there must have been in heaven! How the angels must have crowded around Him! How warm must have been the embrace that He received from His heavenly Father! The best part of any trip is getting home—now Jesus is home at last. No more cruelties—no more injustices—no more misunderstandings—no more beatings—no more sweat, blood and tears. Gethsemane is over—Calvary is past—the tomb is empty and the Son is at home. He has gone from the agony of earth to the adoration of heaven. He has gone from the bruises of earth to the blessedness of heaven—He has gone from the Cross to the Crown—He has gone from the ghastliness of earth to the glory of heaven—He has gone from the hell of earth to the heaven of the Father's house. Thank God, because of His grace some day you and I, too, shall be free from the earth and all of its sorrows and will forever be at home with Him.

> Amazing grace! how sweet the sound,
> That saved a wretch like me!
> I once was lost, but now am found—
> Was blind, but now I see.
>
> 'Twas grace that taught my heart to fear,
> And grace my fears relieved;
> How precious did that grace appear
> The hour I first believed.
>
> Thro' many dangers, toils and snares,
> I have already come;
> 'Tis grace hath brought me safe thus far,
> And grace will lead me home.

> When we've been there ten thousand years,
> Bright shining as the sun,
> We've no less days to sing God's praise
> Than when we first begun.

What were the disciples doing all this time? They were looking their eyes out. They would not believe what they had seen. Then someone tapped them on the shoulders, and they looked around and saw two heavenly messengers in white standing nearby. "Ye men of Galilee," they said, "why stand ye gazing up into heaven? this same Jesus, which is taken up from you into heaven, shall so come in like manner as ye have seen him go into heaven" (Acts 1:11). Then they came to themselves. They remembered their mission on earth and they went off to await the promised power and to witness for Him until the end of their days.

I believe that Jesus is coming back some day. Acts 1:11 is enough to tell me that. There are some who criticize those who preach about the Second Coming. They say, "You fellows are always looking for His coming, and never doing anything." They are wrong—the promise of His coming is our greatest incentive to service. That is why the disciples worked so hard. They did not want to be ashamed when He came back. Nearly every great soul-winning church in the world today has a preacher who preaches the Blessed Hope.

IV. THE PRAYING. Verses 12-14

Where did the apostles go after Jesus left? Did they go to the baseball game, to a concert or some other place of amusement? No, they went back into the city, into the Upper Room to pray. I believe this was the room where they ate the Last Supper with Jesus, the room where Jesus appeared unto them after the resurrection. What tender memories must have flooded their hearts! It was there they had eaten with Jesus. It was there that He said, "Let not your heart be troubled" (John 14:1). It was there that He had said,

"I will pray the Father, and He shall give you another Comforter" (John 14:16). It was there that He had said, "My peace I give unto you" (John 14:27). It was there that they went back to meet Him after the resurrection. It was there that they crowded around Him and felt the sweetness of His presence. It was there that Thomas saw the prints of the nails and cried out, "My Lord and my God" (John 20:28). And in this place of tender memories, they prayed. That is where you and I ought to go daily, to the place of prayer.

One of our soldiers overseas was in great danger. He promised God that if He would bring him safely home he would serve in a better way than ever before. When he returned to the states, he wired his parents saying, "Do not meet me, there is somewhere else I would like to go before I come home." He arrived home at the midnight hour and walked around to the church which he had always attended, and where he had been saved. The front door was locked, but the side door happened to be open. He found his way to the altar and fell upon his knees and thanked God for bringing him safely home. Yes, all of us need to find the place of prayer, for it is only in the place of prayer that we can receive strength and power for the battles of life.

We note that when the apostles prayed they were of "one accord" (Acts 1:14). What if our churches could be like that today? There are many differences among us. Some like the pastor, and some do not—some like the deacons and some do not—some like short sermons and some like long sermons. Some think the sermon is good and some think it is poor. Some people tithe and some use all their money for themselves. What if we submerged all this in prayer and in love for Christ? What if we prayed for God to bless our church and to save souls and transform lives through her ministry? Oh, what churches we could have, and the power of them would be felt to the ends of the earth!

What was the basis of their harmony? First, they loved Jesus—second, they loved each other—third, they had a great story to tell—fourth, they were willing to give their lives for the Gospel—fifth, they wanted to see Jesus again. Oh, that we might have that accord in all of our churches today!

We note, also, that they "continued . . . in prayer" (Acts 1:14). When we pray we say, "God, please do this or do that" and then we forget about it. Some people pray only when they are in trouble. If we lived in the atmosphere of prayer, how much more the Lord could do for us and in us!

V. The Picking. Verses 15-26

Now we read that "Peter stood up in the midst of the disciples" (Acts 1:15). Since Jesus has gone it seems that he takes over the leadership. There are at least 119 others there with him. "Now," says Peter "I want to take up with you the matter of a successor to Judas. He was one of us, but he betrayed the Master. His conscience smote him so hard that he went out and killed himself. We must replace him." Some people ask, "If Jesus knew everything from the beginning, why would He choose a man whom He knew would betray Him?" Well, everything Jesus did was a fulfillment of Old Testament prophecy. We are told in prophecy that there would be one who would betray Him and here we see this perfect fulfillment. In every way we know that God's Word is always true. Now Peter tells the requirements that an apostle must have. He must be one who had walked with Jesus and who had been a witness of the resurrection. Two men were selected—Barsabas and Matthias. Then the believers prayed, asking the Lord to show them which of these men should be chosen. When they cast lots the choice fell upon Matthias, "and he was numbered with the eleven apostles" (Acts 1:26). The church of today is here shown how it should pick its leaders. We should ask God to select them, for God has a man for every place. He had a Joshua to take the place of Moses—an Elisha to take the place of Elijah—and here we see Him choosing Matthias to take the place of Judas.

A certain church that I know of was preparing to call a pastor. Two men were being considered. Very little prayer was offered, but there was much hot "politicking." On the day the vote was to be taken all the telephone lines were busy, but the line of prayer between the church members and God was idle. That night the church took the vote after much quarreling and after many hard things had been said by the members. The man who won out by a very narrow margin accepted the call and came upon the field. In a little while the church was torn to pieces—large groups were going out to join other churches—the people were very unhappy and the strong church had become a weak one. If the people had just prayed more, this might not have happened.

Now just one thing about this man Barsabas. He was one of the candidates, but he was defeated. We do not read that he became angry and quit the church. I am sure that he went on serving and doing the best that he could and that he was happy in his place of service. Why? Because he was a real Christian. Today in our churches we find many people who get in a "huff" and quit everything. Do they have Christ within them? ". . . by their fruits . . . ye shall know them" (Matthew 7:20).

Matthias had a place to fill and so do you. Do people see Christ or Satan in you? You are His representative on earth, for He said, "As my Father hath sent me, even so send I you" (John 20:21).

When a business house sends a man out on the road,

this man must believe in his product. He must believe in the policies of the firm and must stand up for these policies. Are you doing this for Jesus? Do you believe in the product? Christianity is what the world needs. Are you trying to sell this product to the world? Do you believe in the policies and the principles which He taught? You can find them in His Book—are you living by them? Do you stand up for Jesus and His church wherever you go? If it is a choice between His work and anything else on earth you should always say, "I choose Jesus." Suppose that you were a salesman for a clothing firm. Would you wear a shabby suit, a slouch hat, dirty shoes, and whiskers a half inch long? No, of course not. Suppose you were selling fountain pens—if you took down an order with a stubby pencil you would not make a very good impression for your company, would you? Then let me tell you that you will never make a good representative of Jesus if your life is shabby, sinful and neglectful.

A man who ran a restaurant in the old days advertised for a boy to help him. One boy came in and applied for the place. The man told him that he would pay him $10.00 per week and meals. "How good are the meals?" asked the boy. The man patted his big stomach and said, "I eat here." He was a good ad for the restaurant and the boy immediately took the job. Are you a good ad for your church? What are some of the most beautiful ads that you see today in the various magazines? They are the liquor ads. They paint marvelous pictures about "Four Roses," "Three Feathers," "Two Fingers" and "Old Grandad." Jesus said that "the children of this world are wiser than the children of light." If evil men present their product in the most attractive way, why should not Christians do the same thing? The best way for us to present Christ is not in lofty buildings, nor stained glass windows, nor stately services—we can present Him best through everyday, consecrated Christian lives.

A traveling salesman represented an Ohio firm. He was a good-hearted fellow, but he was not a Christian. His wife was a consecrated Christian and prayed earnestly for his salvation. They had one little girl. One day when he was away on a trip a telegram came saying that his wife was very ill. He hurried to her bedside, but as he flew along in the plane he began to think about what a good wife and a good Christian she had been, and how she had prayed so earnestly for him. When he walked into the sick room she smiled up at him and said, "Charlie, I could die happy if I knew you were saved." Then she lapsed into unconsciousness and died a little later.

After the funeral the man took the little girl out for a walk in the garden. He tried to think about the flowers and the birds and the blue sky, but the birds did not sing, and the skies were gray, and the flowers drooped their heads in sorrow. They went back into the house and the little girl came over and put her arms around her father's neck. "Daddy," she said, "mother always prayed with me. Let us pray now." And in the gathering twilight, with the little girl's arms around him, this man asked God, for Jesus' sake, to save him. Of course He did. The man and the little girl became radiant Christians. The good wife had prayed in such a way and had lived such a consecrated Christian life that the husband and daughter came to know Jesus.

In the Book of Acts the apostles prayed and lived and witnessed—other people saw Jesus in them and believed on His Name. God help us to be like them, too.

Chapter Two

"SPIRITUAL INTOXICATION"

Acts 2

In the first chapter of Acts we saw a waiting Church. Christ had given His commission and blessing and had ascended into heaven. Judas' place in the apostolic group had been filled by Matthias. Now, the believers are waiting and praying. At first they were probably a little impatient. They had witnessed a Man come back from the grave, they had felt the touch of His heavenly power—they had seen Him go into heaven. They had a marvelous message and now they are eager to give it to others. But Jesus had said, "Wait for the power, the witnessing power of the Holy Spirit." Now the obedient believers are waiting. The second chapter of Acts, verse one, begins with these words, "and the day of Pentecost was fully come." Pentecost was the Jewish harvest festival, the time when the Jews came before God, making their offerings and thanking Him for the harvest. The word means "fiftieth day." They started counting at the Passover and counted off seven weeks or forty-nine days—then the next day was Pentecost. Jesus, the true Lamb of God was slain at the time of the Passover. He came back and remained forty days, the believers prayed ten days, and now on the fiftieth day Pentecost has fully come and God is ready to send His power on them.

I. The Spirit. Verses 1-4

1. *The Promise.* Joel 2:28: "And it shall come to pass afterward, that I will pour out my spirit upon all flesh; and

24

your sons and your daughters shall prophesy, your old men shall dream dreams, your young men shall see visions." *John* 14:26: "But the Comforter, which is the Holy Ghost, whom the Father will send in my name, he shall teach you all things, and bring all things to your remembrance, whatsoever I have said unto you." *John* 15:26: "But when the Comforter is come, whom I will send unto you from the Father, even the Spirit of truth, which proceedeth from the Father, he shall testify of me." *John* 16:7-11: "Nevertheless I tell you the truth; it is expedient for you that I go away: for if I go not away, the Comforter will not come unto you, but if I depart, I will send him unto you. And when he is come, he will reprove the world of sin and of righteousness, and of judgment: Of sin, because they believe not on me; Of righteousness because I go to my Father, and ye see me no more; Of judgment, because the prince of this world is judged." *Acts* 1:8: "But ye shall receive power, after that the Holy Ghost is come upon you: and ye shall be witnesses unto me both in Jerusalem, and in all Judaea and in Samaria, and unto the uttermost part of the earth."

When Jesus was here He had all power. He knew that He was not going to stay here, yet He knew that His followers would need this power. So He repeatedly gave the promise that the Holy Spirit would come to take His place and would give them power to accomplish the will of God.

2. *The Procedure.* We find all the believers in one place, and all of them are of one accord. In order for Christians to get the blessing and the power, they must be in the right place —they cannot get it out in the world. But praying and seeking a blessing with other Christians in the church they have a right to expect it. Some people say, "I can be a good Christian and never go to church." You may live a good moral life without ever going to church, but you will never live a Spirit-filled life. I am not saying that the church is the only

place where you can receive the power of the Spirit, but it is the most likely place. I know invalids who are great Christians. They do not get to attend church, but they make a shrine of their sickroom. They pray—they read their Bible—they live close to God. They worship there—but a healthy person seldom does that. Yes, it is among God's people that you receive the blessing and the power. That is the reason that I do not hesitate to urge people to attend church, even though I am the preacher. I know that there are blessings there which they can never get elsewhere. Suppose Peter or James or John had been absent on the day of Pentecost—they would have missed the blessing and they never could have been the men of power that they were.

We note also that they were of one accord. God never works in strife and confusion, but in the place of harmony and unity. We have hundreds of different personalities in our church, but they must be in perfect accord spiritually if God is to work among them. If we have factions and divisions we need not expect the blessings and the power to come. God help those who foster these divisions, and who sow the seeds of discord and strife. Does God love everybody? In a general sense we can say that He does. But we are told in Proverbs 6:19 that He hates somebody. Here it is—"he that soweth discord among brethren." I do not want to be in that category, do you?

Now, as they waited there in the house, they heard a strange sound. It came not from the market place, not from men, but from heaven. This thing which is going to happen is coming down from God. Everything that God sends down from heaven is good. He sent His Only Begotten Son and this was the best gift man has ever received. Now again He is going to send a wonderful gift from heaven. The sound they heard was like that of a rushing mighty wind. We who live in the Southwest certainly know something

about that. You cannot see the wind, but you can hear it
and feel it. So it is with the Spirit. He did not stop at the
doors, although they were probably locked, but He came
in and filled the house with His presence. Oh, that He might
fill the house of God every time we come together! Then
above every man's head they saw a strange thing. A flame of
fire like a cloven tongue sat upon each of them. Fire cleanses
and warms and empowers—here every Christian is being
cleansed, warmed and empowered. Why did God send the
Holy Spirit into the world? In a general sense He sent Him
to take Christ's place on earth and to do His work until He
comes again. But we are told some special things that He
would do.

(1) *He came to bring all things that Jesus said to their
remembrance.* He taught them for three and a half years. He
wanted them to put it all down in the Bible for us, so He
said that the Spirit would make them remember these things.
Now they do remember and understand and we can believe
that there were no errors in their teaching or their writing.
He makes us remember, too. We remember a Christian mother
and a praying father. We remember the experience of grace
which we had with the Lord. This memory keeps us clean and
close to God. The Holy Spirit is the One who causes us to
remember. One day a Christian is greatly tempted, but the
Holy Spirit goes to work—he remembers that he is a child of
God and he is able to withstand the temptation. The time
comes when it seems that trouble overflows his life, then the
Holy Spirit causes the Christian to remember that God has
always brought him out and has taught him to know that
"all things work together for good to them that love God."
Yes, the Holy Spirit causes us to remember.

(2) *He came to convict men of sin, righteousness and
judgment to come.* No man is ever saved if the Holy Spirit
does not do this work. The world sees a man deep in sin, lost

and going to hell. God's Spirit shows a man his sin, his lost condition, his destiny in hell and then points him to Christ, the Saviour. The man heeds the voice of the Spirit, accepts Jesus and is saved. Now, the Spirit can be resisted. A man can say, "No," when he is convicted, but to do so is to commit spiritual suicide.

I have often preached and have seen sinners go away unconvicted. Then some dear brother would say, "I don't see how they held back this morning." The sermon may have been all right, but the Holy Spirit just did not convict them. It is not the pastor who brings conviction—it is the Holy Spirit.

(3) *He came to comfort.* Jesus was a great comforter of the disciples, but one day He had to say, "I am going away." Of course, they were very sad. But then He cheers them by saying, "I will not leave you comfortless. I will send you another One who will abide with you forever." So when our hearts are sad, we have the Holy Spirit within us who speaks comfort to us. We go to the cemetery, we put away the one dearest and best to us, but as we ride home every turn of the wheel seems to tell us that it is all right. We know that God's grace is sufficient. We know that all is well. It is the Spirit Himself who tells us these things and brings comfort to our hearts.

(4) *He came to empower us for service.* A man may be eloquent and brilliant and persuasive, but he needs more than all of this. If we are to turn men to God the Holy Spirit must do the work. I have come to the pulpit many times with a message which I thought was well prepared. We would have a good attendance in the chrurch and yet there would be no response. At other times I have felt something different—I have felt the power of God in my life and have had a great response. It simply means that the Holy Spirit was there and that He was giving the power.

You need His power in your service, too. If you must teach a class, sing a song, make a talk, or do personal work, do not try to do it in the power of the flesh, but ask for the help of the Holy Spirit.

The congregation gathered one Sunday morning in a certain church for the regular worship. At 11 o'clock the pastor did not enter the pulpit. The people were there— the choir was there, but the preacher did not come in. After they had sat fifteen minutes one of the deacons went up to the pastor's study. As he stood outside the door he heard the man of God agonizing in prayer, saying, "Oh, God, I cannot go down alone! You must go with me. You must give me a power that is not my own." The deacon tiptoed back into the auditorium and told the people to wait just a few minutes more. Soon the preacher came in with a look of heaven upon his face. When he began to preach men cried out, "What must I do to be saved?" Others came confessing their sins and getting right with the Lord. Oh, that is the power that we need in service!

(5) *He came to guide the Christian.* We come often to the crossroads, and we ask the question, "Which way shall I take?" We do not have to ask a fortune teller, or gaze into a crystal ball. We can go to God in prayer and tell Him all about it and the Holy Spirit will take us by the hand and lead us in the right way. James 1:5: "If any of you lack wisdom, let him ask of God, that giveth to all men liberally, and upbraideth not; and it shall be given him."

There have been times when I did not follow that Guide, and oh, the bitter consequences and sorrow of it all! But when I have followed Him, even though the way seemed dark, I was soon walking in the sunlight and I felt the presence of my Saviour by my side.

When you are born again the Holy Spirit says, "I will abide with you forever. I will give you peace of mind, I will comfort your heart, I will guide you and empower you; when you come down to old age I will cause sweet memories to fill your heart, and when you come to the end of the way you will be able to say, 'I have fought a good fight, I have finished my course, I have kept the faith; henceforth there is laid up for me a crown of righteousness . . . ,'" (II Timothy 4:7, 8).

Dwight L. Moody was preaching in New York City. He was saved and the Holy Spirit dwelt within him, but he felt that he needed more power. He prayed earnestly for this power. One day as he walked along the street the power came upon him. He rushed to his hotel room and fell across the bed. He testified later that this power came upon him in such measure that he had to cry out for God to stay His hand. Oh, that this power might so come upon the pastor and the people of our church!

II. THE STRANGERS. Verses 5-13

Jerusalem was at the crossroads of the world—men of every nation gathered there. God wanted them to be saved, and He wanted them to go back to their own people with the message of the Cross. So what did He do? He empowered these 120 from the Upper Room. They spoke in other languages so that all of these could understand the Gospel. Some people get the authority right here for speaking in "unknown tongues." But this was not an unknown language. These languages were known to these foreigners. Paul said, 1Cor. 14:19: "Yet in the church I had rather speak five words with my understanding, that by my voice I might teach others also, than ten thousand words in an unknown tongue."

Suppose that we had here this morning some Russians, Italians, Chinese and Japanese. Suppose that God gave one of us the power to preach the gospel in Russian—another to preach the gospel in Italian, and so on. This would give us a small picture of Pentecost. God gave these people this peculiar talent for a purpose. He is a God of order and he would never have hundreds of people running around jabbering in a tongue no one could understand. He is not that kind of a God.

Some of the strangers were amazed and said, "These are all Galileans, but here they are speaking in our own language." Others mocked, saying, "These people are drunk." Yes, they were intoxicated with the Holy Spirit. I wish that we were all so intoxicated. But here is the way that the Gospel is always received. Some are amazed and some mock.

III. THE SERMON. Verses 14-36

Peter again assumes the place of leadership, saying, "These men are not drunk since it is so early in the day." It seems that in those days men did not get drunk before nine o'clock in the morning. It is apparent we are living in more sinful times since both men and women get drunk all hours of the day.

Peter said, "This is the fulfillment of prophecy." He was a good preacher—he backed up his sermon with the Scripture. He quoted the prophet Joel, telling about how the Spirit would fall upon the people, and that all who called upon the Name of the Lord would be saved. There are three points in Peter's sermon: first, Christ was crucified; second, Christ was raised from the dead; third, Christ was in heaven now, lifted up by the Father, and the Holy Spirit was here in His place. It was a great sermon because it was full of Christ. No sermon, however eloquent or forceful, can be called great unless Christ is the center of it all.

IV. THE SALVATION. Verses 37-41

Now notice the effect of the sermon. "They were pricked in their heart . . . " (Acts 2:37). It was not their intellects, nor their minds, but their hearts which were stirred. Some people do not believe in emotion in religion, but here it is. We have too much cold formalism in our churches today. If we had a few more tears over our sins we would be better people.

Now comes the question from these people: "Men and brethren, what must we do to be saved?" They were convicted of their sin. The Holy Spirit was at work. "We realize that we are sinners," they said, "we are lost, we crucified Christ, what must we do about it?" When you get a man to that point it is easy to win him. The answer comes back, "Everything has been done. Jesus upon the Cross has done everything that is necessary for your salvation. All you need to do is to enter into this salvation—repent of your sins and put all of your faith in Jesus Christ and you will be saved."

Verse 38 presents a problem to many people. "Repent . . . be baptized . . . and ye shall receive the gift of the Holy Ghost." This causes some people to say that it takes repentance and faith and water baptism to save a sinner. From other Scriptures we know that water has nothing to do with salvation—baptism is an outward thing and salvation is a thing of the heart. Scholars tell us that the correct translation should be "repent and be baptized because of the remission of sins." We often use the word "for" to mean "because of." We say that "he wept for gladness," when we really mean that "he wept because of his gladness." So we can assume that these people were baptized because their sins had been remitted and they had been saved.

Peter had preached Christ—he had given an invitation and had exhorted his hearers to trust the Saviour. What were the results? They received the word gladly—they were saved—they were baptized and three thousand were added to the church that day.

You may say, "That was a mighty sermon—Peter was some preacher." But I would have you to remember that before he preached, 119 other Christians witnessed and testified for

Christ. If we had 119 consecrated Christians in this city witnessing for Christ and doing personal work every day, we would have a Pentecost in our church every Sunday.

V. THE SIGNS. Verses 42-47

How do we know that these people were saved? Let us look at the signs of their salvation.

1. *They "continued steadfastly"* (*Acts* 2:42). I like that. These people did not say, "It's all over, let's go back to our old way of life." They continued steadfastly in the new way. God give us faithful, continuing people!

(1) *They continued steadfast in doctrine.* To be something, you must believe something. Some people say, "It doesn't matter what I believe, just so I am sincere." A certain man one night reached into the medicine cabinet for a bottle of cough syrup. He drank several swallows of the medicine. He was sincere in believing that it was cough syrup, but it happened to be a poisonous liquid, and he died just the same. It does matter what you believe.

(2) *They continued steadfast in fellowship.* They had a wonderful time with those who believed as they did. Christians often seek their happiness on the outside, but they will find the sweetest fellowship among those who love the same Saviour they do.

(3) *They continued steadfast in breaking of bread.* This means the Lord's Supper. Jesus said, "This do in remembrance of me" (Luke 22:19). They came to the table as we do and the Holy Spirit made them remember. As they partook of the bread and the wine they thought of His broken body and spilled blood. The Lord's Supper was a fresh reminder of the crucified Christ and the coming King. Some church members have not met Christ at the Lord's table in years. No wonder they are spiritually weak.

(4) *They continued steadfast in prayer.* They believed in the prayer meeting. Many folks believe in going to church

on Sunday morning, but they never come to prayer meeting. They are missing "The Sweetest Hour of the Week."

2. *They shared everything they had as each man had need.* This definitely is not communism. The government did not take it away from them. They were not slaves of the state. This was Christianity—the love in their own hearts for Christ and others compelled them to share what they had. If we have the same love in our hearts we will share our blessings today. But man's greatest need is spiritual and we should share the gospel with him. Today as far as possible we are to help every other man in every way that we can. They had three thousand members on their roll. My guess is that everyone gave something. The rich gave much and the poor gave little, but all of them gave something. What mighty things we could do if all of our people gave in this manner!

3. *They went to church.* There is no need to comment on that. If you are a Christian you cannot keep away from God's house.

4. *They went from house to house.* It was a visiting church. They ate with each other and took their religion into their homes. We know they were happy because we read that they "did eat their meat with gladness and singleness of heart." Their hearts were single toward Christ— He had the first place in their lives. When we put Him first we get all we need, and happiness is added unto us.

The result of all of this was that people were added to the church every day. This is a picture of an ideal church, where the results are always glorious. Would not you like to belong to a church like this? Well, you can make your church like this one by being like these people.

There is a cure here for backsliding. In every church there are great numbers who must say, "My name is on the church roll, but that is all." Surely Christ and His church ought to mean more than that to those who have been redeemed. Well, if you will do the four things that these people did, your backslidings will be healed. You are to go to church, give God His part, observe the Lord's Supper, pray and attend prayer meeting. Then your backsliding will be cured and joy will fill your heart. There is an old song which says, "Where is the blessedness I knew, when first I met the Lord?" I will tell you where it is—it is back there where you quit doing these things. Come back to these Christian obligations and responsibilities and you will find the joy of salvation which you have lost.

Do you want to have an infilling of the Holy Spirit? You can have it if you empty your heart of worldly things and of wrong attitudes—if you will surrender completely to Him and invite Him to fill you. "If ye being evil know how to give good gifts unto your children, how much more shall the heavenly Father give the Holy Spirit to those who ask Him."

Out in the Rockies some years ago an engineer was taking his fast freight train over a steep mountain grade. Suddenly something went wrong with the air brakes, and soon the train was out of control. Just ahead was the river and a bridge which would not stand the impact of this wild train. The fireman jumped to safely on one side, and the conductor jumped to safety on the other side. When the train hit the bridge, the bridge gave way and the train plunged down into the water. Later on all the crew was found except the engineer. They said that he had probably run off into the woods. But his grey-haired mother said, "No, my boy was faithful. He never left that train. When you lift the wreck you will find him there." It was even so, for when they lifted the engine they found him at his post and his hand was still on the throttle.

My friends, this is the kind of faithfulness that we owe

Christ and His church. God help us so to live that Christ will always be able to say, "I know where he is—he is on the job for Me." Then at the end of the way He will welcome us and we will hear Him say, "Well done, thou good and faithful servant."

CHAPTER THREE

"SPIRITUAL RESTORATION"

Acts 3

As we come to the third chapter of Acts, we see the Church in full swing. Its members are rejoicing in Christ, witnessing to everyone they touch, and winning many souls. We remember that Jesus has now gone home to heaven, where He will sit at the Father's right hand until the time of His return. The Holy Spirit has fallen upon the believers, and now He is here in the world, taking the place of Christ. The membership of the Church has grown to at least three thousand one hundred and twenty souls.

I. THE ATTENDANCE. Verse 1

Peter and John went to church. These two men had walked with Jesus, they had seen Him die, they had seen Him rise again, they knew that He was the conqueror of life and death, the mighty God. Then the Holy Spirit had fallen upon them and had given them great power, yet they still felt that they ought to go to church. It seems that the deeper experience a man has, the more does he feel the need of worship and communion with God. The sad thing today is that millions who have confessed Christ never go to church. Is it because their experience has been so shallow?

Jesus set the example for all of us in church attendance. He knew all things—He knew in advance all that would be said or done in any service, yet we find Him in the House of

God each Sabbath day. Maybe you say that you can be just as good a Christian by absenting yourself from church. I cannot and I know you cannot. It was while I was in the church that I felt the guilt of my sin, I felt the need of my Saviour, and there I rejoiced when I came to Him. We still need to go to church. There we are made to feel the need of Christ and His cleansing. There we are inspired to live for Him. The soul is like a plant which needs water to make it grow—my drooping spirit needs refreshing which it receives only when I come to worship Him. Gladstone, the grand old man of England, when he was aged and quite deaf, still attended church twice every Sunday. Although he could not hear, he said that he felt the need of getting in an atmosphere of worship.

A certain pastor asked a man to teach a class of fifteen-year-old boys. The man refused. His wife told the pastor that he refused to take the class because he played golf every Sunday and did not feel that he should teach a class as long as he did this. Finally he was convinced that he ought to give up Sunday golf and teach the class. Five months later this man walked down the church aisle with the sixth boy whom he had won to Christ. This was the last unsaved boy in that class. The pastor said to him, "Has it been worth while or would you like to go back to Sunday golf?" Tears of joy sprang to the eyes of the man and he said, "This is the greatest time of my life. I would rather spend time telling others about Christ than anything else on earth. I am sorry that I did not start teaching years ago instead of wasting my Sundays on worldly things." Yes, the place for everyone of us on Sunday is in God's house, doing God's will.

We note here that Peter and John were teaming up. They had both been very close to Jesus—they felt the same way about Him in their hearts. Yet the two men were vastly different. Peter was old and John was young. Peter was poor and John was well off. Peter was practical and John was visionary. What does this tell us? We learn here that people who are vastly different in temperament can work well together if first of all they love the Lord Jesus. So let Him be first in our hearts, in all of our plans let us seek His glory, and together we will be able to do good things for Him.

The gate they entered was called "Beautiful." Yes, all the beauties of God are revealed in His house. It may be just a one-room shack, but if it is dedicated to Him, if His Gospel is preached there, if His spirit fills the house, it is always beautiful. The beauties of forgiveness and strength and comfort and grace and communion are seen and felt in God's house. Surely we ought to attend church regularly.

II. THE ASKING. Verse 2

The Gate was Beautiful, but nearby we find a tragic circumstance. A lame man, a man who had been afflicted all his life, was brought every day and put down there where he might beg for his living as the people passed by. Why did he choose this spot for his begging? Because the people who passed here were going to church, and he expected them to give more than others. The world just naturally expects more of Christians than it does of others. We are told that 98% of all money which is given to charity in the United States today is given by church members. This man was lame, but he had sense enough to know where to find the best begging place.

This man was a type of a lost sinner. First, he was lame from his birth. The sinner was born in sin and all of his life he has been a sinner. "All have sinned, and come short of the glory of God" (Romans 3:23). Second, this man was helpless. He could not make a living—someone else had to bring him down to the temple each morning. Likewise the sinner is helpless. He cannot save himself—he cannot lift himself up to heaven by his own deeds and good works. And then, this man was hopeless with divine aid. He never expected to walk. He expected to continue the old life of begging. Likewise the sinner has no hope of heaven unless the divine hand of mercy reaches down and lifts him up.

I can imagine the dreary life this man had lived. When he was a little boy he could not go out and play with others. He could not go hunting and fishing. He never took long walks through the fields. When some great thing happened, he sat at home by the window, and someone else had to tell him about it. When he was old enough he started begging. He sat in the same spot all day long in order that he might have a few coins at the end of the day. The great choir in the Temple sang, but he was on the outside and could not hear the words. The Temple was lighted with glory, but he had to look upon it all from afar. The sinner's life is a dreary one, too. What does he have to live for? There is no peace, no joy, and no happiness in his life. His worldly pleasures last for just a little while. He is waiting for the end and there is nothing out there for him but eternal doom.

What did this man say to Peter and John when they passed by? "Give me some money—I am poor and needy and you are well and strong. Give me something." He has been disappointed often—will these men go on into the Temple and pay no attention to him? Again this man was like a lost sinner, who says to the world, "My heart is empty and hungry, give me peace and joy." But the world cannot give him these things. Philosophy cannot—philosophy can tell him about the various systems of wisdom, but it cannot fill the aching void in his heart . . . science cannot help him—science can tell him why many things exist and how they operate, but science cannot tell him where he can have his sins forgiven . . . infidelity cannot help him—infidelity can wonder about spiritual things, but cannot tell him about the Lamb of God . . . modernism cannot help him—modernism can tell him what a good man Jesus was, but cannot tell him that the ". . . blood of Jesus Christ his Son cleanseth us from all sin" (I John 1:7).

Oh, the pity of it all! Today men are groping in darkness, seeking satisfaction, trying out everything under the sun, and finding only disappointment—while Jesus still stands with outstretched arms saying, "Come unto me, all ye that labor and are heavy laden, and I will give you rest" (Matthew 11:28) . . . He still stands at the door, knocking and saying, "Let me in—I will bring all the joys of heaven and earth to your heart." . . . He still stands with the cup of life in His hands, saying, "Come and drink this water of life and you will never thirst again." Oh, that men would ask Christ for help instead of seeking in the world something to satisfy the soul!

III. The Advice. Verse 4-6

Have you ever gone by a poor blind man or a crippled beggar on the street, and then had such a wave of pity pass over you that you went back and put a coin in his cup? Well, this is what happened to Peter and John. They looked into his eyes and said to the man, "Look on us" (Acts 3:4). There was something magnetic about Peter's voice which made the man forget everything else and look to him.

We are told the "there is life in a look at the Crucified One." Moses said to the children of Israel, "Look ye unto the brazen serpent and live." Jesus said, "Look unto me and be ye saved, all the ends of the earth" (Isaiah 45:22). We may look upon a mountain scene and have our breath taken away. We may look upon the ocean and realize the might and power of a great God. We may look into the starry heavens and cry out, "The heavens declare the glory of God. . . "

(Psalm 19:1). We may look upon the face of one whom we love and say, "God has been good to me in giving me this one." We may look into the face of a new-born babe and say, "This inspires me to live a better life."

"But, oh, how wonderful to look into the face of Jesus Christ! That face looked upon a lost world and Jesus decided to give His life for that world. It was a face which made sinners shrink and kings tremble—it was a face which smiled upon little babies, frowned upon the Pharisees, and softened in forgiveness toward a sinful woman. Oh, the face of Jesus!

> Look and live, my brother,
> Look, look and live.
> Look to Jesus now and live.
> 'Tis recorded in His word, hallelujah!
> It is only that you look and live.

The lame man gave heed to the apostles, expecting to re-receive something. Yes, when the poor sinner looks up to God's man he has a right to expect something. Thank God, we have something to give him—we have a hope in Christ which we can give him. God pity the preacher who has nothing to give to his people! If he does not believe the Bible to be the Word of God, if he has doubts about the Virgin Birth, if he sees Christ as a mere man and not as a God, with power to save, he has nothing to give. John Milton heard some of the preachers of his day and said, "The hungry sheep look up and are not fed."

A naval chaplain sat one day at his desk in an office with several other chaplains. A boy came in and sat down to talk with one of these other chaplains. He was under deep conviction for sin and he needed help. This modernistic chaplain said to him, "You've been going to church too much. Quit worrying about all this—take care of your naval duties and live a normal life and you will be all right." The boy soon went out of the office—with despair written on his face, for his problem had not been solved. This other chaplain could hardly contain himself. He waited until the boy had gone out of the door. Then he ran out and caught him. They went out behind the barracks and the faithful chaplain told him of Christ, the One who could save and forgive and bless. They knelt in prayer behind the barracks and soon the boy was rejoicing in Christ. Yes, the real preacher does have some help for sinners.

Now Peter says to this man, "Silver and gold have I none . . ." (Acts 3:6). There was a time when Peter did have money, for he ran a prosperous fishing business. Now he has left all to follow Jesus and he is poor in worldly goods. He mentioned this to Jesus one time and Jesus said, "I will make it up to you one hundred times over." And all those who follow Jesus will find that He keeps His promise . . . a man is not necessarily rich because he has silver and gold. Some men have these things, but they have no peace, no happiness, no hope. Some men can say, "I have millions— I have all that money can buy." But the child of God can say, "I am richer than that— I have Christ." If you are a child of the king you have riches untold.

Peter now says, "I shall give you something better than silver and gold—in the Name of Jesus Christ of Nazareth rise up and walk." If he had given the man money, this money would have lasted but a day—he gave him something that will last for time and eternity. If a man today could give you one hundred million dollars, that would be fine. If you had to make a choice between that and Christ, you had better let the money go.

A Bishop of Rome was talking about this incident, and as he thought of the riches of the church, he said, "We do not have to say now, 'silver and gold have I none . . .'" (Acts 3:6) and someone replied: "Neither can you say, 'rise

up and walk,' (Acts 3:6) either." Many poor churches cannot offer you magnificent buildings, golden altars and stained
glass windows—but they can offer you Christ, which is the
important thing. God help us always to make this our main
business!

Peter took hold of the man's hand, and as he started to
lift the man, strength rushed into his feet and ankles and he
was able to stand by himself. Do you say, "I cannot live the
Christian life"? Then just come to Jesus—He will lift you
up and give you the strength that you need.

A man who had been a drunkard was gloriously saved. A
few days later as he walked down the street the odor of
liquor from the saloons rushed out upon him. The old
appetite returned and he was almost overcome by it. But,
instead of going into the saloon, he ran all the way home, went
into his room, locked the door, fell down upon his knees and
cried out, "Oh, Jesus, help me now!" God's power came into
his heart and he was able to overcome.

Some years ago I was called to the hospital to see a certain
man. This man had been drinking too much and as I went
into the room he said to me, "I want to make a vow with
my hand on the Bible, promising that I will never drink
again." I told the man of the only One who could help
him. He made his vow and I prayed for him. He did not give
his heart to Christ, however, so his good resolution did not
last very long.

It is only Christ within who can give us strength to overcome the temptations of life. You can make New Year
resolutions and you will be sure to break them . . . you can
make high and holy vows within yourself, and you will
not be able to keep them. In order to overcome sin, you need
the power of Christ within your heart.

We read next that the man stood and walked and leaped
and praised God. Where did he go then? He fell in step

with Peter and John and went into the Temple to worship. Sometime ago I received a telephone call from a man who said, "So-and-so has been saved, I wish you would go to see her." I went to see this person and talked and prayed with her. She said to me, "Yes, I have been saved, but I am not going to join the church." I knew then that something was lacking. When salvation comes to one through Christ it is the natural order for that one to take a stand for Christ and to join His Church. The first thing this man did was to go to church. If you say you are a Christian and you don't go to church, there is something wrong with you. Either you have been greatly deceived, or you are a terrible back-slider.

We next read that the people were filled with wonder and amazement when they saw what had happened to this man. The best advertisement for Christianity is a changed life. When the world sees that change it is always amazed. The shoemaker makes a pair of shoes and holding them up, he says, "This is a sample of my work." The automobile manufacturer rides up in his car and says, "This car is a sample of my work." In like manner, Christ points to transformed lives all over the world and says to us, "These are samples of my work, come unto Me and I will make your life over, also."

V. THE ADMONITION. Verses 11-26

The people ran up to Peter and John, looking upon them in admiration for the great thing which had been done. But Peter cried out, "Wait a minute, do not look on us, we are not responsible for this man's cure, we are just instruments in the hand of God. Jesus Christ, God's Son, did this thing." Oh, the humility of these apostles! They took no credit to themselves. Someone has well said, "You can do a great a-mount of good in the world, if you do not care who gets the credit for it."

Peter now preaches his second sermon. He said, "God sent His Son into the world—you delivered Him up, you denied

Him in the presence of Pilate when he might have freed Him." As Peter used the word "denied" did a sudden pain shoot through his own heart? Did he remember how he had been guilty of the same sin? Probably so—but he could say this, "There is one difference. I went to Him in tears and penitence and He forgave me—that is what you need to do."

In his sermon Peter said, "You killed Him, but God raised Him up. The risen Christ has healed this lame man." These were daring words for him to say in the Temple . . . only a living Saviour could have inspired him to speak in this way. The man who once said to a little maiden, "I have never known Him" now is saying to this great crowd, "You crucified the Lord of glory." Yes, the man who has had an experience with this risen Christ is indeed a different man.

Now comes Peter's exhortation and invitation. " 'Repent . . . and be converted,' " he said, 'that your sins may be blotted out . . . ' (Acts 3:19) —then God will send seasons of refreshing and some day He will send Jesus back for you. A great number of people came to Christ on that day when he gave the invitation.

In the Southwest we live in a desert country. We can look out upon many barren miles of waste space. But our people have done something about it. They have harnessed the rivers and built great dams. Now our farmers turn the water into the fields and the irrigaated portions bloom like a rose and bear their fruits in their seasons. Life without Christ is like this desert waste. But when the fountain of grace is opened up and the water of life flows over the soul, then we are redeemed, our souls are refreshed, and we can bear fruit for the Master's table.

Are you like this lame man? Christ today offers you all that He has. He is anxious to give—are you willing to receive?

A little family lived in a frame shack. The father spent all of his money on drink, while the wife and children suffered for the necessities of life. Finally, the father decided

to break up his home and to send the children to an institution. A good Christian man saw the children of this poor
family sitting upon the front steps Sunday after Sunday, so
one day he went in to invite them to come to church and
Sunday school. When he met the father he told him how he,
too, had once been a drunkard. He told about how he had
spent all of his money in sin, but how God had saved him
and changed his life and given him a happy home. That
night the sinful man said to his wife, "I love you and the
children, but when this awful appetite comes upon me, I
simply must have a drink. If it took the clothes off my back
—if it killed me, I would be forced to have a drink. But God
heard this man's prayer and saved him—maybe he'll save
me, too." He and his wife fell upon their knees and prayed
the old, old prayer, "God be merciful to me a sinner" (Luke
18:13). God heard the prayer and saved the man and his
wife. Today the entire family is living a good useful Christian life, and they have a happy home.

Yes, friends, the Christ who healed the lame man is ready
to do even greater things for you. He is ready to save you
and bless you and put a song of praise in your mouth. "Repent ye therefore, and be ye converted . . . " (Acts 3:19).

CHAPTER FOUR

"SPIRITUAL DETERMINATION"

Acts 4

In the first three chapters of Acts we see the marvelous manner in which God blessed the Early Church. The Holy Spirit had come upon the believers, they had witnessed with great boldness, and on every side people were turning to Christ and being saved . . . Now if the devil hates anything in the world, he hates to see the Church prosper and souls being saved—so he stirs up the religious leaders of that day to bring an intense persecution upon the church. The same thing is true today. When God begins to bless a church, when the crowds are coming, when there is a great spirit among the people, when souls are being saved and people are rejoicing, what does the devil do? He often begins to work through some church members, trouble is stirred up, and God's work is hurt.

From now on there is a definite pattern in the Book of Acts. The Christians go out to witness, a great work is done, then the enemies of the Gospel begin to persecute them. Then as the Christians stand true to Christ, they see God's power coming on them in great measure. There is a lesson here for us—whatever happens we must stand true to Christ. He will bring us out and make us more useful than ever.

I. THE PERSECUTION. Verses 1-4

Peter and John, in the name of Christ, had just healed a lame man. Now the religious leaders become intensely

48

angry. Can you imagine that? Here is a poor man, lame from his birth, begging for a living. Now he is made strong and well, living a godly life, able to take his place in the community and support a family. But these leaders are angry—their hearts are filled with jealousy and malice toward the disciples. Surely the Bible is right when it says that "The heart is deceitful above all things, and desperately wicked" (Jeremiah 17:9).

Here we see the first opposition to the Gospel, but it is not the last. They laid hold on Peter and John and put them in prison. What is their crime? It is two-fold—preaching the Gospel and healing the lame man. There is a similar story in the history of the State of Virginia. That state was settled first by members of the Church of England, a state church. But two humble Baptist preachers had the courage to stand up and preach Christ, and since they had no Episcopal license they were arrested.

Patrick Henry came to the court house on the day of the trial. He defended these men. Standing before the crowd in the court-room and holding up the indictment in his hand, he cried out, "What is the indictment against these men? Preaching the glorious Gospel of the Son of God! Great God! That is the indictment. Are there no thieves going around unarrested and unconvicted? Are there no murderers upon whom to visit the vengeance of the law, that you must indict and try these men for preaching the Gospel?" He made such an impassioned plea that these Baptist preachers were set free.

There is still much opposition to the Gospel today. A chaplain came to my office sometime ago. He had dared to stand up and preach Christ in an army chapel. He denounced the sin in the camp, and would have nothing to do with the drinking parties which were held for the men. His commanding officer called him in and told him that he would be forced to quit preaching in this manner. Yet he was only preaching against sin and about the forgiveness which is in Christ Jesus.

The commanding officer could not stop his preaching, but he had him transferred to a place where his ministry was of little effect and soon the chaplain was out of the service. He told me that the commanding officer sent this word to the Chief of Chaplains, "Don't send us any Southern Baptists—they are too evangelistic." Yes, the world is at enmity against God and the preaching of the Gospel.

The devil is behind all opposition to the Gospel. He began his opposition by forces outside of the church. Later on in the Book of Acts we see this opposition arising inside the church.

Then Satan began to cover up true Christianity by ritualism and ceremony—then he set a wave of infidelity and agnosticism —then came evolution—then came modernism—then came the social gospel—now we have the idea that all men are brothers, that God is the father of all, therefore no man needs salvation. It is still the age-old fight. Satan hates the blood, the resurrection, the forgiveness of sin and the salvation of souls. Wherever the Gospel is preached he is going to oppose it.

We are told that these leaders were grieved over what the apostles had preached. What had they preached? They had preached the resurrection through Jesus Christ. The Sadducees were leading in this opposition—their chief belief was that there is no resurrection, and here we see Peter preaching that Christ was raised from the dead. The Sadducees would have given all they had if they could have gone to the tomb and shown that it was occupied . . . but they could not do it—the tomb was empty and Christ was alive. This is the cornerstone of our faith. If Jesus died as a man, and remained dead, we would not worship Him as

God. But when He came back to life, He proved that He was the Son of God, and that every word He said and every claim He made was true. So we celebrate the resurrection, not simply on Easter, but every Sunday. Thank God, our Redeemer liveth!

Yes, Peter preached Christ. After all, what other message did he have? The death and burial and resurrection and ascension of Christ were fresh on his heart. That message is just as fresh today—it is the only message that we have, the only message that we need, the only message that will help mankind . . . A sermon without Christ is like a fountain without water, a garden without flowers, a heaven without stars, a life without love. It is a barren thing and helps no one.

Some years ago while I was spending my vacation with some friends near Lake Erie, I decided on Sunday morning to go to church and have my own spiritual dynamo recharged. That morning I found a small crowd in a large auditorium. They sang several songs with which I was not familiar, and when the preacher stood up to preach, he talked about world disorder, the dignity of man, the capitalistic spirit. But he said nothing about my Lord, and I went away disappointed. I thought then of how many millions of such sermons were preached, how many wonderful opportunities were wasted. . . . On another Sunday I went to another church. They sang about the Lord Jesus—they sang "All Hail the Power of Jesus Name," and "There is a Fountain Filled with Blood." When the preacher stood up to preach he did not read his manuscript—he poured out his soul. He told of the wonders in Christ, of how He could help us, and how we needed Him in this life and the life that is to come. I came away from that church rejoicing in my heart and saying, "I have been to church this morning. I saw Jesus today."

Yes, they put Peter and John in prison—"howbeit." But what? Here it is—in spite of this imprisonment the number of believers came to be about five thousand. My, how the church is growing! I can imagine these two apostles in the prison that night. Peter was saying, "This is pretty bad, John. Jesus told us to preach the Gospel and we did as we were told. Now here we are in a dark dungeon and we don't know what is coming in the morning." No, that is not what he said. He did say, "Here we are in jail, but we can rejoice because five thousand people have been saved." Today some people can say, "I don't like your sermons,"—but souls are being saved. "I don't like your methods"—but souls are being saved. "I don't like the way you lead the church"—but souls are being saved. Let the devil fight, let the world laugh, let men criticize. As long as we can snatch brands from the burning we can rejoice and believe that Jesus is well pleased.

II. THE PREACHING. Verses 5-12

In the morning the high priest and all of his kinfolks were gathered together. They formed a council to try Peter and John. Jesus had once told them, "Ye shall be delivered up to councils—in the world ye will have much tribulation, but be of good cheer, I have overcome the world." How could Peter and John be so calm—so unafraid in such an hour? They remembered the words of Jesus. "He said this would happen to us," John probably said, "we know now that He spoke the truth and we know that He will be with us, will tell us what to say and will bring us out all right." This was practically the same council which tried Jesus and probably the same court room. Peter and John remembered that Christ had once been in the criminal's place, which they now occupied, and this memory gave them courage. . . . You and I have many rough roads before us. If we remember that Jesus has been down every road that we must travel, if we listen and hear Him saying, "I will never leave nor forsake thee," then we need never fear. He will cause all things to work out all right.

The council asked the apostles this question, "By what power, or in what name, have ye done this?" (Acts 4:7). This gave Peter a chance to preach and he took advantage of it. The last time he was in this judgment hall, a servant asked him if he were a follower of Christ. All his courage oozed out and he claimed that he did not even know Jesus. But listen to him now—he stands before them and without a tremor in his voice he preaches to those prominent and influential leaders, accusing them of killing the Prince of glory. From whence did his power come? Here it is in verse 8— "He was filled with the Holy Spirit." Oh, how the preacher needs to be filled with that power! It was said of one man, that "when he took the pulpit he took the congregation." Every true preacher knows what it is to preach without power. It is like beating against a brick wall. But every true preacher also knows what it is to feel a divine power within him and to preach in the strength of that power.

Listen to Peter as he turns the table on these sinners. They came together to accuse him of a crime—suddenly he is the accuser and they are the criminals. "You ask me how this man was made whole and I tell you that it was through the power of Jesus Christ. You crucified Him, but God raised Him from the dead, and this is a sample of His work."

Now he tells about the rejected cornerstone. Salvation was an important word with Israel. For years they had longed for deliverance for their nation and for themselves as individuals. But here is where they made their big mistake— in erecting the building of salvation they needed a chief cornerstone, and when God sent this stone, the Lord Jesus Christ, they rejected Him and crucified Him. Nevertheless, God made Him the center of salvation, and no one can ever be saved without him . . . You and I are building a life, there are many things we need to put in this life, such as health, education, making a living, friends, and home. But with all of these things life is not complete unless we take Jesus into it. We must let Him be the Head of all things or life is empty and hopeless.

Now comes one of the greatest statements in the Bible, "Neither is there salvation in any other: for there is none other name under heaven given among men, whereby we must be saved" (Acts 4:12). Peter charged his hearers with the crime of crucifixion, but he cannot close his sermon unless he explains the way of salvation to them. It was a good sermon. First, he proclaimed the truth, second, he pressed the fact of sin home on his hearers, then he told them of salvation in Jesus' Name. "What's in a name?" asks Shakespeare. Everything—if that name is Jesus. There was a new body for this lame man in that Name—there was sight for blind Bartimaeus in the Name—there was life for the dead Lazarus in that Name. There was forgiveness for the sinful woman at the well in that Name . . . There was new life for Paul in that Name . . . And for you and me there is salvation, there is a name written in heaven's book, there is adoption into God's family, there is comfort, strength and peace and at last a home in heaven in the Name of Jesus.

Among preachers, John Wesley and Spurgeon and Whitfield and Beecher and Truett and Lee are great names . . . In literature, Shakespeare and Tennyson and Browning and Longfellow are great names. In military circles, Caesar and Alexander and Napoleon and Washington and Robert E. Lee are great names—but in salvation Jesus' Name is the only Name. God has never given us any other saving name. His Name is first and only and always central in salvation. I call upon every other name in the world and there is no response, no answer, no help for the soul. But when I call upon the Name of Jesus I hear Him say: "Here I am, my child, I am ready, willing, and able to save unto the uttermost and give you all that you need." . . . So Peter offered these hardened sinners salvation in Jesus' Name.

III. THE PROHIBITION. Verses 13-22

When Peter ended his sermon these men noted three things. They noted his boldness, which came through the power of the Holy Spirit. They took notice of the fact that these men were ignorant and unlearned and they marveled at Peter's speech. They also took notice of the fact that these men had been with Jesus. They had to say, "These men walked with Christ. We hate Him, but we must admit His greatness. We know that these men are different because they have been with Him." That is what the world needs to see today—Jesus in us. We ought to live today in such a manner that those around us will say, "He is different. He is finer in every way, all because he has had an experience with Jesus."

In the place where you work can they see that you are different from sinners? Can they see it in your social life? In your business life? In your home life? A woman who had not seen her sister for several years came to pay her a visit. When she had been there a few days she said to her sister, "I don't know what's happened to you, but you are much easier to live with." The thing that had happened was this— she had come to know Jesus Christ. Oh, let us so live that the world will know that we have been with Jesus!

We see here that the preacher's power is not dependent upon education or training. These men had no worldly advantages, but they had power. There are certain denominations which will not permit anyone to preach in their pulpits unless they have had college and seminary training. Yet some of the mightiest men who ever preached the gospel were uneducated men. The preacher's power comes not from the schools, but from the Spirit.

When they saw the man who had been healed standing before them, they could say nothing against him. They saw a man, not crippled and begging, but standing and walking. Here was exhibit "A" of Christ's power and they could say nothing against it. Today people look at the hypocrites and back sliders around them and declare that there is nothing in Christianity. But when you and I are changed and live as we should they cannot lift their voices against our religion . . . Paul admonishes us to ". . . adorn the doctrine of God . . . " (Titus 2:10). This means that we are to make Christianity as attractive as possible through living good, useful, consecrated Christian lives.

Here is the prohibition which was put upon these apostles. They could not put them to death because all the people had witnessed this miracle and the leaders were afraid of the consequences. So they were told to go away and never again to teach in the Name of Jesus , . . But you cannot stop a God-called and a God-sent preacher. You might as well tell the sun to stop shining, or the rain to stop falling, or the winds to stop blowing, or the flowers to stop blooming.

So the apostles gave their answer, "You may pass any judgment that you please, you may put any prohibition upon us that you wish, but so far as we are concerned we are under a higher authority. The Lord sent us on a mission and nothing can stop us." My how courageous they were! Then they said, "We have seen and felt some things about Christ. We cannot contain these things in ourselves. We must tell the whole world about it." If you and I have had a vital experience with Christ neither can we keep it to ourselves— we will want to share it with all men. We note that this man was above forty years of age. This is telling us that Christ can save those of any age who come to Him.

IV. The Praise. Verse 23

When the apostles were free they went to their "own company . . . " They sought the company of their fellow Christians. "Birds of a feather flock together." Tell me with whom you associate and I will tell you the kind of person you are. A true Christian feels at home only among godly people. He is miserable with the other kind . . . Peter and John told the brethren everything that had happened and they all rejoiced together. We still rejoice when we hear what Christ is doing all over the world. If your heart does not leap when someone comes to the Saviour, there is something wrong with you. What a good time they had! They talked and prayed and laughed together.

V. The Prayer. Verses 24-31

As these Christians prayed they proclaimed the greatness of God, they thanked Him for what He had done and asked Him to give them boldness to preach Christ, and to help them to do great things in the Name of Jesus. The Council said, "You are not to preach Christ anymore." The apostles prayed, "Lord, give us power to preach more than ever."

When they prayed the place was shaken and they were all filled with the Holy Spirit. The power of prayer has never been withdrawn. If we were like them, if we prayed like they did, God would shake us and fill us, too. Some Christians never go to church—if they prayed they would be shaken and they would take their place in God's House. Some able people never serve the Lord—if they prayed, they would be shaken and they would get busy for God. Some never give anything—if they prayed God would shake them into giving their tithes and offerings. Some have children who are going astray—if they prayed they would set the right example for their children, and their children would be changed. Some are substituting criticism for service—if they prayed their attitude would be changed. Some are neglectful and cold—if they prayed they would become warm servants of the Lord . . . No wonder this was a strong church—they prayed as a church should pray.

VI. The Participation. Verses 32-37

"The multitudes were of one heart and one soul." Is not that wonderful? No wonder they did great things, no wonder their number grew, no wonder someone said of them, "These . . . have turned the world upside down . . . " (Acts 17:6). . . . That was the first Christian church, and it made a mighty impact upon the world. Thousands of such churches have been organized since then and every true church has had its part in transforming life and changing the world. This world would be one big mass of chaos and confusion and the good institutions of life today would be missing if it had not been for the influence of the Christian church. So you and I—as Jesus did—should love the church and give ourselves for it.

I have time to give you briefly a few points mentioned here about this church:

(1) "They had all things in common" (Acts 4:32).

(2) They had great power in witnessing. (Acts 4:33).

(3) "Great grace was upon them all" (Acts 4:33). This made their lives warm, tender, loving and compassionate.

(4) "They spake the word of God with boldness" (Acts 4:31). How many today ever speak out boldly for Christ?

(5) Everybody gave what they had and brought it to the church.

(6) "They were all filled with the Holy Ghost" (Acts 4:31).

This chapter ends by telling us of Barnabas, a well-to-do man, who sold all that he had and brought the money to the apostles. We will hear more of him later. But this act shows that the Gospel was reaching the rich and the poor, the high and the low.

So we find that every time the devil opposed these believers they stood up staunchly for Christ and their beliefs. They won out and God's Kingdom was advanced. This is just what we need today. This is not a time for weaklings and turn-coats in the kingdom of God. This is the time for us to give our best for Christ and His Church. While the world is at its worst, we must be sure to give our best.

When Napoleon's army invaded Russia, they came to a village where everyone had fled except one man. He was a woodsman, with the handle of his axe stuck in his leather belt. They started to shoot him, but he showed such calmness and courage that the French captain decided to save his life. However, the captain said, "We will mark him—we will brand him for life." They heated a branding iron and stamped the letter "N" on the palm of his hand.

"What does that mean?" asked the man.

"That is the letter 'N'," he was told, "it stands for Napoleon —you belong now to our Emperor."

This man had always been a loyal Russian and he felt that it was a time to show his loyalty. He took the axe from his belt, put his hand on the block and cut that hand off at the wrist, saying, "That hand may belong to Napoleon, but I am a Russian and if I must die, I will die a Russian."

Oh, may God help us to cut out of our lives everything that is not honoring to Christ! May we stand up before all the world and give to Him the best life that can be lived.

CHAPTER FIVE

"SPIRITUAL PREVARICATION"

Acts 5

We know that the Church of Jesus Christ is a divine institution, and one of the great proofs of this fact is this —everything in the world has happened to the Church, and yet it still stands. Satan has used against it every weapon at his command and the Church still remains. It will continue to stand until Jesus returns.

In Acts 4 we saw Peter and John imprisoned for preaching the Gospel. The religious leaders were afraid to kill them because of the people and were forced to release them. They were then commanded to go out and to preach and teach no more in the Name of Christ. But they went out to do an even greater work for God and the church grew by leaps and bounds.

The revival tides were running high, the apostles were preaching with great boldness, and scores were turning to Christ. Can you imagine the sensation which all of this caused in Jerusalem? If newspapers had been published in those days, the headlines would have told about the strange things that were happening. The radio commentators would have blared forth their news comments about these matters. If you had met a friend on the streets, he would have said, "Did you hear what happened yesterday? This rich farmer, Barnabas, was converted and sold his land and gave every cent to the church." Another would say, "Did you hear about

Joshua? He has been a cripple all of his life, but he went to the meeting, was converted and completely healed." Another would say, "Do you remember that old blind man who begged every day at the corner of Main and Eighth streets? The apostles touched him and now he can see, and he is going everywhere praising God." Another would say: "Did you notice Sol's Gambling Den, the place where men drank and caroused and where every vice flourished? It was closed this morning. Sol has been saved. A few minutes ago I heard him on the corner, preaching Christ and telling what the Lord had done for him." My what a mighty revival they did have!

Now when the Holy Spirit begins to work, when the high tides of revival power flow over the community, we often see some counterfeit confessions. We also see hypocrisy exposed. In the fifth chapter of Acts we see both of these things in the case of Ananias and Sapphira.

I. THE PREVARICATION. Verses 1-4

These new Christians not only had their souls converted, but they also gave their pocketbooks to the Lord. They brought their money to the church and gave it over to the apostles to be used for the good of the cause and the glory of God. Sometimes men claim to be converted, but their conversion does not cover the whole area of life. True conversion ought to change business life, home life, private life and financial life. Many a man is glad for Christ to save him and to give him a home in heaven, but he does not want to live a heavenly life in this world. He sings, "Jesus paid it all," and is content to let it rest at that. He never pays anything himself. Some church members will say, "Yes, I am saved and I am on the way to heaven," but they have not given a dime to the church in years . . . "It is more blessed to give than to receive," (Acts 20:35) but too many are satisfied simply with receiving. They drink in all the blessings of God like a sponge drinks in water, but there is one difference—you can squeeze a sponge and get something out of it.

Barnabas set a good example in sacrificial giving. The church members said of him, "That was a wonderful gift. Isn't Mr. Barnabas a good man?" Yet in that group there may have been some poor man who was able to give only a meager amount, but who gave it cheerfully and willingly. I am sure that God gave him just as much credit as He did Barnabas, but of course the people talked more about the big gift. In this company there was a couple named Ananias and Sapphira. They had an unholy ambition—they wanted the people to speak of them as they did of Barnabas. They talked about the matter far into the night.

"We could sell our land for a goodly sum," Ananias said, "but that would be too much to give to the church."

"I tell you what we could do," said Sapphira, "we could sell the land and keep most of the money and yet we could take a good sum down to the church. We could tell them that this was the sum which we received for the land. Then the apostles would say, 'God bless this fine generous couple,' then the people would say, 'Why, these folks are just as fine as Barnabas.'" So this couple agreed to follow this procedure.

The next morning Ananias went down to the real estate man and put his land up for sale. It probably was good property and by nightfall the papers had been signed and the money was in hand. That night Ananias and Sapphira divided the money into two stacks, one for the church and one for themselves. I can imagine that Sapphira said, "That's too much to give to the church, Let's put a little more in our stack, we may need it in the years to come." They did not sleep much that night—they took turns watching the money. The next morning they hid their own money away and then got ready to take the other money to the church. Ananias

decided to go to church first and give the money to the
apostles. They would commend him, then Sapphira would
make her entrance, and more praise would be heaped upon
them.

So Ananias goes to church. He walks right down to the
front and lays the money at the feet of the apostles. He
expected Simon Peter to smile and say, "God bless you,
brother Ananias." But instead, the preacher turned on him
with blazing eyes, saying, "Why have you allowed Satan to
fill your heart and to cause you to lie to the Holy Spirit, and
to keep back part of the price of the land?" Ananias was
struck dumb. He could not say a word. How did Peter know
what he had done? He thought that all he had to do was to
fool a mere man, and here is this preacher reading his
heart. The answer was this—the Holy Spirit was filling
Peter and revealing the truth unto him . . . Today men
think that if they can only fool other men, everything is all
right. So they hide their sin from man and forget that God
with His all-seeing eye looks upon everything, whether it is
done in the blackness of midnight or in the brightness of
midday.

You can steal and no one will ever know it—you can
cheat in a business deal and keep it to yourself—you can lie,
you can curse, you can drink, you can hate someone, you can
gossip about someone, but there is a God in heaven and He
knows all about it, and He will call you to account. "Be sure
your sin will find you out" (Numbers 32:23). "The mills of
the gods grind slowly, but they grind exceedingly small."
"Whatsoever a man soweth, that shall he also reap" (Galatians
6:7). Pay day may not come tomorrow, nor the next day, but
just as sure as there is a God, pay day *will* come.

Now Peter said, "You did not have to do this, the money
was yours. Nobody is forcing you to give it—you have not
lied unto man but unto God." Yes, all sin is against God and

He is the one who punishes sin. Peter asked the question, "Why?" Then he answered his own question, "Satan has filled your heart." That is the answer behind all sin, from the sin of Adam down to your sin and my sin. The other believers were filled with the Holy Spirit, Ananias was filled with Satan. This is the great difference in men today. Jesus still stands at the door and knocks. There are some who let Him in and permit Him to fill every area of life. Satan also knocks at the heart's door and there are others who let him in and from that time on he rules their lives.

The pity today is that God's children often let the devil in. They have been saved, they have allowed Christ to come in and redeem them—but then the devil knocks and they say, "I have some room for you, too." So they let him in and they permit the devil to use them while the heart of Jesus is saddened.

How did these two people get into the church? Possibly they were swept in upon a wave of emotion. They were not born again—they were not filled with the Holy Spirit. It was not the preacher's fault that these unsaved people had gotten into the church. Today the preacher does all he can to stir people to a decision. It is not his fault if some come who are not saved. This is your responsibility—if you come to join the church be sure that in your own heart you have had a transforming experience.

I have said that the example of Barnabas inspired the other members to give freely. Ananias and Sapphira were not willing to give freely—they were not willing to make a sacrifice. But they did want to receive the credit for a large gift. They wanted to hear the applause and the compliments of the people.

II. THE PUNISHMENT. Verses 5-14

Ananias never did say anything. He stood there trembling and in a few minutes he fell down—*dead*. Then the young men carried him out and buried him. They had not even a semblance of a funeral service. Now Peter did not kill Ananias, God did. It is an awful thing to lie to the Holy Spirit. The Spirit comes to a man, convicting him of sin, and the man says, "Yes, I'll surrender to Christ." But if he does not do it—he has lied to the Holy Spirit. The terrible thing about it is that some day the Spirit will leave him, to strive no more.

In the nighttime the Spirit says, "Go to that man and straighten out your differences with him." You answer, "I will certainly do that tomorrow." But the next day you say: "No, I'll keep that old hatred in my heart" . . . The Spirit tells you to tithe and you say, "I'll do that—I'll start tithing the first of the month." But you do not do it. You use the tithe for yourself—you have lied to the Holy Spirit . . . The Spirit says to you, "Go to that friend and tell him that you want him to become a Christian." You say, "I will do it." But you do not do it—you have lied to the Holy Spirit and the blood of that friend's soul will be on your hands at the judgment bar. It is an awful thing to lie to the Holy Spirit. When Ananias lied, he died.

Three hours later Sapphira came in—she looked around for her husband and he was not present. She wondered what had happened. She looked up at the apostles, but they gave her no smile of approval. The crowd was strangely silent. She did not understand it, but she knew that something had gone wrong. Peter spoke to her, saying, "Did you sell the land for that much?" and she said, "Yes, that was the price." Peter then said to her, "You agreed with your husband to lie to the Holy Spirit. Your husband is dead and the young men who buried him are ready to bury you." She gave a sob, fell down dead and was carried out and buried by the side of Ananias. They had been together in lying to the

Holy Spirit, now they are together in death and they will be forever together in hell.

I wonder if Sapphira influenced Ananias to do the thing which he did. We call women the weaker sex, but, after all, men are just putty in their hands. A woman can make or break a man. Many a man who is high up in the world can say, "I am here because of a good, godly woman." Many another man who is in the ditch can say, "I was pulled down by a selfish, ungodly, sinful woman." God help you women to be unselfish, consecrated, godly, praying women. That is the kind of wife your husband needs—that is the kind of mother your children need.

The net result of this tragedy was that more people were saved and greater growth came to the church.

Get the weeds out and the flowers will grow. If we exercised discipline in our church, if we cut our roll in half, if we turned out those who are not living their lives for Christ, I wonder if we would not have a more powerful church. The big question is—where would we begin? There is no doubt, however, but that our churches would be stronger today if we could set our standards high and insist upon our members living up to these standards.

Let us look at the effect which this incident had upon the church. First, we are told that great fear came upon the church. The believers said, "We must keep right with God, or this same thing might happen to us." Maybe it would be a good thing if God should bare His mighty arm in our churches today. Second, we notice that the hypocrites did not dare to join this church. Third, we notice that the outsiders were moved. Multitudes were added to the church. When God works in power things really happen. Fourth, the preachers had more power than ever. "Many signs and wonders [were] wrought among the people" (Acts 5:12). A front door revival takes place when many people come down the aisle and join the church. A back door revival takes place when those who should not be in the church are put out. This church had a back door revival, and the after effect was a great ingathering.

Suppose an unsaved man comes to church and becomes interested in his salvation. He is about to take a stand for Christ, then he sees a certain man taking a prominent part. He knows that this man is not what he ought to be and immediately he cools off toward a decision for Christ. He says, "If that man is a Christian, I don't want to be one." The church would be better off without those whose practice does not measure up to their profession. They are stumbling blocks in the pathway of the unsaved.

III. THE PHYSICIAN. Verses 15-16

Next we see the tremendous power of God in a human life. Peter, the former profane fisherman, was so filled with the Spirit that the people brought their sick folks out and put their couches on the streets where Peter walked along, believing that if his shadow fell upon them, they would be healed. We are told that they were healed, yet Peter did not know about it. Because he was filled with the Spirit he wielded a strong, unconscious influence. Somebody is watching you, too. You do not know about it, but you are exerting an influence upon them . . . What a man Peter must have been! What great faith they had in him! God help us so to live for Christ that others will say, "That man is close to God and I want to get close to him."

> Let others see Jesus in you,
> Let others see Jesus in you.
> Keep telling the story—be faithful, be true,
> Let others see Jesus in you.

IV. THE PRISON. Verses 17-28

I have said that the devil hated to see God's work prosper. Now he gets busy. He stirs up the religious leaders and they put the apostles in prison. Now that they have them safe behind bars, they can go home triumphantly. Tomorrow they will strike the decisive blow, they will put these men to death, and stamp out Christianity. "But"—ah, the difference that little word makes! But what? But the angel of the Lord opened the door and led them out. How encouraging that must have been! Now they know that the Lord is with them—now they know that nothing can stop them. The angel told them to go back to the temple and to start preaching again. At the first glimmer of dawn, as the people begin to stir in the streets, the apostles are out proclaiming Christ again.

Early that morning the council gathers. The high priest puts on his severest air. All the council members are very stern and dignified. They are going to scare the life out of these poor preachers. Now they send their hirelings to the prison to bring up the apostles. Soon these men come running back—their report shaking all the dignity of the council. "We found the guards watching the prison, and all the doors were locked, but when we went in, not a soul was there." What a funny situation that was! There are the guards marching up and down, the doors are locked tightly, but the prison was empty. My, what an elaborate guard to place over an empty cage! . . . About that time another man ran in. "I know where they are," he said, "they are down at the temple teaching the people and preaching Christ." What will these enemies of the gospel do next? They said to their hirelings: "Go and bring these men to us, but be easy with them. If we hurt them the crowd will be on our necks." So these men went down to the temple and speaking very humbly and kindly to the apostles they said, "Sirs, won't you please come and meet with the council?" And the apostles went willingly. They knew that the Lord was with them and they had no fear in their hearts.

When the apostles came in before the Council, the high priest said to them: "We told you not to preach in this Name—why have you disobeyed us? Now you have filled the city with this doctrine—you are going to bring this Man's blood upon us." They didn't call His Name, they just simply said "this Man." Ah, the blood was on their hands already! When Pilate delivered Jesus to be crucified these people cried out, "His blood be on us, and on our children" (Matthew 27:25). Now Peter, filled with courage and the Holy Spirit, makes his answer. Listen to his brave words, "We ought to obey God rather than man. You can give us all the orders you like, but the Lord told us to preach and we are going to keep on preaching." Yes, when God lays His hand on a man and gives him a message, that man must obey God. He must preach the truth.

Fifteen hundred years later another preacher stood in Peter's same position. Martin Luther, the Catholic monk, was climbing the Sancta Scala in Rome when this great text burst upon his heart, "The just shall live by . . . faith" (Habakkuh 2:4). He had been teaching that salvation was to be found in a church, in forms, in ritualism and outward things. Now God puts this great Truth in his heart and he goes out to preach it everywhere. When he was called before the Catholic council, someone said to him, "Aren't you afraid?" And he answered, "No—if every tile on every roof in the city should turn to a devil and come against me, yet must I go on." When he stood before the council he stated his position, "Here I stand. I can do no other, God help me." By his staunch stand for the truth he started a movement which swept the world back toward God and toward true religion.

Peter proceeds to preach to them, saying, "You and I and our fathers worshipped the same God. He sent His Son Jesus into the world. You killed Him, but God has raised Him up.

He has exalted Him to the highest place in heaven. The Holy Spirit is now here in His place, empowering us to preach forgiveness in His Name." Again the tables are turned. The prisoner becomes the accuser, and the haughty council members become the criminals.

V. THE PLOT. Verse 33

We read next that these men were "cut to the heart." True preaching does that. When a man preaches the truth, when the Holy Spirit is in his message, sinners are indeed cut to the heart. But what did these sinners decide to do? They decided to kill the preacher. But you can not get rid of the truth by killing the one who brings it to you. The sensible sinner says, "You've cut me to the quick, I see my sin—what must I do to be saved?" That is the right way out. But these sinners were not willing to take that way. Instead they said, "We will kill the preacher." Oh, how wicked is the human heart where Satan dwells!

VI. THE PLEADING. Verses 34-39

One of their leaders, Gamaliel, a very influential man, stood up before the council, and made this request, "Put these men outside for a few minutes, and let us confer about the matter." When the apostles had been put outside, Gamaliel said, "We had better be careful about what we do with these men. You remember the man Theudas, who gathered four hundred men, but he was killed and all his followers with him. Then there was a man named Judas who drew away many people after him. He and his followers also perished. The reason these men failed was because God was not in their work. Now if the work that these apostles are doing is of man it will perish, if it is of God, we cannot stop it, no matter what we do. We would simply be fighting against God." This was mighty good advice, and they decided to take it. This is still good advice for the churches of today. You may not like everything that is being done in your church, but let me advise you not to fight it. If it is the work of man it will fail—if it is God's work, all that you can do will not stop it, and you will simply be destroying yourself.

VII. THE PERSISTENCE. Verses 40-42

After this decision the twelve apostles were called back before the council. The first thing they did with them was to give them a severe beating. This was no little thing—they used a leather whip divided at one end into many strips of leather, and all of these strips were filled with lead and other sharp pieces of metal. The apostles were given thirty-nine stripes each and when the punishment was finished these men were almost dead, and their backs were bruised and bloody. They were then commanded to go out and never again to speak in the Name of Jesus.

Can you imagine these poor men, bloody and humiliated, dragging themselves out of the council chamber? Surely they will give up now. Surely they will quit this business of preaching. No—instead of that I read that they went out rejoicing. What did they have to rejoice over? They rejoiced because Jesus let them suffer shame for Him. Could you rejoice over such things? Or would you resent it if you had to be persecuted for His sake? A real Christian can rejoice when all the world is against him, for he remembers that Jesus is always with him.

I wonder if these men remembered the Sermon on the Mount in which Jesus said, "Blessed are ye, when men shall revile you, and persecute you, and shall say all manner of evil against you falsely, for my sake. Rejoice, and be exceeding glad: for great is your reward in heaven" (Matthew 5:11, 12).

> God has not promised skies always blue,
> Flower strewn pathways all our lives through.
> God has not promised sun without rain,
> Joy without sorrow, peace without pain.

> But God has promised strength for the day,
> Rest for the laborer, light on the way,
> Grace for the trial, help from above,
> Unfailing sympathy, undying love.

Gamaliel and Annas sat in their soft chairs—they sipped the warm wine and dined on rich food. But the bleeding-backed apostles, poor in the goods of this world, but rich in the hope of heaven in their hearts, went from house to house, preaching Jesus Christ. A thousand times would I rather be Peter or James or John than these who persecuted them. I would rather any time be the one persecuted, than the persecutor. The centuries have gone by—the council members have sunk down into oblivion. But the names of the apostles shine high in the history of the world, and their spirits enjoy eternal sunshine on the heights of God. Oh, that we might follow in their train!

When General William Booth, founder of the Salvation Army, died, they placed just one word on his tomb—"PROMOTED." God help us to give our souls and lives away for Jesus Christ, and so live for Him that some day we, too, shall receive our promotion into that upper kingdom where He waits to greet us and to give us His "Well done."

Chapter Six

"SPIRITUAL ORGANIZATION"

Acts 6

The age-long struggle in the realm of Christianity has been a fierce fight. On one side, seeking to advance the kingdom of God, we find the Holy Spirit and the Church —on the other side we find Satan and all of his satanic forces. Satan's work began in the fourth chapter of Acts when we see the bitter persecution aimed at the Early Church. But the apostles stood staunch and God came to their rescue. He delivered them and the work of the Church went on.

In the fifth chapter we see Satan working through Ananias and Sapphira. They lied to the Holy Spirit, and death pounced upon them. Fear fell upon the people and great numbers believed. Then the apostles were arrested by the religious powers. They were beaten and commanded to preach Christ no more, but they went out rejoicing, proclaiming the Gospel stronger than ever.

The devil saw that after each persecution the church was stronger than before. Now, he is not only evil, but he is cunning and wise, so he decides to attack from the inside. He starts a campaign of criticism and faultfinding. It works the same way today—we do not fear any persecution from the outside. No one is going to stop us from holding services, no one is going to shoot us for going to church and worshiping God. So the devil does his work through an inside campaign.

One of the disgraces of Christianity today is that we have so many church quarrels and split-ups. When these things happen friends are divided, people are hurt, sweet relationships are broken, many people quit the church, and the young people of that generation are lost to the service of Christ.

There is no need for any church to have these quarrels. They are usually based, not on the great fundamental doctrines of the faith, but on trivialities, on gossip, hearsay and misunderstandings. Never will there come up in a church one single thing which cannot be settled in prayerful conference —*if we have the Spirit of Christ within us*. When Christians go to quarreling among themselves, Satan sits back and laughs. When in loving unity we march forward in a solid line, the devil trembles and runs away.

I. The Murmuring. Verse 1

By this time the number of believers has greatly multiplied. There are two groups in the church, the Jews and the Greeks. In order to help all those who are in need every church member contributed into the treasury as much as he was able—this money was then divided so that no one would lack anything and all would have plenty . . . The church is now so large that this distribution has become a big task. The Grecians felt that the Grecian widows were not getting a fair share, so they began to complain. Now, it will not do for the church to be divided on this question. The devil would be glad to cause a split and to hinder so many from being saved, but the apostles are not going to allow it. So they had a conference and brought up the matter. Peter presided and presented the problem. "Brethren," he said, "here is the trouble. Several of our Greek brethren have made complaints. They say that the Greek widows are neglected. I have investigated this matter and find their complaint to be justified. Now, of course, no one meant to do this, but we have been so busy preaching and teaching and baptizing new converts that this matter has gotten out of our hands. What do you think we ought to do about it?"

John stood to his feet and said, "Brethren, I am sorry this thing has come up, and we must correct the situation. Our church is going along fine and the Lord is really blessing us; we cannot afford to let the devil get the upper hand. If we have a quarrel in our church it will cause our Lord's work to suffer and the world will laugh at us. They have noticed how we love one another—if we start scrapping they will say that we hate one another." Then Philip said, "There are two courses for us to take —we are either to be preachers of the Gospel or welfare workers. You will remember that our Lord told us to go and preach the Gospel. I think that we ought to give our time to the ministry, and have the church elect someone else to take care of these material matters." Thomas now says, "Brethren, I believe that Philip has the solution to this problem. I make a motion that we ask the church to select seven good, wise, spiritual, faithful men to look after this work." Andrew seconded the motion and it was unanimously carried. Peter was instructed to take the recommendation to the church in conference.

That is the New Testament method—the method that every church should use. The pastor and the deacons or the committees pray over certain matters. They fully discuss these matters and decide what they think is for the best interests of the church. Then they bring the recommendation to the church, and every member has a right to discuss the matter and a right to vote on it.

We note here that the apostles put the redemptive side of the Gospel above the social side. They said, "It is all right to feed people and to help them to have better living conditions, but the most important part of the church's work is to preach the Gospel and present Christ to the people." It was just a few years ago that the social gospel came into prominence.

Some religious leaders said, "The old-time Gospel is out of date. We are not to preach blood salvation, heaven and hell and all of these outmoded doctrines. We have been trying to get men ready to die—now we must help them have a better time in this world." So they began to preach on better living conditions, shorter hours, better wages, world peace, tolerance, and racial prejudice. Brethren, I submit to you that these are the by-products of Christianity. We must preach Christ and Him crucified. We must get men into right relationship with God and then all of these things will work out beautifully.

II THE MULTITUDE. Verses 2-4

The church is now called into conference and Peter makes this statement, "Brethren, there has been some murmuring in our midst. We find that some of the widows have been neglected in the daily ministering of needed things. We have thought and prayed about it, and we are bringing you a recommendation. It is not right that we preachers should give up the more important task of preaching in order to serve tables, so we recommend that you pick out seven good men among yourselves to look after this matter, and we will give ourselves to our ministry."

We read next that the "saying pleased the multitude." I can imagine a dear old brother moving that the recommendation be adopted. There were several seconds, the vote was taken and the recommendation passed unanimously . . . I want you to see the beauty and the harmony and the goodness in all of this. If it had been brought first to an open meeting, all kinds of accusations would have been hurled, some people would have talked out before thinking the matter over, feelings would have been hurt, and all manner of confusion would have resulted. But this small group of good men prayed it out and talked it over. The crowd saw that the apostles were doing what was right for the church.

There were no hard feelings and when the vote was taken everybody was pleased. I think this is the right way to transact church business.

III. THE MEN. Verses 5-6

The word "deacon" is not used here, but all the greatest Bible scholars say that these men were deacons. B. H. Carroll says so, Scofield says so, Alexander McLaren says so, R.B.C. Howell says so—I think these men are right. Later on the deacons are mentioned, one time in Philippians and four times in First Timothy. They are shown to be church officers. There is no place outside of the sixth chapter of Acts where we are told that such men were appointed, so we have every right to believe that these seven men were the first deacons.

What kind of men were to be chosen? (1) They were to be proven men. Deacons are not to be elected until the church has every reason to believe that they are fit for the office. They are to prove their worthiness by their good lives, their faithfulness to all church life, their tithing, and their cooperative spirit. (2) They are to be consecrated men. "Full of the Holy Ghost. . . " (Acts 6:3). (3) They are to be sound in Scripture principles. "Holding the mystery of the faith in a pure conscience" (I Timothy 3:9). We should not have deacons who do not believe the Bible to be the Word of God, along with all the other doctrines included in this belief. (4) They are to be men of intellectual capacity. "Full of wisdom." It is not necessary for them to be college graduates, but they should have good common sense. (5) They are to be men of unswerving loyalty. They are to be loyal to Christ and their convictions, they are to be loyal to the church, they are to be loyal in their serving and their giving. They are to be loyal to their pastor, if he is a worthy man; if not, they should set about to get another one.

Many churches have had troubles which were caused by deacons. Why? Because the church did not go by these Bible qualifications in selecting the deacons. I know certain men who drink freely, but they were ordained as deacons because of the money they could give to the church. If every church would go strictly by these Bible qualifications, we would have a better brand of deacons and our churches would be much better off. There are some people who object to calling the deacons a "board of deacons." They feel that that term means that the deacons are given a certain authority. However, I am sure that those who use the term do not use it in that way. The word "deacon" comes from the word which means "servant"—they are servants of the church. We note here that they were elected to settle a quarrel—not to start one. Deacons should go the limit to keep peace and harmony in the church.

We often get men on the deacon group who do not belong there. This is where the beauty of the rotating system comes in—when their terms run out the church does not have to re-elect them. As your pastor, suppose that I did not come to preach Sunday morning and Sunday night—suppose that I did not attend prayer meeting, I did not tithe, I did not visit the sick or conduct funerals. Would I have the right to be called your pastor, and to receive a salary? Well, there are some deacons who have not been to church in years, they never give, they never serve, their lives are not counting for the Lord. We need a system like this to get them out of office and to give a chance for a good man to serve for God's glory.

The church in Jerusalem is now ready to elect its deacons. One member whispers to another, "I know one man who surely ought to be a deacon." His friend answers, "You must be thinking of Stephen—his was the first name that popped into my mind when Peter brought his recommendation. . ." So he stood up and said, "I nominate Brother Stephen as a deacon—he fills every qualification and there isn't a better man among us." Over there at the end of the pew I see Stephen, bowing his head in humility, while a tear steals down his cheek. The other men were then elected, Philip, Prochorus, Nicanor, Timon, Parmenas and Nicolas. The church did a very wise thing—the complaint had arisen from the Greeks and every deacon elected was a Greek. That is bigness . . . that is the Christian spirit. Christians ought to be "wise as serpents, and harmless as doves" (Matthew 10:16).

When we think of this division of labor, we think of an Old Testament incident. When Moses was snowed under with work, his father-in-law said to him, "This strain will kill you—I advise you to select some able men to help you. Let them judge all the small matters, and you can judge the larger matters." Moses took his advice and the plan worked out mighty well. I tell you, the Bible is the most sensible book of advice in the world.

What did the church do next? They set these men before the preachers and the preachers ordained them. How did they do it? They did it by praying for them and then by laying their hands upon the heads of these men. That is exactly the way that we ordain deacons. We try to do everything in the New Testament way.

IV. THE MULTIPLYING. Verse 7

Here we see the results of the deacons' election. The Word of God was preached, the apostles had more time for it now, and many more people were saved. Even a great company of Jewish priests accepted Christ. This ought to happen in every church. The more good deacons we have, the more souls we ought to see coming to Christ. If all of our deacons would go out to witness as they should, and bring other men into the church where they could hear the Gospel message, we would have a revival in the church every Sunday.

V. THE MOB. Verses 8-15

Now the deacon sometimes becomes a preacher. It happened
in the case of Stephen. He was one of the greatest figures in
the Early Church, he was the first Christian martyr. When
he began preaching he had great power and God prospered
his work. A group from the synagogue began to dispute with
him. This particular synagogue had many Grecians in it.
Stephen himself was a Grecian and here we see his aggres-
siveness in carrying the Christian message straight to his
own countrymen. Saul of Tarsus was probably the Rabbi in
this synagogue. He was a trained speaker, a great thinker and
logician. He debated with Stephen. What a battle of
mental giants this was, with Stephen on one side and Saul
on the other!

What was the subject of their debate? Stephen spoke of
the new order of things which was taking the place of the
old order—the old things that Saul spoke of had been nailed to
the Cross. Stephen spoke of the greater things—he spoke of
a greater person than Moses, a greater sacrifice than all the
bullocks, sheep and goats offered on Jewish altars, he spoke
of a greater day than the Sabbath. He preached the superiority
of Christ to all things in the Old Testament dispensation. Saul
in later years came to believe these things, but at this time
he argued against them. What was the outcome of the debate? Stephen won the debate—Saul and the others were not
able to resist his wisdom and the Spirit which filled him.

These enemies of the Gospel became angry. They had
been badly beaten. A deaf man once went to a big debate.
Someone asked him why he went, since he could not hear.
He said it was always interesting to watch the man who
lost. "For," said he, "the one who gets whipped always gets
mad." This happened after Saul lost this debate to Stephen.
After the debate, Stephen was brought to trial. They hired
some false witnesses, brought Stephen before them, and ac-

cused him of saying blasphemous things about the laws and customs of Moses.

Stephen stood there and listened. He was facing death, but he had no fear. The members of the Council looked steadfastly upon him, and his face looked like an angel's face. Oh, when Christ is in a man's heart as he was in Stephen's heart, a man even becomes different on the outside! If you want to have the new look, the look of the shining face, just come to the Cross. Come to Jesus, open up your heart to Him, let Him come in and possess you and He will make a different person of you. There is more to be said about Stephen, but these things will come in the next sermon.

Oh, I wish that all of us could have what these seven deacons had, as typified by Stephen. I wish that we would all turn our backs upon sin and indifference and say, "Lord Jesus, from now on I am going to be a different person. You can have my best. I will be faithful. I'll put you and the church first in all things." A fine woman in our church, who has been a Christian for just a few years, is very active in the work. She said to me sometime ago, "I must make up for lost time." Do not you, also, need to make up some lost time? Is not it time that you left off some other things and got busy for God?

On one occasion Fritz Kreisler had several hours to spend between trains in a certain city. He decided to walk around and see the sights. He stopped in front of a music store, and saw in the window something which he wanted to purchase. He went into the store and laid his violin case, with his name on it, on the counter. The shopkeeper saw the name on the case and thought that the famous musician's violin had been stolen by this man. He excused himself and going back to the office, called the police. Soon they came and accused this man of stealing Kreisler's violin. He insisted that he was Kreisler, but they would not believe him. Finally he said to the shopkeeper, "Do you have one of Fritz Kreisler's recordings in your shop?" "Yes," replied the man. "Please play this number for me," said Kreisler, "and then I will play the same number on my violin." The record was put on the machine and they listened to the music which had been recorded by Kreisler. Then he picked up his violin and played this same number. The shopkeeper and the policeman stood in amazement. They knew now that this was Kreisler, so they apologized to him profusely, and let him go. You see, his *performance* measured up to his *profession!*

That is what we need today. We profess to be followers of the Lord Jesus Christ. God help us to live up to our profession, even as did the deacons in the Early Church!

CHAPTER SEVEN

"SPIRITUAL ILLUMINATION"

Acts 7

Acts 7 is a drama of intense interest, with Stephen as the chief actor. He had been ordained as a deacon, and later on he had felt God's call to preach. We are told that he was full of faith and power—this was a gift of the Holy Spirit. God spoke to him in such a way that the enemies of the Gospel could not resist him. He defeated the brilliant Saul in debate. Since they could not defeat Stephen in this way, they decided to kill him and get him out of the way. Oh, I tell you, Satan did everything in his power to keep the good news of Christ from being spread!

At the end of Chapter six we find Stephen on trial. His enemies had hired false witnesses to testify against him. They said that he had uttered blasphemous things against Moses and the law. As the members of the council looked upon him they saw a strange thing. His face lit up—it looked like the face of an angel. We will see what happens next as we move into Chapter seven.

1. THE SERMON. Verses 1-53

They gave Stephen a chance to speak for himself, but he did not speak in his own behalf. He forgot his own danger, he preached on the unbelief of Israel, and climaxed his message with the Crucifixion. We notice this about all these men—they did not seem to care what happened to themselves—

83

they were bent on telling people about Christ. Christ told them to preach the Gospel, and they felt if they did what He said, He would take care of them. Is not it always so?

The Queen of England called upon one of her subjects to go on a very important mission for the crown. "But," said the man, "my business will suffer." The Queen said to him, "You serve me, and I will take care of your business." The man went away upon this mission for the Queen. In turn she used her influence for him and the man's business prospered more than ever. I wish that our business men would learn today that if they will serve Christ in the right way, He will take care of them.

Yes, you do what God wants you to do, and He will take care of you. Often I hear a young man saying, "The Lord has called me to preach, but I have a family and other obligations and I can't give up my job and go to school." I have always said to them, "If God has called you to preach, you go right ahead on faith, and God will open up the way for you." I can testify that He did this in my case and He will do it for all those who step out upon His promises.

Now, let us see what Stephen said in his sermon. He began with Abraham, the father of these people, and gave a running review of Israel's history. He showed them that they were not remembering the Scriptures by the way that they acted. They were strong for Moses—and he told them how Moses had prophesied that God would send a prophet like unto Himself, even Jesus. They believed the prophets—and he told them how every prophet had foretold the coming of Christ. He told them how their forefathers had rejected every leader whom God had sent them. He told them how in their sin and disobedience and blindness they had crucified the Messiah, the Lord Jesus. He told them finally how they were rejecting the Holy Spirit, who came to take Christ's place on earth. He ended his sermon by saying, "You are a stiff-necked and unregenerate people. Your forefathers resisted everything a loving God did for them. You are doing the same thing—you are just as bad as they were." Believe me, this was plain, pointed, pungent preaching. This is the kind we need to-day. The preacher needs to say, "Thou art the man—this is what you have done—repent and come to God and beg for His mercy."

II. The Sinners. Verse 54

Look at the twofold result of this sermon. First, they were cut to the heart. The Word of God is like a sword— Stephen had used this sword, thrusting it right into their hearts. He did not argue, he just gave them the Word, and they had no comeback. When men hear some sermons they can say, "The preacher was wrong about that matter." But if every statement is backed up by the Bible, they must admit that they have no further defense for themselves.

Some years ago a man who traveled for a New York firm was in Chicago. He had been stealing small sums of the firm's money until the total now amounted to thousands of dollars. He tried to stifle his conscience by working hard all day and going to places of amusement at night. One morning in his hotel room he was stropping an old fashioned razor. He looked for a piece of paper on which to wipe the blade, but since he could find nothing, he tore a page out of a Bible placed by the Gideons. Suddenly his eyes caught these words, "The wages of sin is death" (Romans 6:23). He smoothed out the piece of paper and read the remaining words of the sentence, "The gift of God is eternal life through Jesus Christ our Lord" (Romans 6:23). Startled by this text he opened the Bible and read for two hours. Then he fell down upon his knees, poured out his heart to God, and rose a new man in Christ Jesus. He went back to New York and confessed his theft to the head of the firm. They decided not to prosecute him, but permitted him to keep on in his work and to pay this money back month by month. You see in this instance the power of God's Word. This is the thing that cut the sinners to the heart when Stephen preached.

The second result was this—"They gnashed on him with their teeth" (Acts 7:54). They were cut to the heart, they were guilty before God and man, but instead of confessing their sins to God, and crying out for forgiveness, they got mad at the preacher. Sinful human beings are like that. It is easier to be angry than to humble yourself and cry out, "God be merciful to me a sinner" (Luke 18:13). But, after all, the best friend is the one who shows you your condition before God and urges you to get right. This is the task of the preacher.

Remember the case of David. He was God's man, but one day temptation knocked at his heart, and David fell into sin. God called on His preacher, saying, "Nathan, go to David and confront him with his sin." Nathan replied: "All right, Lord, I'll tell him a good story and in the end I'll bring him face to face with his sin." Nathan goes down to the palace and says, "Good morning, King David." "Good morning, Brother Nathan," said the King. "I want to tell you a case that has come to my attention," said the preacher. And then he told his story, painting the picture of the villain in the story. When he had finished the king cried out, "Who is this wicked fellow? Tell me who he is and I will see that he is killed." "Thou art the man," (II Samuel 12:7) said Nathan. Then David saw his sin and felt his guilt and cried out, "I have sinned" (II Samuel 12:13). Nathan quickly said to him, "The Lord also hath put away thy sin" (II Samuel 12:13). David did not get mad at the preacher, he saw himself guilty, he cried out unto God, and God forgave him. These sinners at Jerusalem were not as wise as David. They knew they were guilty, but they took it out on poor old Stephen.

III. THE STANDING. Verses 55-56

They gnashed their teeth, but Stephen paid no attention to them—he was looking upward. He was looking toward Someone else—the One to whom we all should look in time of trouble. Oh, that we might be as wise as Stephen. We look at all the circumstances and troubles, we get discouraged —we find no hope in the world—what we need to do is to look up.

When Jesus bade Peter to walk on the water, he stepped out upon the waves and began to walk toward the Master, but the minute he took his eyes off Jesus he began to sink. Always we are to "keep looking up."

An earthly court was trying Stephen, but he knew he was not accountable to them. He looked up toward the heavenly court, the Supreme Court of the universe. He knew that his case was before that Court, and he looked there for vindication. And what did he see? Oh, the wonder of it! He saw God on His throne and Jesus standing at His right hand, the place of authority and power.

When Jesus went back to heaven we are told that He sat down at the Father's right hand, where He is to remain un- til His return to earth. But here we see Him standing up. Oh, the glory of this scene! Some say that He stood in honor of the first Christian martyr, but a deeper truth than this lies behind it all. Stephen needed help, and he looked toward heaven for it. When you expect someone to help you, you do not expect him to sit down. So here we see Jesus rising, stretching out a hand of help in the time of crisis . . . Oh, my friends, he will always do that! Are you lost? Call upon His Name and He will reach down and save you. Are you groping in doubt? Tell Him all about it, and He will reach down a hand to assure you. Are you carrying a heavy load? Just appeal to Him and He will get under that load with you. Are you under a deep sorrow? Look to Him and He will give you comfort and peace. Are you approaching the end of the way? Put all your trust in Him and He will be waiting for you. Yes, He is a wonderful Saviour! When you need help, you will find that He is always ready.

We see here, also, that heaven is interested in earth. Stephen was down here, and Jesus was up there, yet He was interested in what was happening on earth. He was standing ready to help. He stands ready to help us, too. There is a song which has the title, "I Walk Alone." This is not true if you are a Christian. The world may forsake you, but if you are trusting Him, you have a Divine Companion. He has been all along the way of life, and knows how to help us.

We are told that in Africa a group of people who are going to make a journey always send some "bushbeaters" a-head of them. These natives scare out the wild animals and make the way safe. Jesus does more than that. He not only makes the way safe, but He goes along with us. We can say then with Job, "I know that my Redeemer liveth" (Job 19:25). And with David we can say, "Though I walk through the valley of the shadow of death, I will fear no evil: for thou art with me" (Psalm 23:4). Yes, Jesus is in heaven and we are here, but He is interested in us.

Here is another thought—heaven is ready for us. Jesus said, "I go to prepare a place for you" (John 14:2). The home is prepared and He is ready to greet us and take us in. When I was a boy I lived in a small town forty-eight miles from Atlanta. One summer I had the privilege of going to the big city. I was a bit scared as I began the journey. The city was a strange place to me—I knew nothing about it. But my elder brother had gone before me . . . He met me at the train and guided me about the city. He knew his way around—he knew exactly what to do, so I was not a stranger long. Heaven seems to be a dim, distant place, but we have an elder brother, Jesus, Who has gone on before. He is waiting for us and when we meet Him, we know that we will be home at last.

What a comfort it must have been for Stephen, that he could look up and see Jesus standing in heaven. If you will only look up to the Cross and see Him dying there, and will accept Him as your Saviour, some day you will also go up to heaven, and you will find Him waiting there for you.

IV. THE STOPPING. Verse 57

Stephen told the men what he saw, saying, "Behold, I see the heavens opened and the Son of man standing on the right hand of God" Acts 7:56). When he said this the people cried out, they stopped their ears and ran upon him ... People still stop their ears to God's truth. When you tell them how wonderful they are, they will listen. When you tell them that they are poor guilty sinners and need to come in humility to God, they will say, "None of that for me'"' —they stop their ears, they close their hearts. Christ knocks, but they will not let Him in. At last He will turn sadly away and they will go headlong down into hell. Jesus says, "If you have ears, listen to the Spirit." Some of you are Christians, but the ears of your hearts are not open to Christ. He is telling you to put Him first, to be faithful, to give your best, to have Christ's spirit of love for others in your heart. But you will not listen—you have stopped your ears. God help you!

Sin is a progressive thing. It began here with hatred in the heart and grew until the cry rises: "Let's stone him—let's put him to death." So they rushed upon him, they took him out of the city and stoned him. These men are red-hot with anger, and they eagerly set to work. They took off their robes so that they might have more strength and liberty. Then they went to work on a man at whom they were not even worthy to look. What did they do with their robes? They put them at the feet of the young man, Saul. This shows us that he was the leader—all that was done was under his supervision. This is something that Saul never forgot. The time will come when he sees Jesus, falls before Him, and gives his whole life to the Master. The time will come when like Stephen, he, too, will die for Jesus' sake.

VI. THE SPIRIT. Verse 60-a

I want you to see here that Stephen had the spirit of His Master. As death came upon him, he cried out, "Lord Jesus receive my spirit" (Acts 7:59). He looked up into Jesus' face and said, "Lord, the stones are hard, the enemies are strong, but it does not matter, all I want is to come and be with Thee. I know that Thou couldst save me from all of this, but I know that it is better for me to depart and be with Thee." How will it be with you when you come down to death? When Admiral Grayson told Woodrow Wilson that he was dying, Mr. Wilson said, "I am ready." Will you be able to say that? Can you say, "I am ready, Lord, I have trusted Thee as my Saviour, I have tried to live for Thee, and now I long to come home and be with Thee?" Or when you come to the end of the way, must you cry out, "My God, give me a little more time!"

Will you Christians have to say, "I trusted Thee as my Saviour, but I have not lived for Thee, and I am ashamed to meet Thee"? Stephen was ready—gladly did he go up to meet Jesus. I can imagine that all the angels, gathered at the gate, sang their grandest song of welcome as Jesus greeted Stephen, and escorted them as Jesus led Stephen to his mansion in the sky.

As Stephen dies, he kneels down and offers his last prayer, "Lord, lay not this sin to their charge" (Acts 7:60). They were putting him to death, but he was praying for them. Where did he learn to pray in this manner? I know. I see a Cross on a lonely hill . . . I see a man dying there for me. He looks down upon the crowd, then looking up to heaven, He prays, "Father, forgive them; for they know not what they do" (Luke 23:34). Stephen tried to live like Christ—now he is dying like Him. It is probable that he died on Calvary, where Jesus died. This hill was outside the city, and was the ordinary place of execution. Remembering all of this, he exhibited the same spirit that Jesus had.

Stephen knew that in two minutes he would stand before Christ, the Great Judge. Why did not he pray for himself? Why did not he spend this time getting ready to face the judgment? Ah, he had done that long ago! He had no fear for himself, for he knew that he belonged to Jesus, and that he would soon be with Him. When you come to die, what will be your prayer? Will you have to ask forgiveness for your sins, or is it well with your soul now? Death may come sooner than you think. Now is the time to get ready for it. Trust Christ and you will have no fear in that hour.

Stephen prayed for those who killed him. The days went by and his prayer was answered. Saul, the chief persecutor, was saved. Stephen's prayer and Stephen's spirit shook him to the depths. God was preparing Saul for his conversion. God help us to have such a spirit that others will be shaken and will want to know our Christ.

VII. THE SLEEPING. Verse 60-b

With this wonderful vision rejoicing his heart, with a tender prayer for his enemies, Stephen fell asleep. Jesus often spoke of the Christian's death as a sleep. And what a wonderful sleep it is! We go to sleep here at night and when we wake in the morning we face the same old trials and troubles. But this is a sleep from which none ever wake to weep. We fall asleep and we wake up in heaven. Stephen fell asleep, but his soul went winging home to glory. The stones of the slayers were changed into jewels for his crown. There is no loneliness in such a death. Heaven's court opened to receive him. Jesus was there to welcome His faithful friend. Oh, how blessed, how victorious, to die in Christ!

Stephen was one of the few Bible characters about whom we find no regrets. He had no period of early persecution like Paul. He had no flame of anger like John, no doubting like Thomas, no cowardice and denial like Peter. He was so completely given up to Christ that we find no stain nor tarnish on his character. If we are going to influence the world for God, we ought to be like Stephen, because he was like the Master. We may have splendid church buildings, music that charms and delights, eloquence in the pulpit, respectability in the pews, but unless we have something of the same spirit of Stephen, it is all in vain.

However, before we can be victorious in the outer life, there must be an inward goodness and a spiritual heart. Before we have the shining face, we must have the glowing heart. Before we can have the outward change which is seen by men, there must come the inward change which is caused by Christ. Stephen had it, and so can we if we give Jesus the rightful place in our hearts.

A rich man of France dearly loved the song of the nightingale. He wanted some of these birds singing in his own gardens, so he set about to get some of them to come and live in these gardens. He reasoned that if he made the grounds comfortable and happy for the nightingales, they would come. So first he banished the cats and the hawks and the owls, enemies of the nightingale. Then he plowed the ground and filled it with the kind of worms of which the nightingales are especially fond. He studied all the literature he could find about nightingales, and did everything to make a paradise for them.

During the first year none came. It was the same during the second year; but as the shadows fell in the late afternoon of a day during the third year, he was greeted with a delightful song of a pair of nightingales. This was the first pair, but soon others followed and his garden came to be known as "The Garden of the Nightingales." Oh, if we want the Spirit of God to fill our hearts with heavenly music, we must banish all evil from them. We must prepare the soil in earnest prayer, and we must invite the heavenly Spirit to come in and possess us as He did Stephen.

Stephen lived a glorious life and died a glorious death. What kind of a death are you going to die? A prisoner in a Pennsylvania prison contracted a dread disease. He asked the doctor, "Is there any hope for me?" And the doctor answered, "No, there is no hope." The man looked up into the sky and cried out, "I can't go out there alone—God is up there waiting for me." The chaplain told him that God was merciful. He tried to help him, but it was too late. He had hardened his heart against the Holy Spirit so long that he could not even listen to the message of hope. He said, "I can't face God alone—send for my old father—he will be glad to die for me." The father came, but he could not help his son. He had to stand by and see him die. The last thing that the son said was, "I can't meet God alone."

What a contrast to the victorious death of Stephen! Stephen knew that God was waiting for him, too, but he had no fear. He went out to meet Him with great delight in his heart. God is waiting for you, too. How will it be when the time comes for you to go·out to meet Him?

CHAPTER EIGHT

"SPIRITUAL DISSEMINATION"

Acts 8

According to the dictionary the word dissemination means "spreading abroad, as of ideas and beliefs." In Acts eight we see the beginning of the dissemination of the Gospel. Since the Holy Spirit came the message has been confined to Jerusalem—now is the time for the Gospel to start flowing out towards the ends of the earth. Jesus said, "Go ye into all the world" (Mark 16:15). Again He said, "Ye shall be witnesses unto me, both in Jerusalem, and in Judaea, and in Samaria, and unto the uttermost part of the earth" (Acts 1:8). They had witnessed in Jerusalem—now is the time for them to spread out. It is strange that the Spirit had to use persecution to get them to go elsewhere preaching the Gospel.

I. THE SORROWS. Verses 1-3

These Christians had great joy in Jerusalem. It was there that they accepted the Saviour, it was there that the Holy Spirit fell upon them, it was there that God had done great things for them, it was there that they had enjoyed the sweetest fellowship. But they had had sorrows, also. The man is wrong who thinks that he will have nothing but sunny days if he becomes a Christian.

One sorrow that they had was the loss of Stephen. He was a good man, a blessing to the church and a power in

94

the work. But his enemies snatched him away, took him out and stoned him to death, then we read that he was buried, "and [they] made great lamentation over him" (Acts 8:2).

The world is always poorer when a good man dies. Some men die and no one takes note of it. Such men live for themselves, they make no contribution to the world, and when they leave it no one is better off. If you want to live on in the hearts of others after you are dead, you must live for Christ and others, then your works will follow you. Jesus died, but He lives on in the hearts of men. Paul died, but he lives on in his great teachings. Truett died, but he lives on in a great church. Scarborough died, but he lives on in a great school. Stephen died, but he lived on in the hearts of the believers. When a great tree falls in the forest, the entire forest is shaken. When a good and great man dies, the world feels it. How will it be when you pass on? Will the world miss you? Will others be sad? Or will your name just take up another line in the obituary column? Be careful how you live—you must die some day.

After Stephen's death other sorrows came. Saul directed Stephen's death, then went all out in a bitter campaign of persecution. He organized persecution groups, he went into every house in the city where Christians could be found, took them off to prison and put many of them to death. I can imagine a little family in a humble home: the father, the mother and the two children sit by the fireside reading the Scriptures, talking about Jesus, and praying. Suddenly the door is broken open. Several strong men rush in. They grasp the Christians, separate them from each other, and hustle them off to prison. Maybe they never saw each other again in this world, but they were safe in Jesus and surely they had a happy reunion in heaven. We do not read of one case where any Christian denied Christ in order to save his own life. They stood true even though it meant death. Would you stand true?

We read that Saul "made havoc of the church" (Acts 8:3). This is a tragic thing to do, but in this modern age we still have those who do the same thing. The devil uses people in an effort to destroy the work of the church. Some members are not content to see the church going well, and people happily serving God, so they try to hurt the church. God will take care of them—I do not want to be in their shoes. It is easier to tear down than to build up—I want to be a builder. The years went by and Saul the persecutor, became Paul the preacher. He looks back in sorrow upon those days, saying: "beyond measure I persecuted the church of God" (Galatians 1:13). I do not want to have any memories like that. I never want to be forced to think that I did anything to keep the church of Christ from being what it ought to be.

II. THE SCATTERING. Verse 4

Stephen, the first Christian martyr, had met death at the hands of the enemies of the Gospel, and had gone on to glory. Now these enemies waxed bolder. They said, "We've killed one of their leaders—now let's get them all. Let us find every Christian and put them to death, and soon we will stamp out Christianity." Poor deluded souls! They believed like many people believe today. They believed that Christianity was a human thing, and that if you killed the people who believed you killed the Gospel. Oh, Christianity is more than human— *Christianity is Christ* and no one is able to destroy Him! Christians may die, but Christ lives on. He takes them up to heaven, but He raises up other Christians to stand in their place.

"The blood of the martyrs is the seed of the church." Where one dies for the faith, five spring up to take his place. The greatest growth of the church comes, not when

she is at ease in Zion and filled with plenty, but when hardships come and the devil drives. Why is this true? Because
in times of trouble men come closer to God than ever before,
and the closer they get to Him the more courage and more
power they have to serve Him.

Now the persecution begins—every Christian in Jerusalem
is hounded down and many of them are put to death. The
others fled and were scattered to all parts of Judea and
Samaria. We note that those who went out were not
apostles, but laymen. Why? Maybe they felt that they should
stay in Jerusalem and keep a strong home base, sending missionaries out to the ends of the earth. How can we do our
part to send the messengers of the Cross around the world?
We can keep a strong church at home, we can keep faithful,
we can build up a home church that will be a supply
station, sending out the Gospel to all parts of the world.

Why did God allow this suffering, why were they scattered?
It is time for the Gospel to move out. The Gospel carriage has
been in a rut, the preaching has been to the Jews only. Now it
is time to get on the main line, the line that leads to every
nation under the sun. The first stop was at Samaria. These
are the people that the Jews hated. They would cross the
Jordan to the east and go many extra miles out of their
way to keep from putting foot in Samaria. But God is saying
to these Christians, "You are followers of Christ now, and
there is to be no more racial prejudice. I love these people
as much as I do you. Christ died as much for them as He
did for you. Go and tell them of your Saviour." Humbly, and
with the spirit of their Master, they put their prejudices
aside and went to Samaria.

What did they do when they arrived in their new homes?
They told their neighbors about Jesus. They had something
in their hearts which they could not keep to themselves.
They loved Christ, they were filled with the Holy Spirit,

they were bursting with the good news. Oh, if you have had a vital experience with Christ, you are impelled to speak out for Him. You do not have to mount a pulpit, but you do have to witness. Some husbands and wives have lived together for years, yet one will say of the other, "I dont' know whether he or she is a Christian." A boy who was converted one Sunday night said to the pastor, "I am afraid of what the boys at the shop will say and do when they learn that I have become a Christian." The pastor said, "You go right ahead and live for Christ and we will be praying for you." The next Sunday night the pastor asked him how he got along that week, and he answered, "Fine, they never even suspected that I was a Christian." It will not be that way if you have had a vital experience with Christ.

When these folks left Jerusalem, they took their Christianity with them. Many people move away from home and leave their Christianity back there. There are thousands of unchurched people in our city, people who left their religion in a little church or a little cemetery back in the country. Just think of how our churches would be strengthened if these people would line up and go to work. A certain family in a town where I was holding a meeting said this, "We like the pastor and the church and the people, but haven't placed our membership in this church, because we don't know whether we will be here permanently or not." When they were asked how long they had been there, the reply was, "We have been here twenty years." Twenty years wasted! Think of what these people could have meant to that church if they had lined up for the Lord. When you move to a new place you ought to take your Christianity with you as these believers did.

Today we are prone to say that it is the preacher's job to spread Christianity. We notice here that the ones who went out to do this were not preachers, but laymen. In the work of Christ we are not to make a distinction between ministers and others. The layman is under the same obligation to witness as is the preacher. Every converted man is to teach what he knows—all who have drunk of the living water should become fountains of blessing. Our churches will never be what they ought to be until all of us get on the firing line as soldiers of the Cross. So here we see the Christians scattered everywhere, and it is all for a purpose—that they might carry the good news of Christ to men. Those who drove them out meant to put out the fire—Christ let it all happen so that the fire would spread!

III. The Success. Verses 5-8

We come now to another great figure in the Early Church—Philip. Stephen's name was first in the list of deacons, he became a preacher and the first martyr. Philip's name was next. He stepped into Stephen's place and went out to carry the Gospel. Where did he go? He went to Samaria, the capitol of the country which the Jews hated. Jesus had been there and had preached the Gospel there—Philip was the next one to do it. What did he preach? He preached Christ unto them. I imagine that he drew great crowds—the people were curious about him. They said, "Here is a man who was driven out of Jerusalem—let us see what he has to say." He did not tell them about conditions back in Judea, nor about capital and labor, nor about what the government was doing. He preached Christ, a thing which we wish every preacher would do.

His preaching accomplished miracles. Unclean spirits were cast out and the sick and the lame were healed. God gave him power to do these things in order to back up the Gospel story, and to prove that all of it was true. The Samaritans knew of God's power and feared Him. Philip told them that God loved them, and that Christ had died for them, also. When they heard the message, the whole city was filled with joy. One of the deepest longings of the human heart is to feel sure that the great God of the universe sympathizes with us and loves us. Philip made these people feel that. He made them know that if they accepted Christ, they would share all of the blessings and be assured of eternal life. He told of a Saviour who was rich, but who became poor in order that they might become rich. He told of a Saviour who wore a crown of glory, but who laid this crown aside and wore a crown of thorns, that they might have a crown of life. He told them of a Saviour who died that they might live forever. Surely no one ever brought as sweet a message to any people.

Yes, great joy came to the city, for souls were saved, lives were changed, and homes were made over. Suppose I had the power to go into every home in our city where there is a drinking father, a sinful son, or a worldly daughter—suppose that I could take Jesus with me and introduce Him in such a way that these people would come to love Him. All the power of sin would be cast out, these lives would be transformed into active Christian lives, and oh, what a joy there would be in our city! Happiness and joy and hope would take the place of tears and sorrow, and life would have a new meaning for thousands.

Someone asked an old man if he had lost anything when he became a Christian. He replied, "Yes, before I was saved I had an old slouch hat, a ragged suit, and holes in my shoes. I lost them all long ago. I drank to excess and quarreled with my wife—I lost all of that. I had a wicked heart and a hardened conscience—I lost them. I had a thousand guilty fears—I lost them. My wife had an aching heart—she spent sleepless nights worrying about me, she did without the necessities of life—all that is past. Yes, I lost many bad things when I accepted Christ." The Samaritans lost these things, too. Great joy came to the city, for Jesus had visited in their midst.

IV. THE SORCERER. Verses 9-25

In Samaria there was a sorcerer, an evil magician named Simon. He told all the people that he was a great man, and they believed him. They said, "This man is the great power of God" (Acts 8:10). He had thousands of followers in the city. When Philip came to Samaria, he talked not of himself as Simon did, but he talked of Christ. The people immediately saw the difference. Philip did things which Simon would not even attempt. Soon Simon's crowd left him—they listened to Philip and believed on Christ. Now we read that, "Simon himself believed also" (Acts 8:13). After his baptism he followed Philip around, watching all the miracles that he performed. Was Simon a saved man? There is much doubt about it—probably he just went along with the crowd. It is certain that he was more interested in the miracles than in learning more of Christ.

About this time the apostles in Jerusalem heard about the great revival in Samaria and sent Peter and John to the city. When they saw what had happened, they rejoiced in the salvation that had come to the Samaritans, and prayed for them to receive the Holy Spirit. Now we are taught that the Holy Spirit comes into the hearts of people when they believe on Christ. Possibly here it means that these people did not possess the fulness of the Spirit, or they had not received the Spirit's power to do the works which Philip was doing. So the apostles prayed, laid their hands upon these people, and they received the Holy Spirit.

When Simon saw what had happened he said, "That is what I want—if I could have power to bestow the Holy Spirit upon people, I could make all kinds of money." He envied Philip—he wanted Philip's power. He had not received this power when he was baptized, so he decided to buy it from Peter. "Peter," he said, "here is money—sell me this power." The angry apostle blazed out, "Your money perish with you—you are a fool to think that you can buy God's gift with your money. Your heart is not right, repent and ask God to forgive you." Did Simon admit his guilt? No, he simply exhibited fear. Instead of praying for himself, he asked Peter to pray for him. There is no evidence that he ever repented. He is an example of those who believe in the power of God, who would like some of the blessings, but who will not come in the only way a man can secure these blessings—through humility, repentance, and heart-felt faith.

You cannot buy the things which God gives freely. You cannot buy salvation, forgiveness, heaven, or spiritual life with the coin of this world. A rich man would like to live for the world and at the end of the way buy his ticket to glory, but he cannot do this. A lazy man would like to buy spiritual power, but he cannot do it. A sinful man would like to buy forgiveness, but he cannot do it. In the old days the Catholics sold indulgences. If a man wanted to commit a certain sin, all he had to do was to pay, then go right ahead and everything would be all right. But it is not all right.

All the blessings that God has for us are free so far as material things are concerned. We pay for them in penitence, in humility, in confession, in prayer and full surender. You can send a big check to the church treasurer, but this will not buy a great Christian life or the blessings of God. But when you come in humble, contrite surrender, all God has is yours.

V. THE SEEKER. Verses 26-35

Philip was in the midst of a great revival in Samaria. He was a popular preacher and attracted great crowds. He was an effective preacher, and many people were saved. One day when he started out to preach, God said to him, "Arise, Philip, leave the city and go down into the desert." Philip was puzzled. Did he ask God why he should do this? Did he say, "Lord, look at my crowds, I am doing a good work, why should I go into the desert?" No—God's voice was his authority. He left the city behind and started toward the desert . . . Sometimes the captain of a ship receives sealed orders. He leaves port and sails out to a certain latitude and longitude. There he opens his orders, and only then does he learn his destination. So Philip goes out under sealed orders—he goes a hundred miles before he knows why God had sent him in this direction.

Then one day as Philip walked along the desert road, he saw a bright chariot. This chariot contained a prominent man, a man who was surrounded by servants and retainers in other chariots. Who is this man? He is a man of great authority—treasurer of the Queen of Ethopia. What is he doing here? He has been to Jerusalem to worship. Probably he was a Jewish proselyte who had been to Jerusalem to attend the great feasts. But somehow these things did not satisfy. He went to the Holy City longing for living water, but he was still thirsty. He went there hungry for the bread of life, but he was still hungry. So as he rides along in the chariot he opens his Bible and reads the Word of God, hoping to find peace for his heart. He is an earnest seeker after truth. I can imagine him saying, "How can a hungry soul be fed? How can I find peace for my heart and forgiveness for my sin?" Seek, oh, treasurer, your salvation is nigh . . . No one ever turned to God in vain!

The Holy Spirit now says to Philip, "Go near and join thyself to this chariot" (Acts 8:29). Now the preacher knows why he was sent into the desert. Here is a man needing salvation, a man who can take the Gospel to his entire country.

There is a Providence that shapes our ends. God plans everything from the foundation of the world. It was His plan for these men to start out, ignorant of each other, and then to come together at this spot, in this hour. God has plans for you, too. Maybe God sends you to church some morning that your heart and the message might meet—and that you might have one more chance to be saved. Be careful how you treat God's providences.

Philip doesn't ask whether this man is rich or poor, prominent or obscure. He runs to the chariot of the Ethiopian. We note that the word "Ethiopian" comes from two Greek words meaning "to burn the face." This indicated that the Ethiopians were colored people, but this does not matter to Philip, nor to any true child of God. He will sit down by any man, white, black, brown, yellow or red, if he can only lead him to Christ. The man was reading, "He was led as a sheep to the slaughter; and like a lamb dumb before his shearer, so opened he not his mouth: in his humiliation his judgment was taken away: and who shall declare his generation? for his life is taken from the earth" (Acts 8:32, 33). Philip said to him: "Do you understand that Scripture?" And the man replied: "No, I don't understand it, I need someone to guide me. Is the prophet talking of himself or of some other man?" What did Philip do? He seized this opportunity and preached Jesus to the eunuch. He said: "Isaiah was talking about Christ, the Messiah, God's own Son. He sent Him down into the world and Christ died on the Cross for our sins. If you will believe on Him, accept Him as your Saviour, you will be saved." God bless that faithful preacher! He found a soul seeking satisfaction and salvation, heaven and happiness, but he did not tell him to do the best that he could do, to do good works, to treat others rightly—he preached Christ. He told him that the only hope he could ever find would be in Him.

VI. THE SALVATION. Verses 36-40

As they rode along, they came to a body of water, and the man said, "Here is water, why cannot I be baptized?" Philip had told him how to be saved—the next step was obedience in baptism. Baptism has nothing to do with salvation. Philip said, "I am ready to baptize you if you believe in Christ." The man cried out, "I do—with all my heart I believe. I am ready to follow Him forever."

Stop the chariot! A man has been born again and he is ready for a preacher to baptize him. See him as he gets out of the chariot. The Bible tells us that he went down into the water and was baptized.

We read that when they came up out of the water, the Spirit caught Philip away and took him to another post of duty. The man got back into his chariot and went on his way rejoicing. He had something to rejoice over—he had Jesus in his heart, his name was written in the Lamb's Book of Life, he had a Friend to walk down every lonely road with him, and to help him in every task.

Oh, friend, take Jesus as he did, and you will have joy in your heart, too. You will have something that the world cannot give and cannot take away. The Spirit took Philip away, but the man had Jesus left. If Jesus is in our hearts, we may lose health, we may lose wealth, we may lose our loved ones, we may lose our friends, but we can still have a joy that surpasses anything that the world can give.

So the Ethiopian treasurer went happily on his way. He went back to Ethiopia with the Gospel and used his life and influence for Christ. In later years Ethiopia became a great Christian country, greater far than Samaria, where Philip had been holding the big meeting. May God be thanked for this faithful Gospel preacher and this earnest new convert! And thanks be to God who causes His Gospel to be carried to a lost world.

A ship was wrecked not far from shore, and a man and his wife and little girl were thrown into the water. The man was a good swimmer. He started toward the shore with his wife clinging to one arm and his little girl to the other. Soon he felt his strength ebbing away—he knew that he could not make the shore with both of them. Which one should he leave behind? He must do that or all three would go down. It was a heart-breaking decision for him to make, but finally he shook off the little girl and swam away with her mother—away from the little child's pitiful, dying cries.

Bless God, Jesus never had to make a choice like that! He can save everyone who comes to Him by faith. He saved the Ethiopian. He can save you. Trust Him today and He will bring you safely home.

CHAPTER NINE

"SPIRITUAL TRANSFORMATION"

Acts 9

Paul the apostle was a Roman citizen, born in Tarsus, a Hebrew of the Hebrews, a Pharisee of the Pharisees. He was the most self-righteous man who ever lived, yet he was the chief of sinners. He was the worst enemy of Christ and the Church, putting thousands to death, yet he became the greatest servant of Christ the world has ever known. He probably suffered more for Christ, worked harder for Christ, and won more souls to Christ than any other Christian. He was a man of marvelous personality and of the mightiest Christian experience. He was a prolific writer of some of the world's greatest literature, and the most convincing preacher of the ages. Let us study his conversion in Acts nine."

I. THE MADMAN. Verses 1-2

At the close of chapter eight Philip was going everywhere evangelizing. Chapter nine begins with a bitter contrast. We see Saul going everywhere persecuting Christians. One sought to lead people to Christ, the other sought to destroy Christians. One was filled with the love of Christ, the other with a hatred born in hell. The more people accepted Christ, the madder Saul became. He vowed in his soul that this would not go on, that he would stamp out Christianity if he had to kill every believer on the face of the earth.

Before this time the Sanhedrin had been persecuting the believers in Jerusalem. But this was not enough for Saul. He took over the leadership and pushed the battle, not only throughout Jerusalem, but unto the ends of the Empire.

Saul was a very religious man, but he was an example of a man who had the wrong religion. You have heard someone say, "Any religion is all right, just so you are sincere." That is wrong. Saul was sincere, but his sincerity was in the wrong direction. If his sincerity had been toward the true religion, he would not have been known as the madman, whose chief delight was the killing of Christians. What did Saul have against Christians? Why did he persecute them? What stirred him to such actions?

(1) Saul looked for the Messiah, a Jewish hero who would sit on David's throne, bringing all nations under the royal law. When they called this humble peasant, Jesus, "The Messiah," Saul became furious.

(2) He believed in the Temple and all the Old Testament sacrifices and ceremonies. They said all of this was out of date, and he cried out, "Blasphemy."

(3) He was a proud self-righteous son of Abraham, and they had the effrontery to tell him that he had to humble himself and be born again.

(4) He had a synagogue in Jerusalem, and Stephen's preaching was making inroads upon his congregation. Great numbers were leaving him and going over to Christianity.

(5) He was a proud, well educated Rabbi. He knew that he was a brilliant expert in the Law and the Prophets, yet Stephen had soundly defeated him in debate and his pride was hurt.

(6) But Saul found himself whipped on the inside. He remembered Stephen's shining face, his last prayer, his death. He knew that Stephen had something that he did not have. His conscience would not let him go free.

With a heart filled with poison and hatred, he went out

upon his tour of persecution. He said, "I will get rid of this heavy heart. I will track these Christians down and kill them. I will stamp out Christianity. Then I will go back to the quietness of my synagogue and have peace in my heart." Let us follow him and see what he did.

(1) He "made havoc of the church" (Acts 8:3). The picture here is that of a wild boar in a garden, rooting, gnashing and trampling. That is what Saul did to the Church.

(2) He was "breathing out threatenings and slaughter" (Acts 9:1). Even his breath was filled with murder.

(3) He "dragged them in by violence." Not only did he take people off the street, he went into their homes. A man's home is his castle, but Saul disregarded that right. He would go into a home, snatch a grey-haired mother, a lovely young wife, or a sweet little child and drag them through the streets to their doom.

(4) He scourged them. The customary thirty-nine lashes were laid heavily upon the shoulders of both men and women.

(5) He put them in prison.

(6) He exiled them from their own country, traced them to foreign countries, and arrested them there.

(7) He voted for their death, and probably saw many of them die. Sherman's march through Georgia during the Civil War covered an area seventy-five miles wide. From Atlanta to the sea the soldiers burned and pillaged; they did not leave a house nor a fence standing. This was the type of devastation which Saul wrought upon the Church.

We must remember that everything he inflicted upon others, Saul later suffered himself. He had them whipped, and five times he was beaten. He had them put in prison, and often he was imprisoned. He expatriated them, and later he was driven from his home. He pursued them into other countries, and he likewise was pursued, He had them stoned, and he was stoned. He had them put to death, and he was put to death.

Here we see him going into Damascus. He heard that there were some Christians in the city, and he was going after them, to arrest them and bring them to Jerusalem. He got letters of introduction to the Rabbi in Damascus. He secured some attendants to help him and he set out on his journey. Oh, Saul, you do not know what this journey is going to mean to you! Christ up in heaven has His eyes upon you. You made others suffer—He is going to change your heart and send you out to suffer and to die for Him. Your trip was primarily to Damascus, Saul, but it is the beginning of a journey which will lead to suffering, hardships and sacrifice. But the end of that journey is in the city of God, by the side of the blessed Lord, where joys never cease and glory never fades.

II. THE MASTER. Verses 3-9

The journey to Damascus required several days. Now noon of the last day arrived, and the groves of Damascus were in sight. Saul was planning how he would harry the poor Christians he would find in the city. The head driver of the caravan came to him and said, "Sir, it is time for us to rest. It is the custom at the hour of noon for the men and beasts to stop for rest and refreshment under the shade of the trees." But Saul blazed out, "Not this caravan. You have been paid well. Go on. There will be no rest until we reach Damascus." So the caravan moved on over the hill.

Suddenly there was a blinding flash of lightning. Saul fell prostrate to the ground. As he lay there he heard a voice from heaven saying, "Saul, Saul why persecutest thou me?" Saul knew he was being confronted by God. He knew that voice was the voice of authority.

Half-dazed he called out, "Who art thou, Lord?" (Acts 9:5)

The voice answered, "I am Jesus whom thou persecutest: It is hard for thee to kick against the pricks" (Acts 9:5).

Saul answered meekly, "Lord, what wilt thou have me to do?" (Acts 9:6).

The question that was asked was not, "Why persecutest thou these Christians?" but, "Why persecutest thou Me?" Saul was persecuting Christians, but he did not know he was persecuting God. God gave him to understand that when a child of His is hurt—God is hurt. It is true today. If some servant of the Lord is trying to do the Lord's work and is persecuted, not only is he hurt, but also the cause of Christ, and the heart of God. He who is Almighty will not stand aside and see this done without punishment. Saul came here to learn the greatest lesson of his life. He knew that the Lord was speaking, yet the voice said, "I am Jesus" (Acts 9:5). He came to know that God and Christ are one. He came to know that the Jesus whom he hated was the God he sought to serve. All the time he had been fighting Jesus, he was fighting God. What a rude awakening he had! How he must have been filled with sorrow!

Jesus said, "It is hard for thee to kick against the pricks" (Acts 9:5). In Bible times they used oxen to pull the plows. At first these animals would rebel and would fling their heels back in protest against the beam. So the farmer would use a cruel device. He would put sharp iron spikes on the beam; then when the oxen kicked they would be sharply wounded. Even a very stubborn ox would soon get tired of this and settle down to work.

These pricks had been sticking the conscience of Saul. First, he could not get away from Stephen's angelic face and the sweet spirit with which he met death. He knew that he could not face death as peacefully. Then he had seen these other Christians suffer and die. He saw their heroism, the peace written on their faces, and their hope in the hour of death. He knew they had something different, something his Pharisaism had not given him. He kept asking himself the question, "What inspires these Christians? Could Christ be true? Was He really the Messiah?" He tried to put these thoughts down, but they kept on rising. His conscience was pricking him.

Saul surrendered. He knew that it was all true—he knew that Christ is the secret of the believer's hope. Humbly and meekly he asked, "Lord, what would you have me do?" No longer is he breathing threats. No longer is he the arrogant Pharisee who could not make a mistake. He forgot all these things. He forgot his mission to Damascus, and became a poor humble sinner, asking, "What do you want me to do, Lord?"

One day Jesus said, "Except ye . . . become as little children, ye shall not enter the kingdom of heaven" (Matthew 18:3). Paul came in this manner. It is even so with us. When we come boasting of our own goodness and our own works, there is no welcome for us, When we come simply trusting Him, we can be saved.

> Could my tears forever flow,
> Could my zeal no languor know,
> These for sin could not atone;
> Thou must save, and Thou alone:
> In my hands no price I bring,
> Simply to Thy cross I cling.

All of Saul's tears, all of his grief, all of his zeal, could never save him. But the minute he made his full surrender to Jesus, in that minute he was saved. Ask the average non-Christian today how to get to heaven, and he will tell you that you must be good, you must be kind to others, you must pay your debts, you must give to charity. Thus do men seek to establish their own righteousness. But it avails them nothing—it is Christ who saves us and not ourselves.

> But drops of grief can ne'er repay
> The debt of love I owe:
> Here, Lord, I give myself away,—
> 'Tis all that I can do.

That day on the Damascus road Saul gave himself away and Christ saved him.

We often read the words, "Paul, an apostle of Jesus Christ." One qualification of an apostle was that he must have seen Jesus, and have been a witness of the fact that He rose from the dead. Saul did not see Him in Jerusalem after the resurrection. Where did he see Him? He saw Him right there on the Damascus road. This was not a trance—he actually saw Jesus and the glory of the sight threw him to the ground. Jesus appeared to him, not in the flesh, but in the glory of His risen body. It was a sight that he never forgot, a sight that changed his life.

Jesus told him to go into the city. He opened his eyes, but he could not see, and they had to lead him by the hand. What was it that blinded him? It was the vision of Jesus. If you look in the face of the sun for a few seconds, and then down to earth again, your vision is blurred. Well, Saul looked into the face of One a million times brighter than the sun. No wonder he was blinded! So they brought him to Damascus and for three days he neither ate nor drank. He had had such a shaking experience that he did not want food or drink. Like Jesus, he could say, "I have meat to eat that ye know not of" (John 4:32). Some of us have had the same experience. There have been times when the heavenly things tasted so good that we did not care for the earthly things.

Oh, how different is Saul's entry from what he had planned and expected! Instead of the haughty persecutor looking after his prey, saluted with honor by the Jewish leaders, and looked upon with horror by his victims, we see a broken man, trembling, blind, shocked, helpless. Saul was a poor figure as he made his way into the city, but he knew something, he had something in his heart which had never been there before—a thousand thoughts were flooding his mind.

III. The Messenger. Verse 10-16

Saul was taken to the home of Judas, who lived on the street called Straight. He lay down in an upper room and stayed there for three days and nights. Echoing in his soul was the voice, crying out, "Why persecutest thou Me?" (Acts 9:4). In his mind Saul saw all the Christians whom he had persecuted and put to death. They passed by in a long procession. They looked at him with pleading eyes. Finally he heard the words of Stephen ringing in his ears, and through it all there was the voice of Jesus, echoing, "Why persecutest thou Me?" He had come to realize that inasmuch as he had done it unto these, he had done it unto Jesus.

Down the street was a Christian named Ananias. The Lord called to him and said, "Ananias . . . go into the street which is called Straight, and enquire in the house of Judas for one called Saul, of Tarsus: for, behold, he prayeth. In a vision he has seen you coming to him."

Ananias cried out, "Oh, no, Lord, you can't mean Saul of Tarsus. He is the one who made havoc of the church. He is here to imprison all of your followers. Lord, he will kill me if he sees me."

But the Lord said, "Go ahead, Ananias, everything is all right. He is going to serve Me now, He will not harm you."

One thing here shows that Saul is saved. God said that he was praying. When a man is on his knees or when his voice is lifted in prayer, we cannot be sure that he is really praying. But when God says that a man is praying, it is real prayer, He is a saved man. Do you pray? A real Christian, a child of God, cannot help but talk to the Heavenly Father.

We note that the Lord said two things to Ananias about Saul. First, he is to be a chosen vessel to carry the Gospel to the Gentiles. Second, he will be called upon to suffer many things for Christ's sake. These two things literally came to pass.

IV. THE MERCY. Verses 17-19

So Ananias went straight to the house of Judas. He went in to Saul, put his hands on him, and said, "Brother Saul" (Acts 9:17). How welcome, how soothing, how comforting these words must have been to Saul's wounded heart! That is the tender spirit that we need always to use when we try to win someone to Christ. What else did Ananias say, "The Lord, even Jesus, who appeared to thee on the Damascus Road, has sent me to you, that you might receive your sight and be filled with the Holy Spirit." Notice how he used the words, "the Lord, even Jesus" (Acts 9:17). Saul again was assured that Jesus was God. Then Ananias put his hands on Saul, and how sweet was that touch. Saul had planned to bind those hands and to still that kind voice forever, but now he loved the touch of those hands and the sound of that voice. Jesus had made the difference.

Saul was imprisoned in blindness no longer. He looked into the face of Ananias. Ananias smiled, put out his hand, lifted him up, and gave him the hand of fellowship. Saul went out and was baptized. We never hear of Ananias again, but he had done his part in leading Saul to Christ, and he will have a high place in heaven.

We are told that Saul spent some days with the disciples in Damascus. What rejoicing there must have been in his own heart, and in the hearts of the believers! He came hating them—now he loved them. He came to kill them—now he caressed them. He came to destroy them—now he dined with them. He came to slay them—now he served them. Yes, Jesus makes the difference. If you are not altogether a different person since you met Christ, something is wrong. He changes men. So we see here the mercy of God. Saul had no mercy, but God had mercy on him and saved him.

VI. THE MINISTER. Verses 20-31

Saul did not immediately begin to preach. There must first be a period of preparation, so he went into Arabia and spent three years in school. What school was it? It was the school of Christ. There he received training from the same Teacher who taught the other apostles, even Jesus. We learn all of the facts of the Gospel from the Bible, Saul learned by direct revelation from Christ.

Elijah went to this same mountain and came back with a new message. Moses went aside and received the call to deliver Israel. John the Baptist spent thirty years in the wilderness in order that he might preach for six months. Even Jesus did not begin His ministry until He was thirty. I am not saying that a college education is needed before one preaches, but I am saying that one needs to have been alone with God to get His message.

Saul came back to Damascus ready to preach Christ. He went into the synagogue and preached, proving that Christ was the Son of God. Everybody was amazed. They said, "Isn't this the same man who destroyed Christians in Jerusalem? Now he claims to love Christ—he believes that He is the Son of God." Soon the Jews said, "This man has gone out from us—he is turning many people to the way of Christ —we must get rid of him." Now Saul's predicted suffering begins. They set a guard at every gate to catch him, but the disciples placed Saul in a basket, let him down outside the city wall at night, and he made his escape and went to Jerusalem.

When Saul arrived in Jerusalem, he did not go back to the Sanhedrin, but to the Church of Christ. The Christians would not take him in—they were afraid of him. They could not believe that the persecutor had become a preacher. They said, "Memories of this man fill every corner of the city. Many Christians are dead today because of him." Then up stepped one of the best men told about in the Bible. Barnabas said, "I know this brother, it is true that he was the church's worst enemy, but the Lord has transformed him. All the powers which he used for the devil, he now uses for Christ. He is a saved man, and a powerful preacher. I move that we receive him." The disciples did receive him on the recommendation of Barnabas, and Saul began his work with them. The thing that was true of Saul ought to be true of us: we ought to give as much of our lives to God after we have been saved as we did to the devil before we were saved.

Saul was the best moral man of his day. He could say, "I am free from all outward sin, vice and sensuality. I keep the law perfectly, I am snow white as far as my life is concerned." Yet, he needed to be born again, and so do you. All of our own works and goodness will not save us —we need to come to Christ. Paul said, "Yes, I have changed, I am on the way to heaven. I do not deserve Christ and eternal life, but by the grace of God I am what I am." You and I do not deserve any credit either. If we get to heaven, it will be all because of Christ, and not because of self.

VI. THE MIRACLES. Verses 32-43

This chapter closes with two miracles performed by Peter. At Lydda he found a man named Aeneas who had been in bed eight years with the palsy. He said unto him, "Jesus Christ maketh thee whole" (Acts 9:33). The man was completely cured. In Joppa there lived a good Christian woman by the name of Dorcas. She did a lot of sewing for the poor people and her life was full of good works and alms-deeds. Dorcas became sick and died. Someone sent word to Peter and he came immediately. When he arrived at the home of Dorcas he went into the room where she lay in a casket. The poor widows of the city stood around weeping. They showed Peter the garments which Dorcas had made for them while she was living.

Some of these days *you* are going to die. Will those who are left behind be able to show any good thing that you have done? Can they say, "He was a Christian and he was ready to go?" Can they say, "He was faithful to the church?" Can they say, "His life was lived for others?" Can they say, "He did many good works?" What kind of memories will you leave in the hearts of others? You do not have long to live —are you living for Christ?

Peter took up the dead hand and spoke into the dead ears. "Arise," he said. She arose, and was restored to those who needed her and went back to work for them.

Once you and I were dead—dead in sin. Christ came, He took us by the hand, He lifted us up and saved us. What kind of work are you doing? Are you serving Him and others? Surely, if Christ has saved you and given you life, you ought to be busy for Him.

After a fierce battle a chaplain walked out upon the battle-field, his Bible under his arm. He found a boy, wounded and dying. "Would you like for me to read you something out of the Book?" asked the chaplain. The boy replied, "I am so thirsty, I would rather have a drink of water." The chaplain hurried off and soon returned with water. Then the boy said, "Could you lift my head and put something under it?" The chaplain took off his own overcoat, rolled it up and placed it as a comfortable pillow under the boy's head. Then the boy said, "I'm so cold, I wish I had something over me." The chaplain took off his other coat and wrapped it around the boy. Then the boy looked up into his face and said, "Oh, sir, if there is anything in that Book which makes a man do for another what you have done for me, let me hear it."

Yes, there is something in the Book. It is Christ. Let Him come into your heart. He will transform your life, stand by you in death, and take you home at the end of the way. Do not *you* want to know Him?

CHAPTER TEN

"SPIRITUAL MANIFESTATION"

Acts 10

The greatest change that can come in any man's life is a spiritual change. Some people have been changed greatly physically: once they were strong, but now they are weak; once they had good hearing, but now they are deaf. Some people have been changed greatly mentally: once they were ignorant, but now education has broadened them and they have a great knowledge of the things of the world. Sometimes it is the other way around: once they were brilliant, but now they have lost their minds.

However, the greatest change is a spiritual change. God can create a greater change than anything or anybody. In the ninth chapter of Acts God changed Saul from a sinner to a saint, from a persecutor to a preacher. In the tenth chapter of Acts He changed Peter from a narrow, selfish, prejudiced Christian, who believed that Christianity was for the Jews only, into a man with a world-wide vision, who came to know that Christ was the Saviour of all men who put their trust in Him.

If you are lost, I pray that the Spirit will convict you of your sin, point you to the Saviour and cause you to surrender to Him. If you are a Christian and living for self alone, if you are not giving Christ and His Church a big place in your life, I pray that you will say today, "I will live a better, more faithful, more active Christian life."

I. THE PRAY-ER. Verses 1-2

In the city of Caesarea there lived a man named Cornelius. He was a centurion, which means that he was just about the same as a captain in our army. You will remember that Caesarea was a Gentile city, and that the Jews hated the Gentiles. You will remember, also, that they hated the Roman army, which was a symbol of the world power which held Judea in its grip. But instead of anything bad about Cornelius, all we know of him is good. Listen to what the Bible says of him in verse two:

(1) *He was a devout man.* This means he was devoted to religious feelings and duties. Today you would not call a man devout who never went to church, nor showed any interest in the things of God. Cornelius did not know all about God, yet as far as he understood he was devoted to God.

(2) *He feared God with all his house.* This means that he recognized God's place and power and that he led his family and servants to have a holy awe of God.

(3) *He gave much alms to all people.* He was not mean and little and stingy, he did not make money his god, he did not look down on those less fortunate. No, he saw their plight and had pity on them, and out of the abundance of his heart he supplied their needs.

(4) *He prayed to God alway.* He knew that his own strength and resources were not enough. He felt the need of a higher being. He wanted to reach out and touch the hand of God, so in the only way he knew how to pray, he prayed.

Are you saying, "This is one of the best men I ever read about; he was devoted to God, he feared God, he helped the poor, and prayed to God. Some Christians today do not do all that. Surely this man doesn't need to be born again. He is all right as he is." Again I would have you to remember that we are not saved by our own goodness, or our right-eousness, or our gifts. You can be the finest man in the world and yet you are on the way to hell if you do not follow the Bible plan and accept Jesus Christ as your Saviour.

There are two opposite types of religion in the world to-day, and each side is represented by multitudes of people. One group says, "Do this and that and the other, go through this form and that ceremony and you will be saved." The other group says, "It is not a case of what we do—Christ has done it all for us on the Cross. We are dead men, dead in sin, and we cannot do anything to save ourselves. We must look up to Him in faith as He alone can save and redeem."

> Jesus paid it all,
> All to Him I owe;
> Sin had left a crimson stain,
> He washed it white as snow.

II. THE POINTING. Verses 3-8

Though Cornelius was not a saved man, he was a seeker. He did want God's salvation and God's peace. One day God sent an angel down with a message for Cornelius. The angel appeared to him and said, "Cornelius."

Cornelius quickly answered, "What is it, Lord?" (Acts 10:4). It seemed that he was just waiting for God to speak to him. He realized that God had taken note of him and his heart bounded with joy.

"Your prayers and gifts have come up before the Lord," said the angel. "He has a preacher in Joppa by the name of Simon Peter. He is lodging with Simon the tanner. You are to send for this preacher and he will tell you what you ought to do."

Why did not the angel tell Cornelius how to be saved? He was on the spot and Peter was a day and a half away. By the time the men were sent after him and the return trip was made, three days would have gone by. The angel knew the story of redeeming love, but never do we find a place in the New Testament where an angel was permitted to tell this story. All he did here was to tell Cornelius where he could find the preacher who had God's message. This seems to be the reason: the angels in heaven have never sinned, they have never fallen, they have never needed redemption; so God pushes the angels back and gives you and me the matchless privilege of proclaiming the Gospel. We can proclaim it better than Gabriel himself, because Gabriel cannot say what we can, "I am a sinner saved by grace." God wants men today who will witness for Him. Peter could witness because he had had an experience with God. He had sinned, then he had sought forgiveness, now Jesus was very real and very precious to him. One reason many church members are not able to witness today is that they have had no vital experience with the Lord. Oh, it is when men get alone with God and have a vital touch with Him that they can come back and say, "The Lord did this for me."

Cornelius lost no time. He was eager to see Peter and hear the message God was sending through him. I wish that men today were eager to hear the same message. I wish that lost men would crowd our churches and cry out to the preachers, "What must I do to be saved?" Instead they go to the places of amusement and sport on the Lord's Day. They pass Jesus by, they forget the One who has blessed them all the week and has given them a day of rest. But some day they will come to the end of the way, they will feel themselves slipping out into eternity, they will know that God will be waiting for them at the Judgment. Then from the depths of despair they will cry out, "Oh, God, give me back some of the time that I wasted. Give me one more chance and I will make good, I will give myself to Thee, and serve Thee until the end of my days." But it will be too late and they will go to an everlasting death, knowing that it is nobody's fault but their own.

Cornelius did not delay. He did not say, "I will attend to my other business first and then I will seek the Lord." He called in two servants and a devoted soldier. He told them the whole story and sent them to Joppa to find the preacher.

III.THE PREPARATION. Verses 9-16.

The next day at noon these three men were close to Joppa, so God prepared the heart of His preacher, Simon Peter. He convinced Peter and the world that Christ's salvation is not for the Jews only, but for all who call on Him in faith.

Peter was waiting for dinner to be served. The pleasant odors of the kitchen had reached his nostrils and he had become very hungry. He said to himself, "I have a few minutes before dinner, so I will go up on the roof and pray." He went up on the roof and began his prayer. Nearby the waves of the sea lapped the shore. Anyone who has been to the seacoast knows that this makes you both hungry and sleepy. Peter did not get far in his prayer. He went into a trance. God wanted to impart an important truth to Peter. It is always good to pray, but it is sometimes better to listen to God and let Him speak to you.

God sent a vision to Peter, "The heavens were opened and a great sheet was let down." Peter looked into this sheet and saw that it was filled with all kinds of animals and fowls. Remember that he was very hungry. God said to him, "Rise, Peter; kill, and eat" (Acts 10:13).

Peter replied, "Not so, Lord; I have never eaten anything that is common or unclean" (Acts 10:14).

The Lord replied, "What God has cleansed, do not call common." Three times this thing happened. God impressed the matter on the preacher's mind. The sheet was then taken back into heaven.

What did God teach Peter? Well, Peter was an ecclesiastical aristocrat. He felt that everybody but the Jews were outcasts. Surely God did not love outsiders. He was not interested in them. Christ did not die for them. When Jesus said, "God so loved the world, that he gave his only begotten Son" (John 3:16), Peter could not see that the world contained anybody but Jews. He felt that he was God's elect, God's chosen, and that these other people were common and unclean. But God was saying, "You are not to call them common, they are as close to My heart as you are." The Jews believed in the caste system. If a man was not a Jew they would not show him the way if he were lost, nor would they point him to a spring if he were thirsty.

Some churches still have that spirit today. They want no one to join their church but the elite. They care nothing for the great mass of poor, hungry, needy people whom Jesus loves.

A young Methodist preacher went to a certain town to hold a meeting. On the first night he asked sinners to come to the front that they might be prayed for. Poor Mrs. Jones and her son came to the altar. Everything in the church was cold as ice. The people seemed to resent the intrusion of these poor people. After the service, the preacher asked an official about the matter, and this man said, "Every time we try to have a meeting, some people from the South part of town come to church. They lead the way to the altar and keep respectable people away. If we cannot keep these poor people out of our church the meeting will be spoiled."

The preacher was brokenhearted. He did not sleep much that Saturday night. At the Sunday morning service he told the people what the official had said to him and how he had spent a sleepless night. He told them that God would never bless the church nor give them a revival unless they gave these poor people a chance to be saved. He pled so earnestly that their hearts were broken and they went to their knees in prayer and confessed their sins.

That afternoon every poor family in the town was visited by one of the church members. That night when the preacher preached, the Holy Spirit fell. Many poor people were saved and many of the influential people of the town accepted Christ, also.

Oh, we must have a vision and a heart that loves all lost people! We must seek to bring them to Christ. This is the truth that God laid on Peter's heart.

Another thing we note here: God told Peter to do a certain thing, and Peter said, "Lord, I cannot do that, I never did it before." We still have people who feel like that. They never want to advance one inch in spiritual things. The Gospel always remains the same, but not our methods. We must keep up with the times. In an age of airplanes and atomic power we are not still to use oxcart and stagecoach methods. Some people have only one song: "As it was in the beginning, Is now and ever shall be, World without end, Amen."

They sing this song before breakfast, all the day long, and after supper at night. But the successful people are the ones who try something new once in a while.

IV. The Proceeding. Verses 17-33

Peter woke up and was greatly puzzled. He wondered what the vision meant, so God used certain circumstances to show him. There came a knock on the door and a man called out, "Is Simon Peter the preacher, here?"

Then the Holy Spirit said to Peter, "God has sent these men for you. Do not question the matter at all, just go with them."

Peter answered, "All right Lord, I do not understand, but I will go." God bless you, Peter! That is the right attitude.

Abraham had that attitude when "he went out, not knowing whither he went" Hebrews 11:8). Many others have had that same spirit since his time. Here is the thing that we are to remember: when God says, "Go," you do not go alone, He goes with you.

Peter went down the stairs and approached the men and said, "My name is Simon Peter. I understand you are looking for me. What can I do for you?"

One of them replied: "Our master, Cornelius, a Gentile, is a mighty good man. He fears God, he prays, he is well thought of by the Jews. An angel appeared to him recently and told him to send for you, saying that you would have a message from God for him." Now the light begins to dawn in Peter's mind and heart. If God wants him to go and preach to the Gentiles, it must mean that He wants them to be saved. Now he sees the meaning of the vision. All people are precious in God's sight, Christ died for them all.

Remember that Peter is a Jew and that the Jews have no dealings with the "Gentile dogs." But Peter invited these three men in to spend the night. Already the divine change had worked in Peter.

The next morning Peter and the men had gotten up early. Peter had invited some other Christians along to see what was going to happen. They started out for Joppa and arrived there the next day. Cornelius was eagerly waiting for Peter. He had called all of his friends and kinspeople in. If God was going to send him a message, he wanted to share it with others. This shows the fine spirit that he had.

As Peter approached, Cornelius ran to meet him and fell down before him and worshipped him. But Peter immediately took Cornelius by the hand and lifted him up, saying, "Stand up, I am just a man like you are." The true servant of God does not take the glory to himself, but gives it to the Lord.

They went into the house. This was a strange thing for Peter and he hastened to explain his actions, not only for the benefit of Cornelius, but for the Jewish Christians who were with him. He said, "I know it is unlawful for a Jew to keep company with one of another race, but the other day God told me not to call any man common or unclean. So I have come gladly to your house, now tell me why you sent for me."

Cornelius eagerly told his story of how the angel appeared to him, telling him to send for Peter. "Here we all are before God, ready to hear what God has told you to tell us." What a wonderful setting for a mighty service! On one hand we have a spirit-filled preacher, a man with a mighty message from God, a man who had recently had a great experience with the Lord. On the other hand we have a waiting, eager, hungry audience.

I wish that preachers could always have that kind of an audience. If you come to church saying, "Oh, what's the use?" the preacher cannot do much for you. If you come to criticize and find fault, he cannot help you, but if you come believing that God has given him a message for you, if you listen with an open mind, God can use the preacher to bring a blessing to you.

Gladstone said, "Eloquence is the pouring back on the audience in a flood, what the speaker first gets from the audience in vapor."

The sun draws water from every little pool and every little flower, it then pours it back on the earth in a flood. So it is that the preacher draws power from the hearts of his listeners and pours it back in a greater measure into their hearts. Even a mighty man of God has little power in a congregation whose hearts are not open to the reception of truth. But even a poor preacher can preach a good sermon when the people are praying for him and when their hearts are ready to receive the Word.

V. THE PERCEPTION. Verse 34

Peter stood before this crowd a changed man. He confessed "Of a truth I perceive that God is no respecter of persons" (Acts 10:34). This one sentence expressed the great truth that Peter had learned, and which we need to learn today. In God there is no East nor West, no North nor South. Every human being is precious to Him whether he lives in a cottage or a palace, on the avenue or in the alley. Money makes no difference to God as it does to us, education makes no difference, color makes no difference, culture makes no difference. God looks upon a man in mercy. He wants to save all and bless all. We ought to feel the same way. So Peter learned that God wants to bless the Gentiles as well as the Jews.

VI. THE PREACHING. Verses 35-43

Peter did not begin his sermon by eulogizing Cornelius, he did not compliment him on his goodness and his generosity. He did not exhort him to be good and kind and prayerful. No, he preached Christ to him. He told of the birth and the life and death of Jesus, he told of His resurrection, he told of the salvation that He would give to all who believed in Him. He did not try to entertain or amuse Cornelius. He told him what he needed to know.

If your house were on fire and the fire company came to the front of the house and put on a dress parade, and sought to entertain you by showing you how far they could throw a stream of water in another direction, you would be indignant. You would rush up to the chief and say, "Man, my house is burning down. I don't care about all this display. Turn the water on my house before it is too late!" Or if your child were very ill and the doctor came and began a long speech about the advancement of medicine in the last twenty-five years, you would cry out, "Doctor, forget all that. My child is suffering and will die unless he receives help. Do something before it's too late!" So when souls are lost, the preacher has no time to deal in pious platitudes. He must tell a man of his sin and point him to the Lamb of God. Peter did not waste any time. He gave God's message to the crowd at Caesarea.

VII. THE PARTAKING. Verses 44-48

While Peter spoke the Holy Spirit fell upon this group. They put their faith in Christ. They were saved. Cornelius had done the best he could; now he received further light and acted upon it. He did not fall back upon his good deeds, his money, or his prayers. He trusted Christ and depended upon Him alone for salvation. The Jews who came with Peter were astonished. They saw that the Holy Spirit had fallen upon the Gentiles as He did upon the Jews, and they knew that a new era would begin, an era in which the Gospel would not be confined to a few, but would flow out to all the world.

Peter said, "These have believed and have received the Holy Spirit, can anybody forbid baptism?" He looked at his Jewish friends, and they offered no objections. God had changed things. Cornelius and all those who believed in Jesus were baptized.

One wonderful thing about the whole matter is that Cornelius brought his family in with him. Oh, if you mothers and fathers would live rightly for Christ, if you would be faithful to His Church, if you would establish Christian homes, if you would bring your children up in the church, you would never have to worry about them.

A reporter was standing on the rear platform of a train with the conductor. The conductor said, "We will pass my home in a few minutes, and I want you to look in the window as we go by." When they passed the home, the reporter looked in the window and saw three little children kneeling by the bedside in prayer, with the mother standing beside them. The conductor explained, "They go to bed at nine o' clock. My train passes here at nine every night. My wife has the children kneel and as we pass I can see them."

"Do they pray for you?" asked the reporter.

"Yes," the conductor replied, "they pray that I will be good and clean and never come home drunk as I formerly did. I have a hard life and many temptations, but I love my wife and children, and when I think of them kneeling there praying for me it keeps me straight." That is what we need today—Christianity in the home. If we had more of it we would have fewer children going astray.

If I had met Cornelius the next day I would have said, "How was the service in your house yesterday, Cornelius?"

He would have answered, "Ah, it was wonderful! Peter preached Christ to us, and as he told us that we could be saved only through faith, I felt my heart strangely warmed. I surrendered to Jesus. The peace of God entered my soul, and the Holy Spirit came to abide in my heart."

I can imagine a scene fifty years later. Cornelius is an old man now, and he has retired from active service. His little grandson will climb up in his lap and say "Grandad, tell me a story."

"I don't know any more stories."

"But Grandad, tell me about the time when you were praying and the angel came and told you to send for the preacher."

"Oh, do you want to hear that story again?" And then

Cornelius, with the light of heaven upon his face, will begin, "It was a long time ago, and your father was just about your age." Then he will go on to tell the wonderful story of how the preacher came and told him about Jesus.

"Was what the preacher said true?" the little boy will ask.

"Yes," Cornelius will say. "Jesus saved me and I have tested Him for these fifty years and all that Peter told me about Him is true."

Then the little boy will say, "Will Jesus save a little fellow like me?"

"Yes," his grandad will reply, "I learned that day that He will save all those who put their trust in Him."

"All right," the little boy will say, "I will give my heart to him right now." And old Cornelius will hug the boy to his heart and rejoice that long ago he learned of the sweetness and mercy of Jesus Christ.

Have you given yourself to this wonderful Saviour? Very few men out of Christ are as good as Cornelius, yet he needed Christ and you need Him, too. Why not give yourself to Him?

A man who ran a rescue mission in New York told of his conversion. From drinking a cocktail now and then he became a habitual drunkard. One night he went down into a low place where the other men tolerated him because they were too drunk to eject him. He sat on a whiskey barrel and thought of his life. He grieved over twenty years of dissipation. Then he suddenly remembered something that he had heard when he was a little boy; it was this, "Come unto me, all ye that labor and are heavy laden, and I will give you rest" (Matthew 11:28). Then he thought within himself, *I have heard that if a sinner looked to Jesus he would be saved. But where can I find him?* At this moment he felt himself falling from the barrel and he said, "I will fall toward the Cross." He fell upon his knees, poured out his heart to God and was saved.

The old Cross is still there. Jesus still has His arms open, saying, "Come unto me." Why not accept His invitation today?

CHAPTER ELEVEN

"SPIRITUAL IDENTIFICATION"

Acts 11

In the eleventh chapter of Acts we see the disciples identified by name. "The disciples were called Christians first in Antioch" (Acts 11:26). In the tenth chapter God appeared to Peter in a vision, teaching him a great new truth, that Christ was not only for the Jews, but for all men, regardless of race or color or station in life. Someone has well said that the word "humanity" never existed until Christ came. God would have us know that His great love is not for one class only, but for all humanity.

A young lady of the Roman Catholic faith came to my study sometime ago. A young man of the same faith stayed after church recently and talked with me. I asked each of them the same question, "Have you ever heard John 3:16, which says: 'God so loved the world, that he gave his only begotten Son, that whosoever believeth in him should not perish, but have everlasting life'" Both of them answered in the negative. How poor anyone is who has never heard this verse! The verse does not say that God so loved Jews or Catholics or Protestants or Americans, but that God so loved the whole world that He gave His Son. Peter learned that. He learned that God loved all men, and that salvation comes to all those who put their trust in Christ.

The Catholics recently gave out the statement that "there

134

is salvation only in the Catholic Church." But they said that men could be saved outside of the Catholic Church if they did not know that the Catholic Church was the true church. Now is not that fine—that gives the rest of us a chance. Thank God, we do not have to go by what a pope or a bishop says. We have a Book written by men who were touched by the finger of God. This Book tells me that any poor sinner of any race or place who comes trusting Jesus for mercy and salvation immediately becomes a child of God, is adopted into God's family, and is on the way to God's heaven.

I. THE ACCUSATION. Verses 1-3

Peter was returning from his memorable trip to Caesarea. He had preached Christ to Cornelius and his household and had seen them saved and baptized. He had gone in and eaten with them and had enjoyed sweet Christian fellowship in that group. When he returned to Jerusalem, the "Circumcision Party" in the church rises up against him. They make this accusation, "You went in with those who are uncircumcised and ate with them." Oh, they were angry, they were ready to throw Peter out of the church!

This group had believed in Jesus, but instead of believing that men are saved by simple faith, they believed that salvation came by faith, plus circumcision and other Jewish rites. They made the mistake that men make today, men who want to add something to God's simple plan of salvation. But the Book says, "By grace are ye saved through faith" (Ephesians 2:8). Again it says, "Whosoever shall call upon the Name of the Lord shall be saved" (Romans 10:13). Again it says, "He that believeth on the Son hath everlasting life" (John 3:36). But so many people say, "That is not enough, we must add something." So they add baptism, the Lord's Supper, church membership, and good works. Christ is able to save you without help from anything else on earth. You are to put all of your faith in Him and not in these outward things.

We see here some more of Satan's work. Too many souls are being saved, the work is going too well, so he tries to divide the church. Heretofore they had been "of one accord." Now we see a new party rising up—the Circumcision Party, the Legalistic Party, the party which tried to bring the Jewish customs of the Old Testament into New Testament Christianity. Paul later found these people to be his bitterest opponents. It is a black day for any church when the people start forming cliques. I have seen it and you have seen it, and the results are never good. If we are to do big things for Jesus, we must stick together and not let the devil divide us.

You notice here that these people did not rebuke Peter for preaching Christ to the Gentiles, but for eating with them. It is usually that way. When a quarrel starts in a church, it is not over a big doctrinal question, but over some trivial thing which cannot compare with the main issue. I can imagine Peter's disappointment. He expected the believers in Jerusalem to rejoice over the souls saved at Caesarea, but instead of rejoicing they jumped on him for eating with the Gentiles. They did not say a word about the good that was done or the souls that were saved. I have seen the same thing happen. I have seen the blessings of God come upon a church, when souls were being saved and lives blessed and when the money was pouring in for God's work. Then I have seen some little, measly, mean, conceited people rise up and start to criticize something that did not amount to much. May the Lord have mercy on such little souls!

II. THE ANSWER. Verses 4-17

How did Peter answer this accusation? He did it in a sweet Christian spirit. He tried to show that every step he had taken had been ordered by the Lord. He proved that God had taken in the converts at Caesarea, and that He had sent His Holy Spirit upon them. If God felt that way about the Gentiles, surely there was no harm in eating with them. Peter now pointed out four facts to show that God's hand was in the matter:

(1) He told of his vision on the housetop in Joppa. He told about the sheet which was filled with many animals and how God said to him, "Arise Peter; slay and eat."

He told how he had answered by saying, "No, I have never done anything like that."

Then he told how God had said, "What I have called clean, that call not thou common."

(2) He told them of the arrival of Cornelius' men, and of how the Spirit commanded him to follow these men. As he wondered about the vision the men came and requested him to go to Caesarea and preach to the Gentiles. Was that a coincidence? If so, it was arranged by God Himself.

(3) He then told of Cornelius' vision. These two visions fitted into each other, God was working at both ends. At one end he told Cornelius to send for Peter—at the other end He told Peter to go down to Cornelius. There is no guess-work with God. He works everything out on schedule and for a divine purpose.

(4) He told how the Holy Spirit fell on the group at Caesarea. He said, "When that happened what could I do? I certainly could not withstand God."

There are many things to be admired about Peter and one thing was that he was so straightforward. He never beat a-round the bush. There had been a time when he was unstable and vacillating, but that is all over now. He is staunch and solid. He preached Christ without apology and he was willing to defend his position with his life. Jesus knew what He was doing when He named him "A Rock."

III. THE ADMISSION. Verse 18

After Peter's explanation and impassioned plea these men had nothing else to say. They glorified God and made this admission, "Then hath God also to the Gentiles granted repentance unto life." Peter gave to the Jerusalem church the most encouraging message any church will ever receive. He told them that souls were being saved at the other end of the line. There is rejoicing in heaven over one sinner that repenteth, and there should be the same rejoicing in our hearts, also.

A telegraph operator in Cincinnati attended a revival service. In his sermon the preacher told how a telegraph operator in Zanesville had been converted. The Cincinnati operator was interested and when he returned to work that night, he decided to call the Zanesville operator and ask him if the story was true. When he did this the man replied, "Yes, it it true. I am the man. Christ has saved me." They talked over the wires for sometime and the Cincinnati man asked the Zanesville man to pray for him.

Before midnight he called him again and said, "Everything is all right now. Your Saviour is my Saviour, too." This was the message that Peter gave the Jerusalem church. This is the reason that they rejoiced and glorified God, after the other matter had been straightened out.

IV. THE AMBASSADOR. Verses 19-23

The scene changed now from Jerusalem to Antioch. When the persecutions had begun in Jerusalem some of the Jerusalem disciples who were scattered abroad went to Antioch. At first they preached to the Jews only, then some of them started preaching to the Gentiles. God blessed their ministry and many were saved. These evangelists were not preachers nor officers of the church. They were the smaller people of the church, but they loved the Lord and when they moved to

Antioch, they wanted to tell their new neighbors about Christ. This is always true, if we love Christ and remember what He has done for us, we want others to know Him, too. This is the very heart of our missionary program and church work. Christ has entered our hearts and blessed us, so we want other people to the ends of the earth to know Him, and consequently we give our money for that purpose.

When a man has material wealth his great desire is to keep it to himself. When a man has spiritual wealth he wants to share the blessings with everybody. What kind of a Christian are you, when you think of Jesus as a Saviour for yourself only and not for others? If the ship on which you were sailing was sinking, could you be content to get into a life boat alone and let all the others go down? If you had a warehouse full of good things to eat, would you be content to let men and women and children starve in the time of famine? What right, then, do we have to withhold spiritual food from those who are dying in sin?

Jeremiah said, "His word . . . as a burning fire [was] shut up in my bones . . . I could not stay" (Jeremiah 20:9). Yes, when Jesus dwells in our hearts, we cannot contain the blessing, we must share it with others.

When the Jerusalem church heard how these people were being saved in Antioch they sent Barnabas, a wonderful ambassador of Christ, down to investigate. When he came and saw how they had been saved and how happy they were in Christ, his great heart was glad. He did not criticize, he did not find fault, he rejoiced with them. It seems he exhorted them that "with purpose of heart they would cleave unto the Lord" (Acts 11:23). When we see people saved, we rejoice with a joy unspeakable, but that is not all, we should exhort them to cling to Christ.

The great tragedy of our churches today is that multitudes join them and then they seem to forget the vows they have made. They never attend church, they never give, they never serve. Barnabas said, "Cleave unto the Lord" (Acts 11: 23). But many people are cleaving to the world, to amusement, to sports, to society, to sin. Oh, I wish that all of our church members would put Christ first and let Him and His Church be the chief joys of their lives!

Verse twenty-four is one of the finest descriptions of a man in the Bible, "He was a good man, and full of the Holy Ghost and of faith: and much people was added unto the Lord." Often when we speak of a man being a good man, it does not mean anything. He may be doing absolutely nothing for God or man, his life is simply a negative life. It is a misnomer when we call him "good." When God calls a man "good," it really means something. This man had been to Calvary, this man had attended God's school, he had been faithful, God had given him a degree. It was not Barnabas the genius, not Barnabas the gifted, but Barnabas the "good." Can you call any man "good" who does not live for Jesus Christ? No, not in God's sense of the word. He gave His only begotten Son for men, and when a man goes through life rejecting Him and putting something else in His place, thus crucifying Him afresh, you can never call that man "good." A good man first of all must be a Christian man.

Barnabas was good as a steward. Right after Pentecost, the church was filled with needy people. More than three thousand had been saved and many of them had been cast out by their families. These were in dire need. Nobody high-pressured Barnabas, but very quietly he sold his land and brought every dollar to the church to be used in helping the needy. That is the sign of a good man, he realizes that God has given him everything and he wants to give something in return.

Barnabas was good as a friend. When Paul was converted he tried to join the Jerusalem Church but the disciples shrank from him. His hands were red with Christian blood—he was the greatest enemy of the church. But Barnabas took his part, he stood up for him and risked all that he had on Paul's sincerity. The Church then received Paul. If this had not happened the icy chill might have so cooled Paul's devotion that he might never have been a mighty preacher. Then later Mark made a failure and Paul said, "Let's send him home." But Barnabas said, "No, let's give him another chance." He helped Mark out and later Mark made good. He wrote the second Gospel.

Barnabas was good as a Christian. We are told that he was "full of the Holy Ghost and of faith." In one place he is spoken of as a man who risked his life for Jesus' sake. During the time of Martin Luther there was another man named Martin, of Basel. He had received the Lord Jesus as Martin Luther had and he believed as Luther did. He wrote out his confession proving his love and devotion for the Saviour, pried a brick out of the wall, hid his confession there, and put the brick back in place. This confession was not discovered until a hundred years later. Who knows anything about Martin of Basel?

However, Martin Luther, as he crawled up the steps of the Santa Scala, found his faith and then went out to proclaim it to the whole world. He turned the religious realm upside down. We remember Martin Luther, but we forget the other Martin. We remember the man who stands for something. Likewise Barnabas stood up for his faith and let the world know where he stood. By that stand he won multitudes to the Master.

The sum total of Barnabas' life was: "Much people was added unto the Lord." It was wonderful for him to look back at the end of the way and see the long procession of those he had won entering the city of God. What will be the sum total of your life? Will it be thus—he lived and he died—he lived for self and is gone—he lived for money and pleasure and now he is gone where these things do not count? Or will people be able to say, "He lived for God and others, his life was a blessing and someone knows Jesus because of him."

One man wrote his own epitaph, to be placed upon his tomb when he died. It was this:

> I reveled underneath the moon,
> I slept beneath the sun,
> I lived a life of going-to-do,
> And died with nothing done.

Time is fleeting, the end is coming. You had better hurry and get busy if you expect your life to count, if you expect a reward at the end of the way.

V. THE ASSOCIATE. Verses 25-26-a, b

Barnabas jumped into the work at Antioch and began a revival meeting. Soon he saw that he needed help, the task was too much for him. He thought of Paul, the man who had been saved on the Damascus Road, the man whom he had stood up for in Jerusalem. "He is the very man I need," he said, "I will go and get him to help me." Down in Tarsus he found him and brought him back to Antioch. For a whole year they had a real revival and scores of people were saved.

Again we see the bigness of Barnabas. He did not have the ability that Paul had and he was the first to admit it. He saw that Paul could do what he could not do, he heard Paul preach as he could not preach, yet not one ounce of jealousy of the younger man entered his heart. At first the two were referred to as Barnabas and Paul. Later on they were Paul and Barnabas. But this did not effect Barnabas, he was too big for jealousy. May God deliver us always from these little, jealous fellows, who spend their time griping because someone else can do a thing better than they can.

Dr. R. G. Lee says that "Barnabas played second fiddle, but he played it so well that the kingdom of God made progress. He rode second in the Gospel chariot, but he did it with such humility and joy and gratitude that heaven will forever rejoice."

VI. The Adornment. Verse 26-c

"The disciples were called Christians first at Antioch." We are told that their enemies gave them this name in ridicule, but they wore it as an adornment. They were proud to be called Christians, which simply means a follower of Jesus Christ. They were glad to have a part of His Name contained in theirs. Why did their enemies call them Christians? Maybe it was because these believers reminded them of Christ. Many of them had seen Him, they had felt the sweetness of His spirit, they knew He was different. So when they looked on these disciples they were reminded of Christ.

Did anybody ever think of Jesus by looking at your life? Did anyone ever say, "If you are a Christian, I would like to be one, for I would like to be like you?" Are you reminding others of Jesus in your home life, in your business life, in your church life? Often we call people Christians when they may be far from deserving that title. I am sure that these believers measured up in every way. I wish that those who are called Christians today measured up. Are you a real Christian— or do you just bear the Christian name?

VII. The Assistance. Verse 27-30

Here we see the Antioch Church in action, responding to the needs of others. Some prophets had come from Jerusalem and had told about a famine which was coming to Judea. Immediately the Antioch Christians remembered the brethren in Judea. They took a liberal offering, no one held back, everyone gave. They sent this offering by the hands of Barnabas and Paul. The true Christian always responds to the cry of the needy. They did not say, "We'll keep our money at home and build a great church for ourselves." No, they said, "Our brethren are in need and we will gladly sacrifice to help them out." Yes, they had the right name—they were Christians all right.

In this chapter we see that an individual Christian, Barnabas, and a group of Christians, the Antioch Church, attracted attention to themselves. How did they do it? Not by advertising, not by boasting of their works, not by the sounding of trumpets. They did it by living good, useful, consecrated Christian lives. This made the world take note of them. I challenge you to live the same way, to put out of your life all the things that ought not to be there, the things that displease God, the things which crowd Christ out. Then I challenge you to follow Jesus Christ and to live at your best for Him and His Church.

If I had met Barnabas in those days, I would have said, "I'm glad to meet you, Brother Barnabas. I've heard so much about you. I know that you are a good man, full of the Holy Spirit and faith, and that by your efforts many have been won to Christ. Tell me the secret of your great life."

I am sure that he would have said, "It is no secret, I am nothing, but Jesus Christ came into my heart long ago, and he possessed me and changed me. If there is any good in me, it is all because of Him." Oh, my friend, He can save and change you, too. He can help you to live and to die. He can give you a place in glory.

When Henry Morehouse was a very young preacher he was holding a meeting in England. One night one of the deacons came to him and said "You will have to close the meeting. There is a rough man in this town by the name of Ike Miller. He is a terrible drunkard. He says that he is going to run you out of town and break up the meeting."

The preacher spent the next day looking for Miller but never found him.

That evening Morehouse came to the pulpit. Every seat was taken except one in the front row. As the preacher waited for the time to preach, he saw a rough man come in. He knew that this man was Ike Miller. The man took the only vacant seat in the house and sat there glaring up at the preacher. Morehouse changed his text and preached on "The Love of God." He made an impassioned plea and gave the invitation. After one stanza Ike Miller stalked out of the house. Later the deacon told Morehouse that he ought not to have preached on the love of God, that he should have scolded Ike Miller for his sins.

The preacher only replied, "I did the best I could—I believe that God led me."

Ike Miller went home early that night. His two little girls heard him coming and crawled under the bed. His wife slipped into a quiet corner. They remembered how often he had come in drunk and had beaten them. But this night when he came in he put his arms around his wife, and said, "I am sorry for the way I have treated you. From now on I will be a different husband."

He asked for the little girls, and the mother called them out from under the bed. Miller put his arms around them and said, "Don't be afraid any more, God saved me tonight and I will always love you and be good to you." They went down upon their knees and Miller poured out his heart to God, thanking Him for saving him, and asking Him to save his little family. The next night all of them were in church, where they made their profession and joined the church. Ike Miller later became an effective evangelist.

The love of God which reached down and saved Ike Miller is still available for you. Just look up to Him in faith. He will save you and make the joy bells of heaven ring for *you.*

CHAPTER TWELVE

"SPIRITUAL SUPPLICATION"

Acts 12

The Book of Acts is a story of the Early Church, and how the Holy Spirit used Christ's servants to advance Christ's kingdom. On the one hand we see these servants, empowered by the Holy Spirit, preaching Christ everywhere. On the other hand, we see all the enemies of Christ, empowered by Satan, seeking to destroy Christianity and Christians.

The apostles had an up-and-down existence. They would go to certain places, preach the Gospel, and God would bless them and give them success. Then Satan's forces would step in and persecution and suffering would begin. But the apostles remained true to Christ and the Lord always brought them out victoriously. The same thing is true today. The faithful servant of Christ will find the world against him. He will suffer many things, but if he remains true to Christ, God will deliver him and richly reward him. In Acts twelve we find an example of this very thing.

I. THE SUFFERERS. Verses 1-4

The persecution in this instance comes from Herod the King. Why? He knew that this band of Christians had stirred up the enmity of the people, he wanted to please the Jews and be popular with them, so he stretched out his hand and killed James with the sword.

146

Which James is this? He was the brother of John, a member of the famous trio whom Jesus counted as His Inner Circle: Peter, James and John. On one occasion Jesus called James a "Son of Thunder." He was a man of fire and zeal. On another occasion his mother came to Jesus and requested that her two sons be given prominent places in Christ's kingdom. Now, after a period of fine service to Christ, James becomes the first of the Apostles to meet martyrdom.

In the same chapter we see God delivering one apostle, yet he allowed James to be slain. Why did He not deliver James, who was a good man and a useful servant? The same type of question is asked many times. I have been called to homes where death has suddenly struck, and have had someone say, "My loved one was good and useful; why did God take him and permit others to live who are worth nothing to the world?" This is a question we will never be able to answer. But we do know this, God never makes a mistake. When He allows a sad thing to happen it is all for the best. Some day we will understand the meaning of it all. We must leave the whole question in the loving hands of a loving Father, remembering that "all things work together for good to them that love God" (Romans 8:28).

When James' mother asked that he be allowed to sit at Christ's right hand, you remember that the Lord said, "Can ye drink of the cup that I drink of?" (Mark 10:38). James said that he was able, but he did not know what it meant. Now he knows. He knows that the cup was a cup of suffering, and he has drunk the last bitter drop. As the sword pierces his heart his spirit goes soaring up to heaven. He had the joy of meeting Jesus. He was the first one of the apostles to get to heaven. I can imagine that this reunion was filled with great happiness, and that James and Jesus sat for many hours side by side talking about the things that were going on down in the world. James lived a short time; his brother John lived over one hundred years. But both of them lived for Jesus and this is the thing that counts. It does not matter whether you live fifty years or a hundred years. The thing that matters is this: are you filling your life with service to God?

When the Jews heard that James was dead they rejoiced greatly and praised Herod, James' murderer. Then Herod said, "If they like that I'll give them some more of the same and I'll become even more popular with them." Oh, what price people will pay for popularity! Even today we see people stifling their convictions, giving in to sin, and walking with the world in order to gain popularity.

Herod has Peter arrested also. He put him in prison and waited for the time when he could put him to death. He knew that Peter was an important man, for he chose sixteen soldiers, in relays of four, to guard him.

II. The Supplicants. Verse 5

Just as soon as Peter was put in prison the word reached the Christians and they called a prayer meeting in Mary's house. They did not pray for a few minutes and then quit. They prayed without ceasing.

Here we see two opposing forces—on the one hand we have Herod and all the power of the Roman government, on the other hand we have this little band of praying people in Mary's house. I wonder what we would have done under the circumstances. Probably we would have wired the governor or our senator asking him to use his influence with someone higher in authority. This little prayer band called on the One who has more power than all the governments of the world.

Oh, the Church needs so many things today! The best way to get them is by prayer. If all of our people came together in one spirit and prayed earnestly, God would provide every need.

We notice that God did not answer these prayers immediately. The days slipped by and the Passover came nearer. After that time Herod was going to bring Peter out and kill him. The faith of these Christians was being tested, but they stood the test and kept on praying. They prayed without ceasing, they hung on to God. Hold on to God! If He does not answer your first prayer, do not give up; be patient and keep on praying.

III. THE SLEEPER. Verse 6

What was Peter doing while all this feverish activity was taking place? He was not worried, he was not afraid because death was staring him in the face. He was *sleeping*. He was bound with two heavy chains, a soldier was sleeping on either side, and other soldiers were guarding the door on the outside. This is a wonderful picture of sublime trust in God. Peter knew that if God wanted him to continue his work He would deliver him and let him live. If not, he was ready to meet his Lord.

The American Baptist Publication Society has on its seal the picture of an ox standing between the altar and the plow. This picture is telling us that the ox is ready to serve by pulling the plow, or he is ready to die on the altar. It was even so with Peter, and it ought to be even so with us. We ought to be able to say, "Lord, I am ready to serve Thee, if that is what Thou dost want. I am ready to die for Thee if that is best."

Someone said that Peter was the only Christian in the city who was sleeping that night. He could sleep because he had left everything in the hands of God. Why should we stay awake all night and worry when God wants us to turn all of our troubles over to Him? A certain man had worried himself sick over a troublesome matter. He simply could not sleep at night. One day while walking through a cemetery he saw this inscription on a tomb, "Underneath are the Everlasting Arms." That night he decided to rest on these Everlasting Arms, so when he went to bed he turned all his trouble over to God and was able to sleep. "He that keepeth Israel shall neither slumber nor sleep" (Psalm 121:4). When God is awake, there is no use for us to stay awake also. We are to do like Peter. We are to trust God for tomorow and for all the days to come.

IV. THE SUPERNATURAL. Verse 7-10

The midnight hour came and Peter was sleeping peacefully. He could sleep because he knew he belonged to God. His conscience was clear, he was confident that he was doing the will of God, and that God would look after him.

Suddenly an angel of the Lord entered the prison and stood by Peter. A bright light shone in the prison, but Peter was sleeping so soundly that the light did not wake him. What did the angel do? He smote Peter on the side and raised him up, saying, "Arise, quickly!" The sleepy preacher started to get up. As he did so, the chains fell from his hands and yet made no noise. The soldiers slept on.

Then the angel said, "Put on your clothes, put on your shoes, put on your coat and follow me." How tender are God's ministering angels! They have all the tenderness and thoughtfulness of a mother. The angel told Peter to put on his clothes. Then he said, "Do not go out without your shoes. Put on your coat, it is cold outside tonight." Then the angel took Peter by the hand and led him out of prison.

They went down the corridor and came to the first gate. The soldiers were there and Peter feared that they would awake, but they remained sound asleep. Then they came to the second gate and passed on through it. Then the big iron outer gate of the prison loomed before them. They stood there for a minute, the gate swung open, and they passed into the city streets. Peter turned to thank the angel, but the angel had suddenly disappeared and Peter was left alone.

We notice that the angel had to smite Peter to get him to follow him. Today God must often smite us before we are willing to follow Him. We go our way, heedless of His call, turning our backs on Him. He lovingly pleads with us, but we pay no attention to Him. He must smite us before we are willing to leave our sins and follow Him.

Sometimes He smites us with sickness. Often when a man becomes sick he must lie flat on his back. The only way that he can look is toward God. He thinks over his life and resolves to get up and live for God. God smites him and he follows the Lord. Sometimes He smites us with a great sorrow. Here is a man who is living for the world, a great sorrow comes, he realizes that he needs a hope that the world cannot give. He is softened and humbled and sees God's hand in it all. God smites him and he follows. Sometimes God smites us with conviction. Here is a man who is asleep in his sins—Through His means of grace God brings this man to repentance and faith. He smites his heart with convicting power, the man sees himself a lost sinner, and turns to Christ.

Some men who are smitten in this manner never follow Jesus. What if Peter, when he saw the angel, had said, "It is only a dream," and had rolled over and gone back to sleep? Or suppose that when the angel awakened him he had said, "It's no use, there are sixteen soldiers here and three iron gates holding me in the prison." He never would have been set free. And so it is that when God smites men with these things they should wake up and turn to Christ. Alas, many men push these things aside! They go on in their sins and come to the end of the way lost and without hope.

We notice that as soon as the angel had led Peter out into the street he left him. Peter could go the rest of the journey alone. He did not need the angel. So we see that God never does for us what we can do for ourselves. Peter could not get himself out of prison, but the angel could. Peter could not smite off his chains, he could not open the gates, but God could send an angel to do this for him. Peter could put on his garments, he could put on his coat, he could follow the angel. God today expects us to do our part. He is not going to send an angel to do for us the things which we can do for ourselves.

In one of Moody's meetings a man stood up and said, "We need $5,000. Let us pray for the Lord to send us this money."

Mr. Moody jumped to his feet and replied, "Why should we worry the Lord about this. Let us give it ourselves." He started the offering, the ushers passed the plates, and soon they had all they needed. If you need a new church God is not going to drop it out of the skies for you. He knows that you can build it yourself if you only will.

We need to grow powerful church organizations which will serve the Lord in a marvelous manner—but God is not going to send us such organizations tomorrow. It is up to us to go out and build these organizations by hard work. It is certainly true that "God helps those who help themselves." He will provide every need, but He expects us to do our part. We are to be "workers together with him" (II Corinthians 6:1).

V. THE SURPRISE. Verses 11-19

Well, when the angel left Peter on the street Peter came to himself and said, "I know that the Lord has done this. He has delivered me." He gave God the glory for his deliverance and so should we. We have been delivered from the guilt and penalty of sin, we have been delivered from many dangerous experiences, we have been delivered from sickness and sorrow. We ought always to say, "I cried unto God and He heard me and delivered me. Praise His Holy Name!"

Where did Peter go? He went to the house where the Christians were praying. So it is that when we have been delivered we ought to seek God's house and God's people. Peter arrived at the house of Mary, who was John Mark's mother. It was past midnight. He knocked on the door and a slave girl named Rhoda came to the door. She was so glad and so excited when she heard Peter's voice that she forgot to open the door. She ran back to the group, and cried out. "Peter is out of jail and is standing at the door!"

"Thou art mad," they told her (Acts 12:15).

But she kept on saying, "It's true, I heard his voice."

Peter was out there, wondering why they did not let him in. He found it easier to get out of prison than to get into this prayer meeting. Finally they followed Rhoda to the door and they found Peter there still knocking. They reached out and pulled him in and smothered him with their welcome, saying to one another, "Thank God! Thank God!" They had prayed fervently and their prayers had been answered. They were greatly surprised. God often surprises us in the same way, and oh, how sweet and wonderful it is!

Rhoda heard Peter outside the door. She knew he was there. The others tried to shake her testimony, but she kept on constantly affirming that it was so. If we have had an experience with the Lord, the world and the devil will often try to shake our testimony. But we must keep on affirming the truth of our experience.

Rhoda did not argue. She just stood on her experience. When they would not believe her she must have said, "All right, go to the door and see for yourselves." So when people question what The Lord has done for us, we ought to say, "All right, try Him out for yourself, and you will see that He can do the same thing for you."

God never forgets even the humblest servant. Here is this slave girl, now one of the Christians, doing just a small thing. Yet God puts her name here in the Book and records for all the ages to come the humble service which she gave to God's servant. There is a lesson here for us. Our place of service may be a small one, but we must be faithful and God will reward us.

One day in heaven there will be a Great Crowning Day. Peter will stand forth and the Lord will say, "Peter, you did a fine work in the world, you preached a great sermon at Pentecost, you won many souls and organized many churches, here is your crown." By the side of Peter there will be a girl named Rhoda. The Lord will say to her, "Rhoda, your place of service was a small one, but you were just as faithful as Peter. Here is your crown." I wonder if there will be any difference in these crowns, for, as Browning said, "All service ranks the same with God"?

The Christians were not the only ones who were surprised to find Peter free. The next morning the jail is in a turmoil —everything is in its place, but the important prisoner is not there. Herod could not find Peter, so after examining the guards he had them put to death. He is sowing the seed now; soon the harvest time will come and he will reap a tragic fate.

VI. THE SMITING. Verses 20-23

This Herod was a man of great egotism. He was fond of display and willing to sell his soul for popularity. We see him in Caesarea on the occasion of a great celebration. The people knew he was very sensitive to flattery. They knew that if they complimented the King, he in turn might favor them. Therefore they set a day for Herod to deliver an address. His throne was placed high above the crowd. Soon he came out clothed in a robe of solid silver which glittered in the sun. The people, knowing his weak spot, greeted him with thunderous applause. Herod, blinded by his own conceit, gulped it all down. The king then made his speech, the people listened attentively, and when he had finished they cried out, "It is the voice of a god" (Acts 12:22). Suddenly something happened. An angel smote the king, he toppled off his throne and died, and we read that "he was eaten of worms" (Acts 12:23).

Oh, how swift and how complete is divine retribution! Herod killed James, he put Peter in prison, he persecuted Christians, he killed the soldiers. Now, one, two, three, and the worms crawl over him and eat into his flesh. *Pay day has come! The king is reaping what he sowed!* It has been the same way ever since. The man who tries to crush the Gospel will be eaten of worms. The great infidels of the world have preached the Gospel's funeral, but today it is still the power of God, and the worms will eat the man who opposes it.

Verse twenty-four tells us that although Herod was eaten of worms, "the Word of God grew and multiplied." It will always be the same. When your pastor seeks to preach the Gospel you can help him as Rhoda helped Peter and receive your reward. Or you can oppose him as Herod did and furnish a banquet for the worms.

I am sure that many people envied Herod. He was the king, a man of great power and great wealth. But that is not the whole story. When you read the last chapter of his life, you see him lying prostrate in the dust, eaten of worms.

Today you look at some wicked man who has prospered greatly and you say, "Just look at that man. He lives for the devil and seems to have everything. I try to live for God and everything goes against me." But wait a minute—the returns are not all in yet. Take the long look and you will see the wicked cast into hell, for God says, "Their foot shall slide in due time" (Deuteronomy 32:35). When they are suffering forever in hell, we will be at home with God in heaven.

In this chapter we see the Lord's angel smiting twice, but with vastly different results. When he smote Peter he brought deliverance; when he smote Herod he brought death. It is the same angel, with the same power, but one touch brought life and the other brought death. In the same manner, the Gospel produces different effects. God smites one man with the truth and that man surrenders. He turns to Christ, is saved and is on the way to heaven. He smites another man and this man hardens his heart against God. This man goes his own way, which proves to be the way of condemnation and death, and finally lands in hell. May God help you to surrender to the Lord when His angel touches you!

I was holding a meeting in Kermit, Texas, which is the center of a great oil field. One night the pastor, the Rev. Strauss Atkinson, was called out on account of the death of one of the oil field workers. A heavy piece of machinery had fallen upon this man and he was instantly killed. The next day the pastor preached the funeral sermon and the church was crowded with men who had worked by the side of this man. They seemed to be deeply affected, and some of the church members said, "Surely now these men will see the mistake of living without God. They will see the imminence of death and accept Christ as Saviour." The pastor did urge the men to come to church and to come to Christ, but in twenty-four hours it seemed that these lost men had forgotten all about the tragedy. They went their way without Christ, although they had received this vivid warning.

Many times God warns men. He sends His angel to smite them. Too often these warnings are forgotten in a little while, and men go on to hell, to spend eternity there. May God help you to respond to His touch so that you might spend eternity with the One who loved you and gave Himself for you.

CHAPTER THIRTEEN

"SPIRITUAL SEPARATION"

Acts 13

Acts thirteen brings us to a great forward step in the matter of spreading the Gospel. Gradually this Gospel had been spreading out from Jerusalem, near where Jesus died to give us a Gospel to preach. Now it was time for the greatest man this side of Christ to carry the Good News far and wide. So we see Paul begin his first missionary journey. These journeys had a mighty influence upon the world. Churches were planted in many places. The influence of Christ was felt by millions of people. The whole world was soon different because of the direct and indirect effect of these missionary journeys.

These journeys were not pleasure trips for Paul. He found himself in prison often, and several times he was beaten with stripes. He was stoned almost to death, he was hated and persecuted, he was shipwrecked, and at last his journey ended in his death. But he said, "None of these things move me" (Acts 20:24). Christ told him that he would be called upon to suffer many things, but he loved Christ so much and appreciated his salvation so much that he was glad to suffer all of these things for Christ's sake.

I. THE SPIRIT. Verses 1-2

In the church at Antioch were five prophets and teachers. Barnabas and Saul were among them; the names of the other three are not important. They were busy for the Lord, but they had seasons when they fasted and prayed. During one of these seasons the Holy Spirit spoke to them in some way, saying, "Separate me Barnabas and Saul for the work whereunto I have called them" (Acts 13:2). We see here that a call to special service must come from God. I firmly believe that God calls men to preach. If I am sure of anything in this world, I am sure that God called me. I certainly had no such idea in my own mind. God, through the Holy Spirit, called me in an unmistakable way.

Sometime ago I talked to a part-time preacher. I asked him about his call to preach. He replied, "Well, after I was saved, I felt that I wanted to serve the Lord in some way, so I decided to preach." I asked him if there was a definite time or definite place when he was called, and he said, "No, I just felt that I wanted to serve the Lord." Every Christian ought to feel that way, but every Christian ought not to preach. I believe in a definite experience of grace and a definite call to preach. This definite setting aside for Paul came ten years after his conversion. The day that he was converted God told him that He had saved him for a purpose. He was to take the Gospel to the nations, but he was not ready for ten years. A time of preparation and seasoning had to come before he was ready. When God calls a man to a task He wants him to get the best preparation possible.

Before the Spirit separates us unto service, there must be in our own lives a separation from the world. There are many things that a Christian can do which will not hurt him physically or morally but they will hurt his spiritual power. Therefore, if we are to have spiritual power for service, we must be separated from the world. You may be able to drink a glass of beer, go to Sunday shows and Sunday parties, smoke or play cards, or do certain other things without injuring your physical and moral life. But you cannot do these things and still have spiritual power. Gasoline and water will not mix and give you physical power. Neither will worldliness and spirituality mix and give you spiritual power.

II. THE SENDING. Verses 3-5

When they knew that the Holy Spirit had called these two men to special service, they fasted and prayed. They laid their hands on them and sent them away. When they went they took a young man, John Mark, along with them. He helped them in every way possible. Here we have an ordination service. It was an official ceremony of the church, setting aside two men to a specific work by prayer and the laying on of hands. God had commissioned Paul. The church recognized that commission and said, "God has called you, now it is our pleasure as a church to send you, a God-called man, out into service."

Today some young man feels that he is called of God. He comes before his church saying, "I have had a definite call of the Lord. I want to turn my back on all else and preach the Gospel." This is a time of rejoicing for any church, a time when the church should thank God for the honor bestowed upon it.

Barnabas and Saul went out as missionaries of the Antioch Church. That threw the responsibility on the church to support them and pray for them. When a church member goes out to China or to the Islands of the Sea to tell the story of Christ, it gives him heart and courage to know that the home folks are backing him up. The deep sea diver puts on his helmet and goes down to the bottom of the sea. Someone up above pumps the air down to him; he is absolutely dependent upon that help. It is the same way in our missionary enterprise. At one end of the line we have our missionaries exploring the depths of sin and seeking the lost. At the other end we have our churches praying for them, and sending them all that they need.

These two men went out to preach Christ in a new territory. They won many souls, and from time to time this news drifted back to the Antioch Church. When they heard it, they fell upon their knees and thanked God for these victories.

As the missionaries of today send back their reports, we are to remember them, not as dead figures, but as stories of transformed lives. Surely this should make us rejoice. Here is a man in China who was an opium fiend—now he is a native preacher. Hallelujah! Here is a man who was a cannibal—now he is a humble Christian. Hallelujah! Here is one who bowed down before idols—now he knows the living Christ. Hallelujah! Yes, we should rejoice when we hear these stories. Here is another one snatched as a brand from the burning. And here is another and another and another. Hallelujah!

The blessed thing about the matter is that everyone of us can have a part. We cannot cross the seas, but we can send others. We can make money and bring our tithes and offerings and put them in God's treasury. Then those who have been called can go because you send them. Yes, you can be a foreign missionary without leaving home. Some day when you are at home in heaven a redeemed soul will come up to you and say, "I want to thank you for what you did. I am in heaven because of you."

"You will say, "I never saw you in my life."

"But you gave your money and you sent a missionary to me with the story of Christ and I was saved. You did it." Then surely there will be more hallelujahs all over heaven.

We want to build a great church and the best way to do it is by obedience to God's command to send the Gospel to the whole world. We can concentrate on ourselves and dry up and blow away. We can develop a great missionary spirit and God will give us a powerful church. The more we do for others, the more He does for us. The greatest churches we have are the ones with great missionary zeal.

A certain young woman was missionary to the lepers. One day she was going to make a trip to tell the lepers about Jesus, but she learned that there were lions along the road, making her trip a very dangerous one. She felt that she just must make this trip. A native Christian begged her to let him go with her. He was a poor, weak fellow, and she knew that he would be of little help in time of danger. So she asked him, "What could you do if we were attacked?"

He answered, "I could give a life."

May God grant that many of our young people shall rise up and say, "I will give a life."

And may those of us who stay behind say, "I will give my money and my prayers as my part of the missionary work."

III. THE SORCERER. Verses 6-13

The apostles came to the Isle of Cyprus. Sergius Paulus was governor of this Island. The apostles went to the city of Paphos, which is said to be the birthplace of Venus, the goddess of love. The Greeks said that she had been born out of the foam of the sea. Hence the worship of the Island was the worship of Venus, which was as vile as any mind could devise.

At Paphos Paul sought to win the governor to Christ and found him greatly interested. In the city there was also a sorcerer, a Jew, who bore the Greek name of Elymas. He had cast aside his Jewish faith and had become a magician. By his deeds he was causing God's Name to be blasphemed among the Gentiles. Men cannot do without some kind of religion, so we find these sorcerers at every Roman court. When Elymas saw that the governor was interested in Christianity, he did everything to divert him from a decision. Paul blazed out at him, and said, "You child of the devil, the Lord will strike you blind." Immediately his sight was gone and someone had to lead him by the hand. When the governor saw this he was astonished. It made such an impression upon him that he gave his heart to Christ and became a Christian.

It often happens that when the Spirit works with a man Satan steps in and seeks to divert that man and to keep him from being converted. A man hears a sermon, the Spirit convicts him, and when the invitation is given someone sitting next to him decides that it is time to leave. He pushes out and the man's attention is diverted, his line of thought is broken. The invitation is soon over and he goes back into the world, lost. Or a man may be listening to a sermon and as the Holy Spirit seeks to convict him, someone near him begins to talk and he is diverted. Or, when he is convicted Satan says to him, "Look at that man up near the front, he is a hypocrite." Or, when the man is just about to go forward, Satan says, "You have plenty of time, enjoy your sin a little longer. You have a long time to live and before you die you can be saved." Yes, Satan does his best to keep men from being saved.

We note that a change appeared right here in the Gospel story. Saul's name was changed to Paul. Saul was a Jewish name. He was proud of his Jewish ancestry and privileges. But he changed the name to the Roman name, Paul. It seemed that he was saying, "I am taking all the worldly things that I am proud of and am wrapping them up in a bundle. I am putting them behind me so that I will be able to reach the ones that I could not reach if I held on to these things." If you want to bless men you must identify yourself with them.

A great teacher became interested in helping the blind. He decided that he would open a school for them. He had himself blindfolded for months, so that he would know just how a blind man felt. When he began his school, he knew the mind and the feeling of the blind and was of great help to them.

This is the reason that God did not send Jesus to earth as a fullgrown man. He allowed him to come as a little babe and grow up as a normal child. He suffered all the things that come to us on this earth and now He knows how we feel and can sympathize with us.

So Paul, the apostle to the Gentiles, adoped a Gentile name. He said "All that meant most to me I have left behind. I am here to help you to Christ. I have become all things to all men so that I might win them." The name Saul means "Desired," and tells of his life before conversion. The name Paul means "Little," and tells of the way that he felt after he met Christ.

Paul's first recorded convert was named Paulus. Paul took his new name from this convert. He thought that the highest honor that could ever come to him would be to win a man to Christ. He remembered it the rest of his life by using the convert's name as his own.

What do you think is the best thing in life? What do you want on your tomb? "He was rich, he was famous, he ran a big business, he wrote books, he was president of a college?" Or would you like to have it written on your tomb that you had "turned many to righteousness." This man Paul could have been all of the above things, but he flung them away and chose to live for Christ. Now he is remembered for what he did for the Lord.

IV. THE SERMON. Verses 14-43

Paul and Barnabas were alone now. For some reason Mark had left them. They went to Antioch in Pisidia. On the Sabbath day they went to the synagogue and sat down in the congregation.

There are three parts to a Jewish service. The ruler reads a portion from the law, then a portion from the prophets, then comes the Midrash, or sermon. If any distinguished visitor was present the ruler would ask him to give the Midrash. You will remember that on a certain Sabbath when Jesus was in the synagogue the ruler read a prophecy from Isaiah, and when he asked Jesus to speak, Jesus told them that the Scripture had been fulfilled that day in their midst.

On this day the ruler turned to the apostles, saying, "If you have anything to say, say on." Paul went to the front and preached his first recorded sermon. What a surprise this was to them! He interpreted the Scriptures all right, but he showed that all of it led up to Jesus Christ.

The results of the sermon were tremendous, not because Paul was a mighty preacher, but because he was filled with the Holy Ghost and because he preached Jesus Christ. What kind of a preacher was Paul? We find the answer in II Corinthians 10:10—"His letters . . . are powerful; but his bodily presence is weak, and his speech is contemptible." They said that he was a good writer, but a poor preacher. However, when he finished that first sermon the Gentiles crowded around him, and said, "We want you to preach for us again next Sunday." A preacher knows he has made a good impression when they invite him back again.

When Paul and Barnabas had left the synagogue and started toward their hotel, the people who had been converted would not give them up. They followed them down the street and the apostles talked with them some more, and exhorted them to stand up to their conversion. The great trouble today is that many have been converted, but few continue faithful. Not all of these go back into sin, but many of them go back into the world and become indifferent to Christ and His Church. God help you who have been recently saved to say, "I will be faithful—I appreciate what Christ has done for me and I am going to be faithful to Him and His Church."

I cannot help mentioning Paul's first recorded sermon. He did not talk about Jesus' good life, His miracles or His teachings—he concentrated on His death and resurrection. He spoke thusly of David, whom they reverenced, "He died and saw corruption." Of Jesus he said, "The one whom God raised saw no corruption." This was the secret of all Paul's power. He believed that he had a living Saviour and not a dead deity.

Martin Luther came to a time in his life when he needed unusual strength. He was sitting at a table with a friend. This friend saw him tracing on the cloth with his finger the words: "Vivit-Vivit," meaning "He liveth-He liveth." That is our hope. Men come and go, but He abides. They die, but He lives. Their lights shine for a while, but He shines forever.

V. THE SPEAKING. Verses 44-45

During the next week the people talked about Paul's sermon all over the city. This was something new and wonderful, especially to the Gentiles. They learned that they could become Christians without becoming Jews and submitting to circumcision and other Jewish rites. The next Sunday the house would not hold the people.

Your advertising in the paper or through the mail may be very effective, but when everyone goes out of a church to tell others about the great services which are being held there it will not be long until the house will be filled. The Jews saw the Gentiles pouring in to hear the new Gospel, and became filled with prejudice and jealousy. They began to fight Paul and the Gospel he preached. We see here a contest of speech, of argument, of logic. On one side we have Paul, contending for the Gospel. On the other side we have the Jews, contradicting everything that Paul said. Men are always stirred to great action by effective speech. During the war we had Hitler on one side and Churchill and

Roosevelt on the other side, goading their countrymen into action by their oratory. But the greatest speaking that ever has been done in the world was done by the flaming heralds of the Cross.

VI. THE SHAKING. Verses 46-52

When the Jews fought against Paul he said something that broke his own heart. He loved his own race, he longed to see them saved, but he had to say, "It was necessary to offer Christ to you first, but since you do not want Him, since you will not have Him, we turn to the Gentiles." This happened every place that he went. In each city he sought out the Jews first and offered Christ to them, hoping that he would find one group which would accept Him. But always and everywhere they rejected his message and he was forced to turn to the Gentiles. This is the reason that he is called, "The Apostle to the Gentiles."

Paul and Barnabas left the synagogue. They went out into the open where they found eager hearts awaiting them. The Gentiles rejoiced that Jesus and salvation were going to be offered to them.

We read that "as many as were ordained to eternal life believed" (Acts 13:48). Is Luke saying here that ordination precedes eternal life? Yes, the whole Bible teaches it. Ordination to eternal life takes place in eternity. Salvation commences with God and not with man, salvation is all of grace and not of works. Paul gives the order in Romans 8:29-30. "For whom he did foreknow, he also did predestinate to be conformed to the image of his Son, that he might be the firstborn among many brethren. Moreover whom he did predestinate, them he also called: and whom he called, them he also justified: and whom he justified, them he also glorified." Salvation starts in the heart of God. He foreknows you, He ordains you, He calls you. The moment that you believe you are justified, and some day you will be glorified.

The result of the work of Paul and Barnabas is shown in verse 49: "And the word of the Lord was published throughout all the region." This roused Satan's anger. He got busy and caused the Jews to stir up the women of the city against Paul and Barnabas. Soon they were expelled from the city.

Paul and Barnabas left the city and as they left they did a strange thing. They shook the dust off their feet. You will remember that when Jesus sent His disciples into a town, they were to go to a house and say, "Peace be on this house." If the people in this house refused to receive them, they were to shake the dust off their feet. Here Paul and Barnabas said to the people, "We bring you peace of heart and salvation in the Name of Christ." But the message was rejected and now they shook the dust off their feet.

This was done as a testimony. These people must meet that testimony again at the Judgment Bar of God. Some day these men will be on trial before God. A little handful of dust will be brought in and each man will say, "What does this dust have to do with me?"

And the answer will come back: "On this very dust God's man stood and preached to you the Word of Life, but you rejected it." Thus will the dust testify against these men.

Today men hear the Word of God and go on in sin. Many witnesses will rise up in the Judgment against them. The Bible will say, "I was there upon earth to teach you the way of life, but you rejected my teachings." The Church will rise up and say, "My mission in life was to point men to the Lamb of God, but you said that you did not need the church."

The sermons that you have heard will rise up to condemn you. Your better judgment and your conscience will rise up and say, "We tried to warn you, we told you which was the better way, but you would not walk therein." The dark providences of God will rise up and say, "We were sent upon you to make you stop and think and see your need of God, but you trampled over us in order to go to hell." The Holy Spirit will rise up to say, "I came into your heart to convict you of sin, but you quenched my voice, and went on without the Lord." At last Jesus Christ will rise up and say, "I died upon the Cross for you, I loved you with an everlasting love, but you turned your back upon Me. Yes, you turned your back upon the only One who could give you help and hope."

The Judgment Day is coming. Let me urge you to leave your sins and come to Jesus now so that you will be safe in that day.

The apostles left Antioch, but we are told that the believers who were left behind were filled with joy and the Holy Spirit. The preachers were gone, the believers were left in the midst of their enemies, and yet they rejoiced. They rejoiced because they knew Christ, their sins had been washed away, and they had a daily Companion. They rejoiced because they had One who would stand by them in life and death and take them home to heaven at last. Thank God, you and I, too, can rejoice in every circumstance of life. Let the winds of adversity blow, let the troubles come, let Satan buffet. We have Jesus and all is well with our souls.

The Christ-rejectors at Antioch remind us of the story of Aaron Burr. At the age of nineteen he was a brilliant student in Princeton University. A revival broke out on the campus. He was deeply convicted. His roommate asked him to accept Christ and he was almost persuaded. He went to see one of his professors and told him about his dilemma. The professor gave him a Bible and said to him, "Go to your room and settle this matter on your knees." Instead of doing this he tried to shake off the power of the Holy Spirit.

Finally in desperation he cried out, "God, let me alone and I'll let you alone." As soon as he said it, all conviction left him. Years later he met a friend whom he admired very much.

"Dr. Burr," this friend said, "I would like for you to meet a friend of mine."

"If he is anything like you, I will be glad to meet him," said Dr. Burr.

"His Name is Jesus Christ," replied the man, "I would like for you to meet Him." The cold sweat popped out upon Burr's forehead. He told about how at the age of nineteen he had said, "God, let me alone, and I'll let you alone."

Then he said, "From that day to this, I have never had one desire to become a Christian."

Do not say, "God, let me alone." Instead will you not say, "Come into my heart, Lord Jesus. I need You now. I will need You when I come down to die. I will need You when I stand out yonder before the judgment bar of God."

CHAPTER FOURTEEN

"SPIRITUAL TRIBULATION"

Acts 14

In the early days of America our land was greatly blessed by the traveling preachers. The little settlements of that day were widely separated and were not large enough to maintain churches and regular pastors. These "saddle-bag" preachers came riding into these small settlements from time to time. They would stay awhile in each place; preaching the Gospel, winning the lost, and ministering to the people. They left a trail of blessing wherever they went.

We can think of Paul and Barnabas as having done the same kind of work. They had been commissioned by God to be missionaries, and in the thirteenth chapter of Acts the Antioch Church set these two men aside to do this special work. Next we see them going from city to city, preaching the Gospel. As the fourteenth chapter opens we see that they went into Iconium on the second part of their first missionary journey.

I. THE DIVISION. Verses 1-7

We see that Paul and Barnabas went into a Jewish synagogue. Paul "so spoke" that a great number of the Jews and Greeks were saved. What is meant by the term "so spoke"? This meant that they not only spoke the truth in Christ, but that they spoke it in a convincing manner. They put the issue right up to the hearts of their hearers. They did not say, "We are telling you about God and sometime it would be a good idea for you to look into the matter of your salvation." Such preaching never would have convinced anybody. It demanded a decision.

This is the kind of preaching we need today. We need to say to men, "Here you are in your sin. Here is the God whom you must face someday. You are not ready now. A sinful man can never face a perfect God. But He offers you a way of salvation. He offers you perfection in Christ if you will only accept Him as a free gift. What are you going to do about it? Will you accept Him and be saved, or reject Him and go to Hell?" That is the clear-cut issue which faces every man today. Therefore our preaching should be clear-cut and should call for a decision.

As usual, when the Lord began to save the people, Satan stirred up trouble. The Jews said things which made many of the Gentiles turn against the apostles. On the other hand, the Lord gave the apostles power to perform many miracles. In a little while the whole city was divided. Some said, "These men are devils." Others said, "These men are wonderful; God must be with them." Christ is forever the great divider. He never divides along horizontal lines, putting some above others, saying that some are better than others. He uses perpendicular lines. On one side he puts the sinner, on the other side the saint. On one side he puts the lost, on the other side the saved. He said, "I came not to send peace, but a sword" (Matthew 10:34). Men divide at the Cross, and it becomes an eternal division.

Christ had been the divider in Paul's life. When Saul came to know Christ, he stood over on one side with Him, and all of his old friends and interests stood on the other side. Christ had made the division. Today a woman accepts Christ and invites her husband to go along with her. He stubbornly refuses. They may live together for many years, but you will find a division there, one is with Christ and the other is against

Him. A young man who has many fast friends is converted. They soon give him up, they will have nothing to do with him. Christ has divided them.

Dr. W. A. Criswell tells of a young Jew who came to his church in Dallas and who gave his heart to Christ. However, the young man would not come for baptism, as he felt that he could not make the final break with his family. One day he came to Dr. Criswell and said, "I am ready for baptism. I will go all the way with Christ. It will cost me my family, but I must follow my Saviour. Right now they are having a little funeral ceremony for me at my house, counting me as dead. It breaks my heart to lose them, but I must follow Christ, whatever the cost."

Jesus said, "A man's foes shall be they of his own household" (Matthew 10:34). This means that one in the home will seek to follow Christ while another will oppose the Christian and do everything to hinder him. But in the same chapter He tells us that if we do not love Him better than all of these, we are not worthy of Him.

Here is a woman who accepts Christ. Her husband makes it hard for her. Then she says, "I want to have peace in my family." She gives up her church, she stays at home with him or goes to the places of the world with him on Sunday. Her religion never means anything to her. She has no influence on her husband, and soon she is drifting down the same stream with him.

But I have seen another type. A woman accepts Christ and although her husband makes it hard for her she says, "This is going to be hard for me, but I will be true to my Saviour." She goes to church, she serves her Lord. She has a mighty hard time, but she tries to keep sweet and keeps on praying for her husband.

She lives such a good Christian life that he finally says, "There is something to it after all." Soon he is interested, and soon he is converted. Yes, Jesus is a divider. But remember that when He draws a line, when He makes the division, He is over on the side of the one who trusts Him.

He not only divides here—He is the eternal divider. People live side by side for years, but out there He divides them forever. His sheep are on one side, and Satan's goats are on the other. In the story of Lazarus and the rich man, you will remember that the rich man wanted Lazarus to leave heaven for a minute and to come down into hell, bringing him a few drops of water. But Abraham said, "There is a great gulf fixed between heaven and hell; when you go to one place you can never get over into the other one."

Dr. L. R. Scarborough tells of preaching one night on the subject of hell and the fixed gulf. An unsaved man sat in his congregation with his wife, who was a Christian. They drove home to the ranch that night without speaking a word. They went to bed at ten o'clock, but they could not sleep. At two o'clock the wife said to him, "Husband, what's the matter?"

He replied, "Wife, we've lived together for forty years. We have been very happy and I don't want to be separated from you. The preacher said that there was a great gulf out yonder in eternity. Is it true?"

"Yes," she said, "I will read it to you out of the Bible." They got out of bed and she read this story from the Bible.

"Oh, wife," he said, "I want to get on your side of the gulf!" They knelt and prayed together and he gave his heart to Christ. The next day, when he came to join the church, he said, "Bless God, I am on my wife's side of the gulf."

Some day you business men will leave your office, your store or your shop for the last time. You housewives will clean your house for the last time, cook your last meal, wash your last dish. You will lie down to sleep for the last time.

Death will creep up on you. Soon your loved ones who stand by the bedside will say, "He is gone."

Someone will make the funeral arrangements. Your body will be carried to the funeral parlor and then to the cemetery. The preacher will say, "We do now commit this body to the grave, to await the resurrection morning." Where will your soul be? Which side of the gulf will you be on? Oh, if you are wise you will get on Christ's side! You will leave your sin and trust Him, so that when death comes you will be ready.

II. THE DELIVERANCE. Verses 8-10

Because of the division and difficulties in Iconium Paul and Barnabas went to Lystra. As Paul preached one day in the congregation he saw a crippled man, a man who had been helpless all of his life, a man who had never walked. It is bad enough to be crippled now, with rolling chairs and modern surgery and scientific inventions to help. How much worse it must have been then when they had none of these things and when a man had to depend upon someone else to carry him wherever he wanted to go. How pitiful it was to see him there with his eyes lifted toward Paul! But he could thank God that someone brought him to this place today. We could do more of that, too. We could bring more helpless sinners to church, where they could receive the help that they need.

We read next that the man "heard Paul speak" (Acts 14 :9). Paul told how God loved lost sinners, how He sent His Son into the world to save them, how Jesus lived a perfect life. He told how Jesus went about doing good, giving sight to the blind, healing the sick, and giving new bodies to the lame. Then he told how Christ died upon the Cross, was buried, rose again and ascended into heaven. Then with a glowing face Paul told of his own wonderful meeting with

Christ on the Damascus Road. He told how his entire life had been transformed by the Lord.

You can imagine how this sounded to the poor crippled man. "If Jesus can do all these things," he said, "if He can even bring a man back from the grave, I believe that He can surely help me." Paul had been watching the man. He saw how his face had lit up, how the hope had risen in his eyes. He knew he had faith to be healed, so he cried out with a loud voice, "Stand up on your feet!" The man never had been able to do this, but he gave no excuses. He started to rise and as he did so, he felt a strange power flowing into his body. In a minute he was not only standing, but he was leaping and walking.

The Lord always does a complete job. He did not just fix the man so he could stand, but he gave him the power to walk and leap like a boy. When He saves you and me, He does a complete job. He saves us from sin: past, present and future. He takes our feet off the slippery clay and plants us on the Solid Rock. He snatches us out of Satan's grasp, adopts us into His own family, and makes us to become the children of God. He closes His hand around us, and no power in heaven or earth or hell can break that grip. He takes us home to heaven at the end of the way. Yes, salvation in Christ is a complete salvation. He saves our souls now, He writes our names in the Lamb's Book of Life.

One day He will come back and redeem our bodies, making them perfect and glorifying them. Then all through the eternal ages we will enjoy a perfect life because of His complete salvation of soul, mind and body.

III. The Deification. Verses 11-18

The people knew this cripple. They had seen him lying about in a helpless condition for many years. Now they saw him leaping and walking. They were tremendously affected. They lifted their voices and said, "See what Paul and Barnabas have done. These are not men—they are gods come down in the likeness of men."

These people worshipped the gods of mythology. Jupiter, who lived on Mount Olympus, was their head god. There were many other lesser gods and goddesses. So they looked at Barnabas, who was the more imposing of the two and said, "He is Jupiter." Then they looked at Paul who delivered the message and said, "He is Mercury, the messenger of the gods." They then rushed into the temple and told the heathen priests about it.

The priests said, "If Jupiter and Mercury are here, we must offer a sacrifice to them." So they took an oxen, put garlands upon his horns and marched down the street. When they found Paul and Barnabas, they were ready to make a sacrifice.

If there was one thing that the Jews believed in, it was the fact of one God. There had been a time when they worshipped the gods of the surrounding nations, but they were cured of that in captivity. They came back, knowing that the Lord God was the one God and the only God. What these people did seemed to be the most awful blasphemy to Paul and Barnabas. They tore their clothes, rushed among the people, and cried out, "Do not do this; we are just men; there is only one God—the God of heaven, and we are His servants." Finally, after great difficulty, they were able to restrain the people.

In his impassioned plea, as he sought to impress upon them the truth of the one God, Paul told them that God had not left Himself without witness. That witness was in nature. Paul said, "Other gods have done nothing for you. Look around and you will see what the God of heaven has done. He has sent you the rain and the sun and fruitful seasons. He has given you everything that you need on this earth."

Everything in nature points to God. "The Heavens declare the glory of God; and the firmament sheweth his handy-work" (Psalm 19:1).

(1) The mountains remind us of the steadfast, unchanging nature of God.

(2) The recurring seasons tell us of His fidelity.

(3) The rainbow tells us that He always keeps His promises.

(4) The clouds remind us of how He led His people toward the Promised Land.

(5) The sea reminds us that He said, "I have cast thy sins into the deepest sea."

(6) The river reminds us of the River of Life that flows by the throne of God.

(7) The troubled waves reminds us of Him who stilled the storms.

(8) The rocks remind us of the Rock of Ages.

(9) The stars remind us of Jesus Christ, the Bright and Morning Star.

(10) The sun reminds us of the Son of Righteousness, shining into our hearts, dispelling all of our doubts and darkness.

(11) The trees and the flowers and the waving grain remind us of the One who gives life and sustains life.

Yes, all of nature unites to say, "God lives, God loves; God provides for every need and fills our lives with gladness."

IV. THE DECEASE. Verses 19-20

We look now upon a hateful picture of vindictiveness. The people in Iconium and Antioch had run the apostles out of these cities. But they were not satisfied with that, they followed them down to Lystra, told all kinds of tales about them, and stirred the people against them. What happened? They stoned Paul and, thinking that he was dead, dragged him out of the city.

Look how the people had changed: one day they were willing to fall down before them and worship them as gods —the next day they were trying to put them to death. Such is the power of gossip and talebearing.

A man may be very good, he may be doing a fine work in a certain place, but a group starts talking about him. Every time they pass a certain tale around, the tale gets bigger. Soon this man and his influence have been ruined. This is one of the biggest faults of Christians today, and the devil is behind it all.

But Paul was not dead. God still had a great work for him to do. His time of death would come later. I believe that God keeps a man going until he finishes the work He sends him to do. Some people are not doing any of God's work. Their time may come sooner than they expect. I can imagine that the disciples stood around Paul saying, "Poor old Paul, he meant well, but he was too zealous. If he had just toned down his Gospel a little, if he had soft pedaled his talk about their guilt, maybe he would still have been living." But as they watched him, they saw him stir a bit. A groan came from his lips, but he rose to his feet and said, "Brethren, God saved me that time, He saved me for a purpose. I must go on about my Master's business."

One outstanding thing happened at Lystra. A grandmother named Lois, a mother named Eunice, and a boy named Timothy were saved. Later on this boy Timothy is going to become a preacher. He will be one of the brightest stars in Paul's crown, and Paul will look upon him as his own son. If nobody else had been converted at Lystra except Timothy and Eunice and Lois, it would have been worth all the suffering that came out of the trip. I am sure that Paul felt that way.

V. The Development. Verses 21-23

Paul and Barnabas moved on to the city of Derbe. There

was no persecution there for them. Maybe God was making things up to Paul for the trouble he had at Lystra. During Paul's stay a famous man, Gaius, was converted.

Now was the time to close the tour and go back to the mother church. It would have been easy for them to avoid Antioch, Iconium and Lystra. They had been run out of the first two places, and Paul had been stoned almost to death in the last one. But they went right back over the same ground. They were not afraid, they had work to do in these places, and they knew that God would be with them.

They did two things in these cities. First, they confirmed the converts. This does not mean that they went through some sort of a religious ceremony. These people had been saved, they had been baptized. This simply means that they were strengthened by the apostles and exhorted to be faithful. They had just emerged from heathenism and they needed this encouragement. We need to do more of this in our churches. It would be foolish to put a new-born chicken in a refrigerator. Yet, just about the same thing happens in our churches. Souls are born into the kingdom of God, they are put down into a cold church and soon lose interest. We ought to do everything in our power to encourage and enlist our new converts.

The second thing Paul and Barnabas did was to ordain elders in these new churches. These churches needed ministers. When Paul and Barnabas returned they found that some of the younger men, like Timothy, had become very active for God. The churches recommended them to the apostles and they were ordained and left in charge of the work in the churches. Then Paul said, "We will have to leave you now, you Christians remain faithful to the Lord and follow your pastor's leadership." Then he led them in prayer, left them in the hands of God, and departed.

John Wesley went through many English mining villages

on his preaching tours. Sometime later Cardinal Newman went through these same villages. He was surprised at what he saw. These villages were not dirty like the other towns. The homes were neat, flowers were planted in various places, the women were tastefully dressed and everybody seemed to be happy. When he asked what had made the difference a villager answered, "Several years ago a man by the name of John Wesley passed through this village." I am sure that after Paul and Barnabas passed through these cities, they, too, were changed. The people were better, they were cleaner, more useful and more unselfish. All this happened because these men brought Jesus with them. He is the One who makes the big difference. I wish that you and I would so live for Him that we, too, would leave a trail of goodness and happiness behind us.

VI. THE DESCRIPTION. Verses 24-28

The first missionary tour was over now and the apostles went home to make their report. The Antioch Church had sent them out, and so to Antioch they returned. We can imagine what happened.

On Sunday the pastor announced, "Sometime ago we ordained Brother Paul and Brother Barnabas and sent them out as our missionaries. We have heard wonderful things about their work. They have been through many difficulties, they have had many narrow escapes, but they will be here Wednesday night in person to tell us all about it. I know that you will want to hear them." Wednesday night every member who was able to walk was present. The house was packed with people. They sang the doxology, and offered a prayer thanking God for the safe return of these two men, then turned the meeting over to the apostles.

Paul insisted that Barnabas would speak first. He made a short talk, but left it up to Paul to tell most of the story. He told all that the Lord had done, about the souls that had been saved and the churches that had been established. He thanked the church for its support and prayers, but he gave all the glory to God.

When the meeting closed, the people thronged the aisles, gripping the hands of these apostles, and spoke words of encouragement and love to them. The hearts of Paul and Barnabas were so filled with joy that they forgot all the hardships and thanked God that they were worthy to be called servants of the Lord Jesus Christ.

When we think of the lives of the apostles and compare them with our lives today, it gives us a sickening feeling. They endured hardships for Jesus and rejoiced in them. They were nearly killed but they did not quit, they went on. At the end of the journey they did not say, "It is time for us to retire;" but they said, "we are ready to go again —anywhere for Jesus."

What do some of you say today? "We work six days a week and we are too tired to come to church on Sunday. We gave the church five dollars several years ago and we are not going to give anything this year. Mrs. Jones is not cordial to me, so I am going to quit. I am on the committee, but they didn't list my name in the bulletin, so I am going to resign. The church sent me a statement and I received it in the same mail with the grocery bill, the telephone bill and the gasoline bill. I'll keep on trading with them, but I'll never darken the door of the church again. I don't like the pastor, or the deacons, or the choir, so I am going to stay at home."

Their lives are not made up of service, but of excuses. At the end of the way, they will not have any sheaves to lay down at Jesus' feet; they will just have a bundle of excuses. Yet they say they are Christians and they talk about Cross-bearing. God pity us! What a sorry lot we are!

A small boy was playing on a pier at a summer resort when

suddenly he fell into the deep water. He cried for help, since he could not swim a stroke. A man who was going by heard his cries, took off his coat, jumped in the water and pulled the boy out. They gave the boy artificial respiration and soon he was all right. He looked up into the face of his rescuer and politely said, "Thank you, sir, for saving my life."

"That's all right son," replied the man, "I was glad to do it, but see to it that you are worth saving." The boy never forgot what the man said. He grew up to be a good and useful man.

Friends, there was a time when we were sinking deep in sin, but Jesus gave His life to save us. May God help us so to live that He will be glad that He saved us. Let us leave the low path-ways of sin and walk with Him on the road of good, useful service. Then at the end of the way He can say, "I am glad I died for you. You tried to pay me back with a worthy life."

SIMPLE SERMONS
FROM THE
BOOK OF ACTS

VOLUME II

By

W. HERSCHEL FORD, B.A., D.D.

Introduction by

ROBERT G. LEE, D.D., LL.D., LITT.D.

ZONDERVAN PUBLISHING HOUSE
Grand Rapids, Michigan

CONTENTS

CHAPTER FIFTEEN

"SPIRITUAL INDOCTRINATION"

Acts 15

God's true preacher proclaims always that salvation is all because of God's grace, and that a man receives salvation through faith in Jesus Christ, and that alone. This is pure Bible teaching. We are to add nothing to God's plan, we are to take nothing away. Here is where the churches divide today. Some teach that a man is saved the minute he puts his trust in Christ. "As many as received him, to them gave he power to become the sons of God. . ." (John 1:12). Others teach that you must add baptism or the Lord's Supper or church membership or good works or something else in order to be saved. In Acts 15 we see the beginning of this issue. We hear the contention of the two opposing groups and we find the clear-cut Bible answer. We need to study this answer again, in order to decide if we are following the Bible way.

I. THE DISSENTERS. Verse 1

In the Jerusalem church there were some nominal converts to Christianity. Privately, and without authority from anybody, they slipped off and went to Antioch. As they spied upon the Antioch Church they saw that the Gentiles were coming into the church without being circumcised and without submitting to other Jewish rites. One day they had the boldness to stand up and say, "You folks can never be saved, you can never get to heaven unless you are circumcised."

Today we hear the same sort of false teaching, "You

13

can't be saved unless you are baptized," they say, "or unless you do this or the other external thing." These people admit that you must trust Christ to be saved, but they say that this is not enough, you must add something else. I tell you that Christ has the power to save men without help from anything else on earth. The worst enemy of Christianity is the man who makes salvation dependent upon external rites. Salvation is an inner thing—all the outward ceremonies and rites are powerless to save. The heart is the thing which must be changed.

Sometime ago I visited a dying man in a certain hospital. As I came out of the hospital room I was greeted by one of the sisters. I told her that this man was dying without salvation. Quickly she said, "Do you mean that he has not been baptized?" When I told her the man had never accepted Christ she quickly sped away to bring someone back who would perform an external rite upon the man before he breathed his last breath. Here was a man who had lived in sin and unbelief, rejecting Christ all of his life. What good would it do at the end of the way to sprinkle a little water on his head? Five billion gallons of water cannot wash away one single sin, no matter who blesses the water. We often read of a criminal who is slated to die in the electric chair. The night before the execution the priest comes in and gives him the "extreme unction". Does that ceremony wash the criminals sin away and give him entrance into the heavenly kingdom? No, the only way to be saved is through an inner heart experience with God through Jesus Christ.

> What can wash away my sin?
> Nothing but the blood of Jesus;
> What can make me whole again?
> Nothing but the blood of Jesus.
> Oh, precious is the flow
> That makes me white as snow;
> No other fount I know,
> Nothing but the blood of Jesus.

II. THE DECLARATION. Verse 2-4

Paul and Barnabas soon learned of the work that these dissenters were doing. The fundamental things which these two men had preached were being undermined. This brought on quite a discussion, which I am sure developed into heated arguments. Paul received his doctrine straight from God. He knew he was right and he had the courage to stand up against these men from Jerusalem. He did not say "The Jerusalem church is full of heresy, the men up there have gone over into modernism." He was wise enough to say, "Let's find out if this teaching is prevalent in the Jerusalem church before condemning them." It's always wise to take this course. Too many of us jump to conclusions. We hear something bad about someone and turn against him, when there may not be a particle of truth in the story.

So the Antioch Church decided to send messengers to Jerusalem to ask them the question, "Have you decided that Gentiles must conform to Jewish rites in order to be saved, or are these men acting on their own authority? What do you believe?" They elected Paul and Barnabas and several other men as messengers.

These men took Titus, a young Christian, along as a test case. He was a full-blooded Gentile. They could present him and say, "Here is a Gentile, a man not descended from Abraham. He is an intelligent man. He gives every evidence of the fact that he is saved. Do you mean to say that he cannot be saved until he is circumcised?"

These messengers began their journey, and as they went along they stopped and visited the various Christian believers. They did not talk about the question at issue, but they just told how the Gentiles were being saved and this news caused these believers to rejoice.

III. THE DISCUSSION. Verses 5-18

When these men arrived in Jerusalem they were graciously received by the church. The church knew of the good work they had done and felt honored to have them present. I have gone to our conventions, have seen the missionaries on the platform and have heard their thrilling stories of how salvation had come to heathen lands. I felt like bowing before these missionaries whom God had so used. However, these men did not lose much time in greetings. Soon the question came up for debate. Paul said, "Certain men have come to Antioch from your church. They say that the Gentiles must conform to Jewish rites in order to be saved. Do you think this is true? Or do you think that men are saved through simple faith in Jesus Christ?" The pastor, the apostles and the other preachers came together to discuss the matter and later the entire church was called in.

The first testimony was given by Peter. Surely no man was better qualified to speak than he. "You remember that sometime ago God sent me with the Gospel to the Gentiles at Caesarea. Cornelius and many others were saved. When you heard about it, you investigated the matter and approved of what was done. Are you now going to repeal the decision which you made then?"

Paul and Barnabas then spoke. They told of how they had gone among the Gentiles, and recounted many instances of marvelous conversions. I wish I could have heard these men speak. Surely everyone there must have been thrilled to the depths.

James was the next one to speak. This was not James the apostle, one of the famous trio of Peter, James and John. He had already been killed by Herod. This James was the brother of Jesus. He was the pastor of the Jerusalem church and therefore he acted as presiding officer. We are told that he died as a martyr, that he was thrown down from the Temple, stoned, and then his brains dashed out with a club. When he was dressed for burial they found great callouses on his knees, showing that he had been a man of much prayer.

These men of old could teach us something about prayer.

They were ringed about with their enemies. Their lives were never safe, but they found refuge in prayer, they received courage in prayer. Today our lives may not be in danger, but we are surrounded by enemies of the soul, and we truly need to pray.

What did pastor James say? "I heard Peter declare that it was God's purpose to take out of the nations a people for His Name." That is what God is doing right now. He is not saving entire cities and entire nations, but here and there He is taking some out and saving them. We are to work towards saving everybody, yet we know that not all will be saved. We are to evangelize the whole world, but we can never Christianize the whole world. If you want to see how God's program is working, just look around you. Great multitudes are passing by the church of God. They are crowding the places of the world. But now and then the Holy Spirit reaches out and saves one. Yes, God is gathering Himself a family.

We are living now in what we call "the church age." God's program is simply this—we are to tell lost men about the Christ who died for them, and we are to try to get them to trust Him. If we want to make a success of anything, we must work with God. We plant our crops according to God's calendar. God sets the seasons and if we do not work with Him we lose out. It is even so with churches and individuals. We must find God's program and work with Him. It is not a program to save society or to save civilization. Many present day preachers spend their time and energy talking about everlasting peace, world communion, racial prejudice, tolerance and world brotherhood. How much progress are they making? They are getting nowhere fast, simply because they are not going according to God's program. The program is for us to tell the old, old story. We are to be faithful in our witnessing and then we can expect some to be saved.

May I humbly tell you about one of the finest compliments

I ever received? A Methodist District Superintendent told me about it. His wife had been sick and during her illness she had listened to our services over the radio. She said to her husband, "He preaches like you used to preach."

"What do you mean?" he asked.

She replied, "He is not trying to save the world nor to get civilization straightened out; he preaches to the individual hearts. He urges individuals to come to Christ and to get into right relationship with God." I believe that is God's program for this age.

A large part of the work which Christians are doing will never amount to very much. Why? Because so much of it does not have any of the redemptive note. We ought not to give our time and money to anything which does not eventuate in the salvation of souls. Our churches can put on a big show and go through many forms and ceremonies, but what does all this mean to Christ? It means nothing. There isn't enough Gospel in some modern churches to save a flea. The people in these churches say, "But we must keep up with the times. It was all right for Paul to go from house to house and town to town, but it's different today." So they build fine churches and say to the multitudes, "Come and get it." Yet there is not one word in the Bible where God tells a sinner to come to church. God says we are to go after them, we are to tell them about Christ—we are to bring them to church. How many of you last year picked out one soul and said to him or to her, "I am praying for you—I want to see you saved. Will you go with me to hear my pastor next Sunday?"

A ministerial student was going home for the holidays. Hitchhiking, he caught a ride with a man who took him far out into the country, and who then said to him, "I turn off here." The man turned down a side road and left the boy stranded.

The boy looked over in the woods and saw a group of men cutting down some trees. He went over to them and asked them about the church in the community. He was told that they did not have a church near this place. "Would you like for me to hold a service here for you?" he said. When they gave their consent he began to preach. He used a pine log as a mourner's bench and in the service he led several of those men to Christ. This young man was working at God's program.

There is only one fundamental thing for Christians to do and for a church to do, and that is to tell the Gospel story and to seek to win the lost. When churches do not do this they fail; when they do it, they win gloriously—they become a blessing to the world and a glory to God. May God help us to work with Him in His mighty program.

Now James quoted some prophecy, as follows, "After this I will return." This prophecy means that Christ will return. Return after what? After He takes out a people for His Name —after He gathers to Himself a family. Some day the last one will be saved, the body of Christ will be complete. The bride will be ready for the Bridegroom, Jesus will return and gather His family around Him.

IV. THE DECISION. Verses 19-21

After all these speeches a decision was made. Pastor James announced it. He said, "We are not to trouble these Gentiles who have come to Christ. We know that this is God's way— to save people who come by faith, and by faith alone." Then he must have declared that these trouble makers were out of line, and the church probably disciplined them. However, he did give the Gentiles certain advice.

First, he told them that they were not to eat meats offered to idols. What did he mean by this? The heathen daily set meat before their idols. Of course, these idols did not eat the meat, consequently every day the left overs were sold cheaply. This meat would be just as good to eat as any other day-old meat. But Paul said that we should not eat meat if that would make anybody stumble. Somebody might think it was wrong, and be offended, so he declared that he would not eat such meat as long as the world stood.

Today people say, "I can do this thing or go to that place and there will be no harm in it." However, through doing this you may lose your influence and harm someone else. Therefore, we should be careful about all of these things.

Second, the Gentiles were advised not to eat blood. In those days certain people ate blood pudding and this prohibition was placed upon them. Third, they should not eat "things strangled." The life is in the blood. If a beef had been strangled the blood would still be in it, and they were not to eat it as it was. It is all right to eat meat, but not the blood. Because the Gentiles were surrounded by the Jews who did not believe in these things, it was felt best for the Gentiles to avoid these things.

Something else happened here which Paul tells about in Galatians. He said that in Antioch Peter and Barnabas mingled with the Gentiles and ate with them, but when the men from Jerusalem came with the idea that the Gentiles could not be saved apart from circumcision, Peter and Barnabas separated themselves from them and would not eat with them. What did Paul do? He tells us that he resisted Peter to his face. He said, "Peter, you are wrong. I condemn you for what you have done. You ate with the Gentiles at Caesarea and God told you that was all right. You are doing wrong in holding yourself aloof from them in Antioch."

Why did Peter do this? It was because of the statement of these men who came from Jerusalem. Since James was the pastor of the Jerusalem church Peter thought that these men came from him and had his approval. This may have caused him to step aside and do wrong. Later he found out that James did not send these messengers. The point I want to make is this—Paul withstood Peter publicly to his face. Some people call Peter the first Pope. If that was so, how could Paul, an independent preacher, rebuke him?

V. THE DELEGATION. Verses 22-35

It seems that the vote was taken and that the entire church approved the stand of its pastor. They decided to write a formal letter and send it to the church at Antioch. They chose two of their chief men to go along with Paul and Barnabas to deliver the letter, namely Judas and Silas. While we know one Judas who betrayed Christ, here is one who was faithful to Christ and who was honored by the church. It is not the name which counts, it is what is in the heart. They journeyed to Antioch, came before the church, and read the letter. The people rejoiced. Judas and Silas, the visiting brethren, were permitted to preach. When it came time for them to go back to Jerusalem Silas said, "I like this man Paul. I have decided to stay and work with him."

I would call your attention to one descriptive phrase in this letter. In speaking of Paul and Barnabas, James said that they were men who had hazarded their lives for Jesus Christ. Later on we hear Paul saying, "I know that bonds and afflictions await me in every city. None of these things move me, neither do I count my life dear unto myself, so that I might finish my course with joy and the ministry which I received of the Lord Jesus Christ." Oh, can we say that? Can we say, "My life means nothing to me—Jesus means everything. I will be happy to suffer and die if I can but serve Him."

I heard of a boy from a non-Christian home who went to church and was converted. The pastor told him he would have a hard time at home if he lived for Christ, but he declared that he was willing to suffer anything for Jesus. The next Wednesday night the pastor started to pat him on the back. The boy drew back and asked the pastor not to touch his back. They then went together to a room and the boy pulled off his shirt. His back was bloody, for his father had beaten him for joining the church. It takes a lot of love and loyalty to stand up for Jesus in that way. But Jesus is worth it. He went to the Cross to save us from something worse—from the pangs of hell. If we will but be true to Him He will repay us a thousand times.

VI. THE DIVISION. Verses 36-41

Some days later Paul said, "Brother Barnabas, let's go back to the cities where we preached and established churches and see how they are getting along."

Barnabas replied, "All right, Brother Paul, but I want to take John Mark with us."

"No sir," said Paul, "he forsook us on the last trip. He is not dependable, we cannot take him."

These two men began to contend with each other and the contention became so sharp that they decided to go separate ways. Barnabas took Mark and Paul chose Silas to go with him.

Now, who was wrong? In a way, both were. Barnabas insisted on taking his cousin. Barnabas and Mark went to Cyprus and we never hear of Barnabas again. He may have done some good work, but he never went again on any great missionary journeys. The ties with his great friend, Paul, were broken. But it seems that Barnabas was right in wanting to give Mark another chance. Mark made good—he wrote the second Gospel. Later on Paul, in writing to Timothy, said, "Bring Mark with you, for he is profitable to me for the ministry." I am glad that Barnabas wanted to give Mark another opportunity to make good.

God is like that. I make my mistakes, but when I go to him in confession he forgives me and says, "Do better now, my child."

I think of Peter and what a mistake he made in denying Jesus. Nevertheless, when Jesus passed by Peter, He gave him a look of love and tenderness which broke his heart. Peter went out and wept bitterly. Jesus took him back into His arms and Peter became as strong as a giant for the Lord.

I am glad that my case does not rest in the hands of men,

but in the hands of God. I know He is a loving God—He recognizes my weaknesses and makes allowances for my mistakes. I am glad, too, that when I come to the end of the way, I will be facing His grace and mercy and not the judgment of man.

The outstanding thing about these men as we find it in this chapter is that they counted themselves nothing, while Christ was all. Oh, that it should be so with us.

> Oh, the bitter shame and sorrow
> That a time could ever be
> When I proudly said of Jesus,
> "All of self and none of Thee."
>
> Yet He found me—I beheld Him
> Bleeding on the cruel tree,
> And my wistful heart said faintly,
> "Some of self and some of Thee."
>
> Day by day His tender mercies
> Healing, helpful, full and free
> Brought me lower, while I whispered,
> "Less of self and more of Thee."
>
> Higher than the highest heavens,
> Deeper than the deepest sea.
> "Lord, Thy love at last has conquered,
> None of self and all of Thee."

A young Swede was converted in Dwight L. Moody's meeting in Chicago. He came to Mr. Moody and asked him what he could do for the Saviour. Moody, seeing that he was awkward and illiterate, said to him, "How would you like to be a sandwich?"

The boy replied, "I will be anything and do anything for Jesus." Mr. Moody told him to report for duty the next morning. When he came to see Mr. Moody the next morning, Mr. Moody strapped two boards over his shoulders. On the front board were painted the words of John 3:16—on the back board there was a notice of Moody's meeting. The young man went up and down the street smiling, feeling that he was doing something for Jesus. The cruel boys along the way threw stones and mud at the board, but the young man never gave up. A traveling man saw the notice, came to the meeting and was converted. He had a good voice and when he went to the various cities he sang in the mission stations. In New York a young Jew drifted in and seemed to be charmed by the traveling man's songs. After the meeting the man went down and talked to the Jew and won him to Christ. The Jew became a missionary to Africa and won many souls to the Lord. Why did it all happen? Because one young man had the spirit of these apostles. He was willing to be ridiculed for Jesus' sake. May God give us the same spirit.

CHAPTER SIXTEEN

"SPIRITUAL REGENERATION"

Acts 16

On the darkest day that ever dawned Jesus died on a cross just outside the city of Jerusalem. For God it was a dark day —for us it was a bright day, for because of that Cross we have a way out of our sins and up to God. The word Gospel means good news. When Jesus died and rose again He gave us a Gospel to preach and the good news to tell. The Gospel began in Jerusalem—as we move through the Book of Acts we see it spreading far and wide. The time has now come for this Gospel to jump Continental boundaries and go into Europe for the first time.

As Acts 15 closed, we saw the great team of Paul and Barnabas breaking up. Barnabas and Mark went to the Island of Cyprus and this is the last that we hear of Barnabas. Paul took Silas with him and began his second missionary journey. The coming of Paul to those places with the Gospel was like fresh rain to the parched soil, like a cooling drink on a hot summer's eve, like a good meal to a starving man, like healing for the fevered brow, like release from pain. Let us follow these servants of God as they moved out upon their journey and entered Europe with the Gospel.

I. THE SERVANT. Verses 1-5

Paul had been to Derbe and Lystra once before. He was stoned at Lystra. He now went back to tell them the decision of the Jerusalem Council—that the Gentiles could be saved without becoming Jews. As he went along on his journey he did two things: he won the lost and strengthened the saved. These are the two ultimate ends of all preaching. Every preacher ought to strive to do both. Every time he preaches he is confronted with these two groups. His message ought to contain a word for the saved and a warning for the lost.

In Lystra Paul met again that remarkable young man, Timothy. Timothy had been converted on Paul's first visit to the city, along with his mother and grandmother. He had been reared in a devout Jewish home and had been well instructed in the Scriptures. When Paul reached Lystra he found Timothy doing a great work for the Lord.

Paul wanted a companion to help him in the ministry, so he decided to take Timothy with him.

A man who is not faithful and active in his own home church will never be worth much to other churches. If he does not win souls at home, he will never win them abroad. I have seen young people go forward and make a surrender for full-time service and yet you could never get them to give any service at home. I have heard them say, "I will give Jesus my whole life in service. I will preach for Him anywhere, or go as a missionary to any country." Yet they were not willing to give Him any service in the home church. When God calls us to serve Him, we ought to serve Him right where we are. If He takes us to a foreign country, then is the time to serve Him there. Paul chose Timothy to go as a missionary because he was faithful and active in his home church. Timothy became a great evangelist, he was dearer to Paul's heart than any other man, and his name was written high upon the records of God.

We note that Paul caused Timothy to be circumcised. Why did he have Timothy circumcised and not Titus? Well, Paul said that circumcision did not profit spiritually, but he felt that Timothy should be circumcised as a matter of expediency. Timothy was a Jew. The Jews believed in circumcision and unless Timothy was circumcised, he would not be able to get a hearing among the Jews. As long as there was no great principle involved, Paul would do anything to get his Gospel to his own people; as he said, "I will become a Jew to those who are Jews, in order to win some of them."

II. THE SPIRIT. Verses 6-11

This little group went to Galatia. The Christians there were mighty good to the preacher, and he said later that if it had been possible they would have plucked out their own eyes and given them to him. This is a wonderful way to feel about the person who has led you to Christ. They could say, "Paul, you can't see worldly things very well, but you have seen Christ and you know Him. Then you saw us in our sin, you came and preached to us and now we are saved. We will do anything for you, Paul. If you had not come to us we would even now have been on the way to death and hell." Let us never forget those who told us of Christ and who minister to us in the things of the Gospel.

When Paul felt better, he decided to go into Asia. But the Holy Spirit spoke, saying, "No, you can't go there at this time." Paul then went down into Mysia and decided to go into Bithynia. The Spirit again spoke, saying, "You are not to go there either." So they stopped at Troas. We see that every step in the extension of the work was directed by the Spirit. Paul wanted to go into Asia, but God wanted him to go into Europe. There are times in our lives when we think it best to go one way, but God hinders us and sends us another way. We think we are just about ruined, but God eventually works the matter out for our good and His glory.

A young woman had prepared herself for missionary service on foreign fields. She had been appointed by the mission board and was ready to sail when she received a telegram saying that her sister had died in a western state. She cancelled her reservation and went home. The sister left four little children and since there was no one to care for them this young woman had to stay with them. Her heart was broken. She had dreamed of being a missionary and now she would never have a chance to go out for the Lord. However, she submitted to the Lord's will and did the best she could for the children. As they grew up, one by one they came to her saying, "Auntie, I feel that God wants me to be a missionary." So instead of one person going out as a missionary, four went out. She came to see, after all, that God's way was the best way.

Now we come to one of the greatest events in history—the carrying of the Gospel into Europe. That Gospel would saturate the continent and later men would sail out to live in the new land called America, taking the Gospel with them and causing America to become a Christian nation. How did God get Paul to understand that He wanted him to go to Europe? In the night He sent him a vision. Paul saw a hungry-hearted man standing on the European shore of Macedonia, with arms outstretched, saying, "Come over into Macedonia and help us."

When Paul awoke he said, "This is it—God would not let me go into Asia and I see the reason now—He wants me to go into Europe. Let's go." Here is a wonderful thing about Paul—when he found God's will he was ready to follow it immediately. He did not say, "I will wait a while. I will wait until I can write a letter and secure suitable quarters—I will wait until I learn what kind of financial arrangements have been made." No, he said, "God wants me over there, and I will go. He will take care of the details."

Macedonia was in Greece, and Greece was in Europe. Greece had beauty, philosophy, art, culture and gaiety. What did Paul have to offer? Only one thing—Christ. Yet we hear the man of Macedonia calling him to come over and help. Today men have the things of the world, but these are not enough. They need help—they need the Gospel, they need Christ. The man of Macedonia was an impersonation of a great need. The whole world today is sunk in sin. Men are dissatisfied, they are unsaved; we have Christ and they are calling on us to come over and help them. Every day we have contact with those whose hearts are hungry—hungry for the peace of God, the forgiveness of sin, the hope of heaven. They look to us with sad, longing eyes. We have Christ. Let us heed their cry and give them this Treasure.

III. THE SELLER. Verses 12-15

The chief city in Macedonia was Philippi, so the party stopped there. They were in Europe now and they were launching a movement which would shake the world. Luke, the beloved physician, was with them. He was a doctor and an evangelist. He could not only help in the preaching, but he could minister to Paul physically. Along the way I have known some good Christian doctors who lived for Christ and who, by their medical skill, sought to help me to be able to perform the work of a minister. So there was the group— Paul, God's big man of faithfulness and service, Luke, the beloved physician, Timothy, the young preacher, and Silas, Paul's shadow, full of devotion and courage. These men were in strange surroundings. They could have spent the Sabbath day viewing many historical and beautiful things. But instead, we find them going out by the riverside where a group of good women are holding a prayer meeting.

In his vision Paul saw a man, but at his first meeting in Europe there were only women present. The leader of the prayer meeting was Lydia, a business woman, a seller of purple. She knew God, she had a worshipful spirit. When Paul and his friends came to the meeting and when they showed by their conversation that they had a revelation from God, Lydia was ready to listen. We are told here that the Lord opened Lydia's heart and caused her to receive the truth. We see here that God does the first work in the matter of conversion. No matter how eloquent a preacher is, God must open his hearers' hearts if the truth is to have its way.

If you will look at the bird's nest in the spring, you will find it full of little half-naked birds. When the mother bird flies down to the nest with a fat worm or a choice morsel, every baby bird's mouth flies open to receive the food. Lydia's heart was filled with a hunger like that, a hunger for spiritual food. God had opened her heart.

Lydia gave her heart to Christ. As she entered the kingdom she did not go in alone, but she took her household with her, her servants and assistants. She had taken a personal interest in them, she had taken them to prayer meeting. When Paul preached Christ, she said, "This is the way. I am giving my life to Jesus and I would like to see you do the same."

"Yes," they said, "we'll do it." Oh, if we would run our homes and our businesses on a Christian basis, we, too, would have a mighty influence for Christ.

It is always good to see a new convert showing conclusive evidences of salvation. We like to see people not only confess Christ, submit to baptism and attend the church, but we like to see changes in their personal habits, in their speech, and in the way they conduct themselves. Look at Lydia. She knew that these four preachers had no money. So she said, "I have a big house with several servants and plenty of food. Please move right in and stay just as long as you are in the city."

Paul answered, "Thank you, Miss Lydia, we knew that God would provide for us in some way."

A real Christian wants to share his blessings.

A mother was reading the Bible to her little boy and she read the portion which tells us that "foxes have holes, and the birds of the air have nests; but the Son of man hath not

where to lay his head" (Luke 9:58). The tears came into
the little fellow's eyes, and he said, "Mother, if I had been
there, I would have given him my pillow."

Every good work must have a beginning, so this was the
beginning of the Gospel's good work in Europe. It was just
a small beginning, with a few women who were saved in a
riverside prayer meeting, but it grew to great proportions. The
growth came, not because of Paul or Lydia, but because of
God. Do we feel that the things we are doing are little in
God's sight? Then we must keep on being faithful, do our
best, and some day it may mean the salvation of multitudes.

A certain Scotch preacher felt that his year's work had been
a failure. He said, "We only had one person saved—that was
wee Bobby Moffatt." But Moffatt became one of God's great
servants and won many to Christ.

IV. THE STRIPES. Verses 16-24

In the city there was a certain maiden who was possessed
of an evil spirit of divination. She was a fortune teller. A few
men saw an opportunity to make money by using her, so they
formed a syndicate, bought her time and talents, and made
money with them. Yes, men will do anything for money. Satan
was the one who possessed her and when he saw Christianity
spreading into Europe, he decided to use her to hinder these
preachers. Therefore, when they went to a prayer meeting
she would follow behind them, crying out, These men are
servants of the most high God, which shew unto us the way
of salvation." In their minds Satan wanted the people to
associate the preachers with this maiden. A preacher can
never win people to Christ if the people associate him with
anything evil or worldly. A certain preacher ran for a
high political office. He slung political mud just as did the
other politicians. He did not win the election, but after that
time, when anyone read his name in the paper or went to his

church, they thought, not of a man of God lifting them toward heaven, but of a petty politician.

Paul stood this interference for a few days, then he said, "I have had enough, we must do something about it." So he went to this girl, and with the God-given power which was his, he spoke to the spirit that possessed her, "I command thee in the Name of Jesus Christ to come out of her." Immediately the evil spirit came out, for no devil can withstand the powerful name of Jesus. What happened next? Her masters saw that they could make no more money out of this girl and they became furious. Touch some men's pocketbooks and you almost kill them. So these men rushed out, caught Paul and Silas and brought them before the rulers. It seems that Timothy and Luke escaped.

The men said to the rulers, "These Jews are causing trouble in our city. They are teaching things which we Romans ought not to observe." They did not say, "These men are taking away our income." They did not even mention the girl. As long as their wicked business was not harmed they cared nothing about the Roman customs. Now that the money had stopped coming in, they were suddenly concerned about customs. The devil works the same way today. If he can't find anything against the preacher, he trumps up some false charge.

A large crowd had gathered by this time and these wicked men, spreading lies about the preacher, incited the mob against them. The magistrates tore off the preachers' clothes and commanded them to be beaten. Paul and Silas were beaten unmercifully. Their backs were soon a bloody mass, and they were so weak that they could not stand up. They were thrown into prison and the jailer was ordered to keep them safe. He took them into the inner prison, put their feet and hands in the stocks, and left them there to suffer through the night.

V. THE SINGING. Verse 25

When the midnight hour came the prisoners were not asleep. The blood was dried upon their backs. Intense pain shot through their bodies every time they moved. Their feet and hands were in the stocks and they were hungry and cold and weary. I say to them, "Paul and Silas, aren't you sorry that you have been so outspoken for Christ? Don't you wish you had stayed in Antioch, where you could have had a comfortable home? Don't you think God has just about forgotten about you, since He permits you to suffer in this manner?" Would Paul say, "You are right, there is no profit in a life like this"?

No, instead we hear him say, "All things work together for good to them that love God . . ." (Romans 8:28). For our light affliction, which is but for a moment, worketh for us a far more exceeding and eternal weight of glory. (II Corinthians 4:19). For I reckon that the sufferings of this present time are not worthy to be compared with the glory which shall be revealed" (Romans 8:18).

A song could be heard rising out of the prison. Paul and Silas were singing praises to God. Thank God for the song at midnight.

Anybody can sing when the skies are clear and when life is full of laughter, but it takes a strong Christian to sing and rejoice and praise God in the midst of troubles. But, after all, that is the time when the world judges a Christian and decides whether or not his religion is a helpful thing. People are often wrecked by fair-weather Christians—the kind who sing when everything is coming their way, but who grumble and complain when trouble comes. If, when we have trouble, we say, "Why did all this come to me—I don't see how I can stand it;" then the world says, "His religion does not bear him up in time of trouble."

However, if in the time of trouble, we say, "I don't know

why this has come, but I know that God has a good purpose in it all and I will just trust Him," then the world will say, "There is something to his religion after all."

Many Christians come to the pastor and say, "I am having such a hard time, it's so bad, it's so hard." Very few ever come and say, "I am having a hard time, pastor, but it's all right, I know Jesus and I know that He will work it out all right. Hallelujah, praise the Lord!"

We can glorify God in our suffering—or we can deny Him. We are to be careful how we suffer.

We read here that "The prisoners heard." Yes, the world is listening to us, they are looking at us. If we stand the test, they will see the value of our Christianity. As Christians, we ought to be able to say, "I have lost all my money, but hallelujah, Christ is left!" "I am sick, but hallelujah, some day I will go to a land where there is no sickness. I have a weight of sorrow, but hallelujah, God will wipe away my tears." Paul and Silas sang at midnight. It seemed that they had nothing to sing about, but they had something in their hearts which no beating, no stocks and no prison could take away.

VI. THE SALVATION. Verses 26-34

When men sing and pray in their difficulties like Paul and Silas did, something is bound to happen. What happened here? God sent an earthquake to free his servants. He may not always answer by an earthquake, but if we keep faithful, if we glorify God in all of our troubles, He will always take a hand. When the earthquake came, the foundation of the prison was shaken. Everybody was loosed and all the doors were opened. The earthquake awoke the jailer, he arose from his bed, and when he saw the doors open, he thought that his prisoners had escaped. Knowing that he would be held responsible, he drew out his sword and was about to kill himself. Paul then cried out with a loud voice, "Do thyself no harm—we are all here."

A man has no right to harm himself. Others may harm him, but he must not do it. Others may bring shame and disgrace to his name, but he must not do it. Others may kill him, but he must not kill himself. Let the world do what it will—man must do right. The man who harms himself, harms others. If the jailer had killed himself that night his family would have awakened to find themselves without a father. They would have stood bare-footed in blood, helpless to face the world. Some men, who find themselves in trouble say, "I will get out of it all." Then they commit suicide, never stopping to think of the grief and trouble which they bring to others, and that instead of getting out of temporary trouble they are getting something worse—hell for eternity.

The jailer called for a light. Someone else had to hold it for him, for he was trembling like a leaf. He brought the preachers out and fell down before them, crying out, "What must I do to be saved?" Why did he ask this question of them instead of the other prisoners? He had probably heard them preach and surely he had heard them singing and praying. He saw that they had something which he did not have. Now he wanted it and asked for it.

Paul's answer is clear-cut, "Believe on the Lord Jesus Christ, and thou shalt be saved." He did not say, "Submit to baptism and you will be saved." He did not say, "Treat your fellow man rightly and you will be saved." He did not say, "Give your money and you will be saved." He did *not* say, "Believe on the Lord Jesus Christ and you *may* be saved." He *did* say, "Believe on the Lord Jesus Christ, and thou *shalt be saved.*"

Surely he was right, for did not Jesus say, "Him that cometh to me I will in no wise cast out"? (John 6:37). Did He not say, "Come unto Me, all ye that labor and are heavy laden, and I will give you rest"? (Matthew 11:28).

Did He not say, "He that believeth on the Son hath everlasting life"? (John 3:36). Surely Paul was giving him the right answer when he told him to believe on the Lord Jesus Christ.

There is a difference between believing something about Jesus and believing on Him. We can believe that He is the Virgin-born Son of God, that He lived a sinless life, that He died on the Cross, that He rose from the grave, that He is coming again—we can believe all these things and still go to hell. We must put our belief into action—we must trust Him as a sick man trusts the doctor, as a drowning man trusts the lifeguard. We must trust Him with our soul and our future as a man trusts the bank with his money.

After Paul told the jailer to believe on the Lord Jesus Christ, he explained the Gospel to him and his household. The result was glorious. All of them believed, all of them were saved, all of them were baptized. Did these people join the church? I am sure that they did. Along with Lydia and the others, they formed the church at Philippi. This church was one of Paul's favorites. They sent offerings to him more than once, and he wrote them one of his finest letters.

There are two evidences here which show that the jailer was saved. First, he washed the stripes of the apostles. He had taken keen delight in beating these men, but now, with penitence and humility, he sought to straighten up the past.

When a man comes to Christ he ought to go back and straighten up the past just as far as possible. If he holds any grudges, if he owes any money, if he has done anything wrong, he ought to try to straighten everything out.

Second, the jailer had these men sit at his table and eat his food. His salvation showed in his service. When we have been saved surely we want to do something for the Lord. We want to serve Him and others. Yes, the jailer was saved. He was a heathen when the sun set, he was a Christian when it rose. He had been lost, but now he was saved, he had been groping in darkness, but now he walked in the light of Christ. He had been ready to commit suicide, but now he was ready to live for Jesus.

In this chapter we note the diversity of circumstances under which men are saved. Lydia was saved in a riverside prayer meeting. Her salvation came as quietly as the dawning of a spring day. On the other hand, the jailer had an earthquake experience in the middle of the night. Today some people walk down the aisle of a church and make a quiet confession of Christ, while others weep and agonize for days before they come to know the Saviour. The one who comes quietly is just as much saved as the one who has an earth-shaking experience. Lydia was just as surely saved as was the jailer.

One day up in heaven, Paul and the jailer and Lydia met at the side of Jesus. They talked about the prayer meeting by the riverside and the midnight experience in the prison. Both the jailer and Lydia said to Paul, "Thank you, Paul, for coming to Philippi. You came to tell us about Jesus even though it caused you great suffering. If you had not come and told us about Him we would not have been in heaven today."

Then I am sure that all three of them turned their glory-filled eyes upon Jesus and said, "Thank you, Lord Jesus, for coming down to earth and suffering and dying for us. If you hadn't done that we would have been lost forever. We will never cease to thank you for saving us."

> When we've been there ten thousand years,
> Bright shining as the sun,
> We've no less days to sing God's praise
> Than when we first begun.

VII. THE SATISFACTION. Verses 35-40

The next morning the officials sent soldiers to the prison to say to the jailer, "Let those men go."

But Paul said, "Oh, no, we are not going to have it that

way. You beat us openly when you knew we had done nothing wrong. We are Roman citizens. Our release must be just as public as was our arrest." When the officials heard that they were Roman citizens they were sore afraid. They knew that they should not have heaped such indignities upon these Romans. They rushed down to the jail, apologized for their actions and released the apostles. Paul and Silas went back to Lydia's house, found Timothy and Luke, and told them all about their experiences.

In this chapter we see again Christ's power to save unto the uttermost all who come unto Him by faith. Spurgeon tells the story of his friend, Brownlow North, who had been a greatly dissipated man, but who was gloriously saved and called to preach. His old companions resented what had happened to him. One day several members of this old crowd came into the church just before North was to preach, and sent a letter up to him. When North opened the letter he found a list of the wicked things which he had done before his conversion. Then the question was asked, "How can you dare to preach to those people, when you have been such a vile sinner?"

When Mr. North stood up to preach he read the letter to the congregation. Then he said, "All this is true—I was a degraded sinner. But, Oh, how wonderful is my Saviour! He has washed all my sins away in His atoning blood. I have come to plead with you to take Him as your Saviour, too."

Friends, I would like to say the same to you. I was a sinner, lost in sin, but Jesus saved and redeemed me. I invite you to come to Him. "Believe on the Lord Jesus Christ, and thou shalt be saved."

CHAPTER SEVENTEEN

"SPIRITUAL ABOMINATION"

Acts 17

As Paul traveled around on his missionary journey, I am quite sure that he did not select the places to which to go, but that he was guided solely by the Holy Spirit. God wanted him to go to Europe, so He had a man in Macedonia appear unto him in a vision, crying out for help. In Philippi, God wanted Lydia and the jailer and others saved. He wanted a church planted there, so Paul was sent to Philippi. As the 17th chapter opens we see that Paul left Philippi and went deeper into Greece. All of this was according to God's plan for spreading the Gospel. Let us follow Paul now to Thessalonica, to Berea and to Athens.

I. The Convert. Verses 1-4

The party passed through two small towns and came to the great seaport city of Thessalonica. Paul always carried the Gospel where the people were. He preached in the great centers of population, many people were saved and Christianity spread like a prairie fire. He stayed three weeks in this city, preaching each Sabbath in the synagogue. He gave the days of the week to personal work.

What was the burden of his message? The Jews believed in a coming Messiah, but they saw him only as an earthly king. Paul sought to convince them that, according to the Scriptures, Christ must suffer and die. Then he told them all about Jesus, His life, His death and His Resurrection. Paul

39

ended his message by exclaiming, "This Jesus whom I preach is Christ, the Messiah." It was not easy for him to go into a Jewish synagogue and preach like that. He told later of the conflict which he had. I imagine that as he preached and quoted the Scriptures, different ones stood up to oppose him.

However, many of the Jews accepted his sermons as the truth from God. In a letter which Paul wrote, he said, "I received my Gospel not as the word of man, but as the Word of God." If a preacher is a true man of God, if he preaches Christ's pure Gospel, that is exactly what his sermons are to the heart—the Word of God. What were the results of this three-week's meeting? A great number were saved, among them some very prominent women. They are going to help the church to become great, for no church ever prospered without the help and prayers of good women.

As Paul preached to these new converts he stressed two things. First, he emphasized practical Christianity. He told them that a Christian must live a holy, Godly life. He must not steal, nor lie, nor wrong his neighbor. He must be industrious and never a busybody. In other words, he told them of the good lives that they should live as Christians. Second, he emphasized the Second Coming of Christ. Paul had had a hard time, and they had lost many of their loved ones. In one of the Bible's finest passages about the Lord's return, he told them that they are not to sorrow like people who have no hope. He told them that God would take care of their deceased loved ones and that some day He would come and take them all up into heaven with Him, to be forever with the Lord.

The experience of these Christians is given in First Thessalonians 1:9-10. They had turned to God from idols, they were serving the true and living God, and they were waiting for His Son from heaven. These three things should be true of us. We have turned to God from sin and as we wait for His appearing we ought to be serving Him with the best that we have.

It is fine to have a great revival and to see many people saved, but we also would like to know how the church is getting along after the revival is over. Paul told us. He said, "You became an example to all the believers in that part of the world. You sent out the word of God everywhere and everybody gave a good report of the fine work you did. These people were in a strategic position. The city was a seaport, so every ship could be used to carry the news of the Gospel. The city was also on all the great highways. The travelers going to every direction could carry the news of Christ and what He was doing in the lives of the people of Thessalonica. Nearly every church is in a strategic position. The heart's desire and prayer of every true Christian is that the news of Christ should go out from their churches to the ends of the earth.

A beautiful thing happened during the latter part of this meeting. The church at Philippi sent a nice offering to these preachers. This was a new church which had just been organized, but they knew how poor the preachers were and sent an offering to help them out. Paul came to love the Philippian church more than any other one, and they came to love him in return. We know it was a good church—for it was a missionary church.

II. THE CONTROVERSY. Verses 5-9

While some of the Thessalonians believed, some of them turned against the preachers and a bitter persecution followed. The Gospel either melts the heart or hardens it. It is a stumbling block or a sure cornerstone. You can build upon it, or be crushed by it. What did these enemies do? They went to the market place, hired "certain lewd fellows of the baser sort," and sent this mob all over the city to stir up the people against the preachers and to make false charges against them.

As we follow this mob, we see that they rushed down the street toward Jason's house. Jason was a good Christian man and kept the preachers at his house. I am sure that Jason was greatly blessed by the presence of these Godly men. When the mob reached the house the preachers were gone. Perhaps they had been warned. The nest was empty, but the crowd had to have its victim, so they seized Jason and rushed him to the rulers, saying, "This man has been housing these men who have turned the world upside down. They are against Caesar. They say that Jesus is the king." They did not care anything about Caesar—they just wanted to incite the Roman rulers against these preachers.

We note here the expression "they have turned the world upside down." In a certain sense the charge was true. Christianity *is* revolutionary. The world today needs turning upside down—or rather it needs turning right side up. This revolution must take place in the *hearts* of individuals. The way to change the world is to change the individuals in it. We will never have a better world until we have better people. When Christ comes into a life He turns it upside down. He does it in the matter of beliefs—the things that we once believed were false, now we believe to be true. He does it in the matter of pleasures. He does it in the matter of home life. He does it in the matter of hopes—from a hopeless life He gives us a hope of heaven and eternal Life. The rulers finally decided to let Jason out on bail. Possibly one of the conditions was that the preachers should leave town. At least we know that they left Thessalonica.

III. THE CONTRAST. Verses 10-14

In order to avoid more trouble the brethren sent Paul and Silas away by night. They went down to Berea, entered the synagogue and preached there. We find a marked contrast here. In the other places where Paul preached the Jews would not reason things out—they ran the apostles out. But we read that the people of Berea were "more noble." When Paul preached they searched the Scriptures to see if his preaching was true. It would be wonderful to have people go home from church, brush off their Bibles and verify the truth of the preacher's sermon. The result here was that a great multitude was saved. This will happen anywhere.

If lost men will listen to the Gospel, then open their Bibles and check on the preacher's message, they must say, "This is right. I must walk in that way." If Christians studied their Bible more we would not see them going off into so many false isms and cults. We read the newspaper and the magazine —we listen to the radio. Why not become familiar with the Word of God?

The peace that the apostles enjoyed in Berea did not last very long. The Jews in Thessalonica heard of the meeting which they were having, came to Berea, and tried to stir up the people against Paul. Can you think of anything meaner than this? But their tribe is not dead; the devil still uses people to hinder the work of the kingdom. Sometime ago I met a man who said, "I am the chief critic in my church." I don't want that man in my church. What we need is fewer critics and more boosters.

Someone says, "It is good to have a little opposition." We expect opposition from the outside, from Satan, but we do not need any opposition within the ranks. If our churches today were one hundred per cent on God's side and on the Bible's side, we would make a deeper impression upon this sinful world.

IV. THE CURIOSITY. Verses 15-21

Paul now moved into the capitol city of Athens. He was greatly impressed, not by the wonderful buildings, not by the art, not by the philosophy, but by the idolatry. The whole city was filled with sculptured idols. There was a god upon every hill top. These gods filled every street and avenue.

Every house was filled with gods and statues of them were in every garden. It was easier to find a god in Athens than to find a man. There were gods to the right, gods to the left, gods in front, and gods behind. Yet these gods were only idols. The people had lost all faith in them. As Paul walked up and down the streets he looked upon these idols. No wonder his heart was moved. His Jewish heart rebelled, for he believed in one God, the God of heaven. So it is that the heart of a Bible-believing Christian is stirred when he sees all the modernism crowding in upon Christianity today.

I began my ministry in 1922. It was an unusual thing then to hear of a minister who did not believe in the great doctrines of the Christian faith. When Fosdick said that he did not believe in the Virgin Birth, that news made the headlines of the New York papers. In the intervening years I have seen many ministers go astray from the Word of God. We can thank God for those who are still true to the Bible, but far too many preachers today are ridiculing the old-time religion.

Paul preached first in the synagogue and then in the market place. It was there that the philosophers met the people and taught them their doctrines. Paul engaged in a debate with two groups of these philosophers. First, there were the Epicureans. They were the materialists and atheists. They believed that the world was ruled by chance. Their motto was: "Eat, drink and be merry, tomorrow we die." We have too many of these people in the world today. They are thinking only of the pleasures of the flesh. The Stoics formed the other group. They believed that the world was ruled by fate. They said, "There is no use to weep over anything or rejoice over anything. What is to be will be, so we will just harden our hearts against everything."

Some of these people called Paul "a babbler." Today some people feel that way about the preachers. They see no earthly use for a man to stand up before a congregation and preach every Sunday. To them it is foolishness. Yet, God's plan calls for preachers and preaching. The Gospel is the "power of God unto salvation." (Romans 1:16). The true preacher has the message from the Bible that is needed. if man rejects that message down through the endless ages he will cry out in hell, "I wish that I had listened and learned and believed."

Others said that Paul was a setter forth of strange gods." It was rather ridiculous for these Athenians to talk about srange gods when their city was full of them, but they had enough and they had passed a law forbidding anyone to introduce any new gods.

They took Paul to Mars Hill and said to him, "Tell us now what you have to say." What kind of a place was Mars Hill? It was a place where the men of Athens gathered to gossip. These men were consumed with curiosity and rushed up to Mars Hill every day to hear the latest gossip or slander. We read that they "spent their time in nothing else, but either to tell, or to hear some new thing." They made no contribution to the city, they helped no one; they just gathered and gossiped and looked for something new. There are certain centers like this in Amercia, places where men are always looking for something new and always inventing some new religion. We have about as many gods today as those Athenians had.

V. THE CHARACTERIZATION. Verses 22-29

Paul now took a stand and preached his sermon. To the people who had many gods he gave a concise characterization of the true God. He said, "I see that you are somewhat superstitious." The correct translation is "somewhat religious." Men may be very devoted to religion, yet that religion cannot save them nor help them. The man who worships the sun is religious, so is the man who bows down to wooden idols, the woman who casts her baby into the Ganges, or the modern man who trusts in the formal ritualism of religion. However, this religion means nothing to life, there is no help or comfort in it, it offers no forgiveness for sin and no hope for the future. The thing which counts is not devotion to a system, but faith in a Saviour, Christ Jesus, the Man who can save and satisfy and help.

Paul went on to say, "I passed down your streets and I saw all the statues which you had erected. I notice that one was erected to the Unknown God." You see, the Greeks had erected statues to all the other gods and felt that in so doing they had appeased them. However, fearing that they had left one out, they erected this special statue, inscribed: "To the Unknown God." Note how daring Paul was as he spoke to these learned philosophers. "In your ignorance you worship an unknown God. I know Him and have come to tell you about Him." Imagine a little man like Paul talking to these learned Athenians about ignorance! He told them that God made the world and all the things in it, that He was the Lord of heaven and earth and that He did not dwell in temples made with hands. Their gods were dead, cold things—his God made everything, sustains everything, and needs nothing from us. It took courage for him to say, "You are all wrong about your gods, let me tell you about the real God."

Now Paul delivered a body blow to Greek pride and prejudice. They believed that they were a race apart and that all other people were barbarians. They spoke always of "the Greeks and the barbarians." This was race prejudice at its worst. Paul said, "God made us all of one blood." He was saying that the Greeks were no better than others, even if they did think so. There is too much class and race prejudice in the world today. We need to remember that we all have the same ancestor, that God made us all of the same blood. This makes every man and woman in the world my brother and my sister. The black man is as close to God's heart as is the white man. In Christ there is no North nor South, no

East nor West. When Christ died on the Cross it was not for any one race or nationality, but for the world. As He loved all people in the world, so should we. So Paul told these Greeks that God made us all, that we all look alike to God.

He also told them that God was not far from any of us. They thought of their gods as living on Mount Olympus, drinking nectar, eating ambrosia, and caring nothing for men on this earth. Paul said "God is close to us—He is nearer than hands and feet and closer than breathing. He loved us and is ready to help us in every time of need." Why do men today feel that God is far away from them? It is because their own hearts are far away from God.

The man who is living in sin says, "There is no God," or "God is too far away to care for me." However, the minute he is willing to turn from his sin and come through penitence and faith in Christ to God, He will find the Father right there, reaching out to touch his hand.

Paul speaks here of men who seek after God, but, alas, there are few who do it. However, God is always seeking after men. In Eden he cried out, "Where art thou?" (Genesis 3:9). When Jesus came into the world, what was He doing? He was simply seeking after men in order to save and bless them. Francis Thompson reverently calls God "the Hound of Heaven." In his poem he tells how he fled from God, and how God kept on following him on the feet of love until He found him and saved him.

God has been tracking some men down for many years. When He surrounded them with love and blessings, He was saying, "I want you." When He gave them health and home and loved ones and a job, He was saying; "I want you." When He permitted sorrow to come their way He touched their hearts and said, "Life is fleeting—I want you." When they were convicted by hearing a certain sermon, He was saying, "I want you." When they became sick and realized that life would not last always, He was saying, "I want you." If you are unsaved today, it is not God's fault. He has called you a thousand times.

You are lost because you won't turn away from your sin and say, "Lord, thy love has conquered, I will give myself to Thee."

A wealthy man sat in the back seat of his car. By his side were his wife and his little baby girl, three years of age. He was not a Christian, but his wife was. The wife's pastor came over to the car and said, "Charlie, God has been good to you. You have a fine wife, God has helped you to make a fortune and you have everything that you want. Now God has given you this beautiful baby. You ought to be a Christian." Just at this time the little baby looked up into the father's face and said, "Daddy, do you love me?" This touched his heart very deeply.

The preacher said, "The goodness of God ought to lead you to repentance."

Three days later the man came to the preacher, saying, "I haven't slept for three nights. I want to tell you that I am giving my heart to Christ. The goodness of God has led me to repentance."

It is true—God is not far away from any of us. When we say, "Lord, I have sinned, and I am sorry," He is near unto us, saying, "I forgive you, my child." He is near us in our loneliness and despair, saying, "I will never leave thee." He is near us when the load seems too heavy, saying, "I will be with you." He is near us when we face failure and loss, saying, "My grace is sufficient." He is near us in the hour of death and we can say, "Though I walk through the valley of the shadow of death, I will fear no evil: for thou art with me" (Psalm 23:4).

God is not far off when we sin. A person can hide his sins from his wife, parents, pastor, friends, but cannot hide them from God. God sees us in the brightness of the midday, or in the blackness of the midnight. When Moses was leading

Israel toward the Promised Land, God gave them a cloud to lead them by day. One day the Egyptians pursued them and caught them near the Red Sea. God wanted to give Israel time to cross over the sea, so He caused the cloud to stand behind Israel, between them and the Egyptians. There were two sides to the cloud—the light side toward Israel, so that they could see what to do—the dark side toward the Egyptians, so that they could not move. So it is, that if we follow the Lord, God's face will be toward us and will shine brightly upon us. If we follow sin, His face will be against us, and He will frown upon us. We cannot expect God's blessings if we are walking in sin.

Paul gave the Greeks a fine characterization of God. He declared that God made the world and all that was in it, that all men were of one blood, that God is close to us all, and that he is not contained in a statue, but that He fills heaven and earth with His power and glory.

VI. THE COUNSEL. Verses 30-34

Paul said in closing, "I am going to give you some advice. God has been overlooking your ignorance up to this point. You know how to paint, how to carve great statues out of stone and wood, how to make speeches and talk of philosophy, but when it comes to God and eternity and heaven you are in ignorance."

This is true today. The places of the greatest culture are the places of the greatest ignorance of God. Most of our great American Universities know little about the true God and the saving grace of Christ.

The apostle now said, "God has not disturbed you in your ignorance, but now you are ignorant no longer. He commands you to repent of your sins and turn to Him."

Why did He call upon these men to repent? Because they were sinful and headed toward judgment; because they were doomed if they did not repent. We can go ahead today and laught at the idea of judgment, but we cannot laugh it away. In the days of Noah God predicted the flood. The people laughed about it, but there was no laughing when the flood came. In the days of Lot, God predicted the destruction of Sodom and Gomorrah. There was no laughing when fire and brimstone covered those cities. In the days of the prophets, God predicted that the proud nation would be brought into captivity. There was no pride and no laughter when Israel was carried away into exile. In the days of the Lord Jesus, He predicted the destruction of Jerusalem. Men laughed at Him, but there was no laughing when Titus came in and destroyed the city. We can laugh now at the idea of judgment, but when we stand before the Judge of all the earth we will find no humor in the situation.

Who will that Judge be? Paul tells them that it will be the man whom God raised from the dead. Yes, Jesus Christ, God's mighty Son, who was with Him when He made the world, who came and lived and died and rose again, He will be the judge. He offers to be your Saviour now, He will be your judge then. You can go on in your sin, you can reject Him, can live without Him. But, oh, what will you say when you face Him at the Judgment? If you were facing trial at an earthly court, if you knew that you were guilty, if you knew that your chances of release were slim, you would want to settle the matter out of court. Oh, beloved, you can do that now. You can come to Jesus Christ now, repent of your sins and trust Him as your Saviour, and you will never come into judgment. Listen to Romans 8:1—"There is therefore now no condemnation (no judgment) to them which are in Christ Jesus."

What were the results of the Mars Hill sermon? A man named Dionysius, a woman named Damaris and others were saved. These were the poorest results Paul ever had. Why? Because he adopted the learned, intellectual way of preaching instead of pouring out his heart for Christ and telling what the Lord had done for him. But Paul went on down to Corinth, fell upon his knees and said, "Lord, I'll never again rely upon human wisdom. From now on I am determined to know nothing but Christ and Him crucified." He had a great meeting at Corinth, but not at Athens.

What do we see in this chapter and in every chapter of Acts? We see a great Saviour seeking to save lost sinners. He is still doing the same thing. He wants to save men today.

On a certain occasion some of John Wesley's people were going to hold a meeting in a barn. Some villagers decided to break up the meeting. They chose one of their number to go to the barn. He was to conceal himself in a sack, and when the meeting was under way he was to open the door, let the mob in and help them to break up the meeting. Soon the people came into the barn. They sang a hymn and the man in the sack liked it and listened to it. Then a prayer was offered and a sermon was preached. The man in the sack was moved and convicted. He began to cry out for mercy. The good people looked around and were astonished to find a sinner in a sack seeking a Saviour. The door was never opened for the mob; the man was gloriously saved.

No matter why you came to church, nor what your sin, Jesus is standing ready to save you and bless you this day.

Chapter Eighteen

"SPIRITUAL ISOLATION"

Acts 18

The title of this chapter is "Spiritual Isolation" because of the one sentence in verse 17—"Gallio cared for none of these things." When matters of religion came up he isolated himself, he turned his back upon them, he just did not care for those things. The world is full of "Gallios" today. Many men are interested in everything else under the sun, but they are not interested in Christianity, the salvation of their souls, forgiveness of sin, judgment and the life to come. These men get by all right in this world, but a time is coming when they must face God. As they stand before Him, they will realize at last the enormity of their sin. They will cry out for mercy, but it will be too late. Every person should give thought *now* to Eternal matters.

I. The Toiler. Verses 1-3

After Paul left Athens he came to Corinth. Corinth was a wonderful commercial center and it was also the sports center of the ancient world. Boxing, foot races, discus throwing and many other games were indulged in by hundreds of people and watched by thousands of others. Of course, all forms of gambling flourished. Venus, the goddess of love, was worshipped by the Corinthians. In her name they engaged in the vilest religious rites. Sodom and Gomorrah at their worst were no worse than Corinth. Sailors coming from the West brought to Corinth the vilest Roman customs; travelers from the East brought the vilest Oriental customs. The Roman Empire was rotten, yet all Rome looked down upon Corinth as a place of the greatest evil. When they saw a man living a lewd, evil, sinful life, they described him by saying, "He behaves like a Corinthian."

Paul was alone in Corinth. His companions had not yet come to the city. He had no money nor any means of support. However, he found in the city the most notable married couple in the New Testament, Priscilla and Aquila. They were fine Christian people. They were also faithful members of the church. Some people claim to be good Christians, yet they give little thought or help to the local church. This couple lived in three places—Rome, Corinth and Ephesus. In Rome the church meetings were held in their home. They were the kind of people who bless a church wherever they go. Paul had been a Rabbi. Every Rabbi learned a trade and Paul's trade was tent making. Priscilla and Aquila were also tent makers, so Paul lived in their home, worked at his trade, and preached the Gospel on the Sabbath. The people of Corinth had not heard the Gospel before this time. If Paul had come and preached and taken a collection, they would have said, "This man is preaching in order to make money." Thus he would have lost his power with them. The established churches today know God's plan. The Bible says that the one who preaches the Gospel should live of the Gospel, and therefore the churches should support the ministers and missionaries and leave them free to do God's work. When Paul later wrote to the Corinthian Church he apologized to them for not taking regular offerings, telling them that this was not best for their growth. If a church could be endowed so that the members would never have to give anything, that church would soon dry up and blow away.

There was a certain pastor who received his living from a real estate business, he accepted no salary from the church for many years and said nothing to them about giving and stewardship. The church was never developed in this grace and when the pastor died he left a weak church. A church which is not taught stewardship never develops into a great church.

May I say here that if a preacher is to have influence and win souls, he must be free from any taint of suspicion about money. A merchant once called me and told me that a certain preacher had given him a bad check. Do you think this merchant would ever want to hear that man preach? If he did go to hear the man preach he would not hear the sermon, but simply the rustling of that bad check. Every man ought to pay his debts and most of all the preacher.

Here we see that Paul lived with Priscilla and Aquila. He toiled at his trade during the week and preached the Gospel in the synagogue on the Sabbath day.

II. THE TESTIMONY. Verses 4-11

Timothy and Silas soon came to Corinth. This made Paul feel much better. He loved companionship, he loved to feel that his bretheren were by his side, backing him up. Nothing in the world helps a pastor so much as to know that the good men of his church are standing by him. Nothing hurts him so much as to know that some of those who are supposed to help him are out criticizing him and stabbing him in the back. A Gospel preacher, called of God and empowered by the Holy Spirit, having the help of good men, can do a tremendous work for God. You can have a vital part in this work and you will receive a rich reward. When these men came to Corinth they brought Paul a good offering from the young church at Philippi. They had heard what Paul was doing, so they said, "It is not right for our preacher to be making tents when he could be winning souls." Paul, having received this offering, could give up tent making and give his full time to Gospel work.

We read that Paul was "pressed in the spirit." In the heart of every genuine Christian there is something which causes him to desire the salvation of lost souls. In Paul the pressure was so great that he could not contain it, so he went boldly to the Jews, testifying that Jesus was Christ, the Messiah. They opposed and blasphemed. Paul then said, "All right, if you will not accept the truth of the Gospel, I will leave you alone." Shaking his robe as a sign he said, "I am clean, your blood be on your own heads, I am going to the Gentiles." A man who is picking apples does not spend his time in a dead tree. He goes where the boughs are laden with fruit. Paul knew that the time was short. He could not spend that time where there was no fruit, so he passed on to riper fields. We waste much time and energy in our churches today on the things which have no redemptive value in them, when we ought to spend the time in fruitful contacts with souls.

So Paul left the Jews, but he did not go far. He stopped next door to the synagogue in the house of Justus. If one of his country men should be touched and if he wanted to know more about Jesus, Paul could be easily located. His heart still yearned for the salvation of the Jews. His strategy paid off. Crispus, the ruler of the synagogue, came over and was saved. When he did this his family followed him, and many other Corinthians believed and were baptized. When a big man takes his stand for Christ, the world takes note of it. If our president and the other high officials of our nation were consecrated Christians, what a mighty power they could be for God!

However, it seems that Paul had a case of the "blues." The best men are often depressed. Maybe Paul felt that he was not accomplishing enough, maybe he was afraid that the Jews would kill him. The Lord, knowing his heart, came to him in a vision in the night, saying unto him, "Do not be afraid Paul. Go ahead and preach. I am with thee. I have much people in this city." When Paul heard that reassuring voice, I am sure that he rose from his bed, thanked God, and took courage. Oh, that is the assurance we need to have! If we can feel that God is close by our side, we need not be afraid of all the devils in hell or all the demons on earth. There were just a few believers in the city up to this time, yet God said, "I have much people in this city." They were there, they were His, but not yet had they been called out. It was Paul's duty to stay and preach. Soon these would be saved and God's people would enter God's family.

Paul stayed in Corinth eighteen months longer and many were saved. His preaching here was different from his preaching in Athens. At Corinth he stuck to one theme—Christ crucified. He laid aside all worldly wisdom, relied entirely upon the Holy Spirit, and preached Christ. No wonder he had such great success.

III. THE TRIAL. Verses 12-17

Up to this time the Jews had not been able to hurt Paul very much. Then a new ruler came along, whose name was Gallio. The people said, "We will seize Paul, take him before Gallio, and see what he will do with him."

This man Gallio was a brother of Seneca, the great philosopher. He was said to be the noblest and gentlest Roman of his day. The Romans called him "the sweet Gallio." He was always superbly dressed, he had gentlemanly manners, there was nothing harsh about him. Seneca said about him, "Everybody in the world loves Gallio, but no one loves him half as much as he deserves."

The Jews now rushed Paul to the judgment seat, saying to Gallio, "This fellow has been persuading men to worship God contrary to the law."

Paul opened his mouth to speak, but Gallio stopped him. "If this man is charged with immorality or some similar crime, I will consider it," he said, "but since it is just a question of words and names and your law, I am not interested. Case dismissed!" When the people heard Gallio say this, they felt sure that he was against the Jews. They wanted to gain favor with Gallio, so they seized Sosthenes, ruler of the Jews who brought the charge against Paul, and beat Sosthenes before Gallio. Then we read this tragic sentence: "Gallio cared for none of these things." He had an opportunity to hear Paul preach Christ, but he cared for none of these things. He talked of names and Paul talked of the Greatest Name, but Gallio cared for none of these things. A man was beaten severely right in front of him, but he cared not at all. What an opportunity this man had! The angels were hovering near and he could have planted his feet on the road to glory, but he cared for none of these things.

The world is full of the same kind of indifference today. There are many men who are good men, like Gallio, but they simply do not care for spiritual things. We find them in our churches. It does not matter to them whether we have Sunday services or not. They care nothing about prayer meeting, nor how many souls are saved, nor whether the budget is raised, nor whether we give to missions. They simply do not care for these things.

In the time of a great battle a soldier was missed from the ranks by his commanding officer. After the battle the soldier was found amusing himself in a flower garden. When he was arrested, he said, "But I was doing no harm." Yet he was convicted and shot.

One day the great King will say to us, "My church was there in the world, why were you not busy, why were you not faithful?"

We may answer, "I was doing no harm." But, fellow Christians, we are doing harm if we are not actively serving God. "To him that knoweth to do good, and doeth it not, to him it is sin" (James 4:17). We will get to heaven if we have been born again, but will be saved "as if by fire" and will lose our reward if we do not faithfully serve Christ.

Life's greatest tragedy is found in those who hear about

Christ, salvation and judgment, but who shrug their shoulders, saying, "I am not interested." Oh, if they knew what Christ could do for them, they would be interested! If they knew the terrors of hell which await them, if they knew the length of eternity, they would be interested.

Jenny Lind was once traveling in Italy. She went to a chapel where Milton had visited on his travels and where he played the organ. The monks at this chapel told her that she would not be allowed to enter. But she smiled and said, "Maybe if I tell you who I am, you will let me in."

"Who are you?", they asked. When she told them that she was Jenny Lind, every head bowed and all the doors were opened. She went into the chapel, seated herself at the organ and played and sang as only Jenny Lind could play and sing. The monks crossed themselves and felt that there had never been such beautiful music in the world.

Oh, if those who are indifferent only knew the joy and beauty which Christ could bring into their lives, they would open the door of their hearts for Him. If they only knew the music that He could bring to the soul and the hope of heaven with which he could fill the heart, they would say, "Come in, Lord Jesus, I do care. Come in."

IV. THE TARRYING. Verse 18

Paul tarried for some time at Corinth. God's power was present in an unusual way and great numbers were saved. Corinth was a very wicked city, therefore many of these conversions must have been remarkable indeed. Here we find a drunkard being saved and becoming a faithful Christian. Here we find the gambler becoming a preacher. Here we find a libertine becoming a loyal layman. The Gospel was having its power. When Paul felt that his work in Corinth was done, he took Priscilla and Aquila and went down to Cenchrea. Here we witness a strange thing. Paul was a strong believer in salvation by grace, but we read here that he took a vow and shaved his head. He was a very wise man, but he was not infallible. He may have "slipped up" this time. We do not know the kind of vow that he took, nor why he took it. Anything that we could say about it would be guess work, so we must leave that among some of the other things which we will not understand this side of glory.

V. THE TRIP. Verses 19-23

Paul went next to Ephesus and as he went into the synagogue, he found a surprisingly warm welcome. They said to him, "Stay with us longer, we are interested in what you have to say." He told them that he could not stay longer at this time, but that he would return if God willed it. He did return and he held a great meeting in Ephesus.

Note here Paul's complete submission to God's will. He said, "I will come back if God wills it." Yes, God ought to be taken into all of our plans. James 4:13-15, "Go to now, ye that say, today or tomorrow we will go into such a city, and continue there a year, and buy and sell, and get gain: whereas ye know not what shall be on the morrow. For what is your life? It is even a vapor, that appeareth for a little time, and then vanisheth away. For that ye ought to say, If the Lord will, we shall live, and do this, or that."

We say, "I am going to do this thing. I am going to that place." But God may have other plans for us. It is better to say, "Deo Volente"—God willing. So Paul left Priscilla and Aquila at Ephesus, went back to Jerusalem, and then on to the home base at Antioch. He did not take any time out for a vacation, but was soon off again, visiting churches and strengthening the saints. Paul was a busy man. He did not travel for fun, but to win souls and to establish the churches of Christ in every place. Today men travel in these same countries. What do they see? They see the Parthenon, the ruins of ancient civilizations, the famous pictures and statues. Paul saw souls, lost in sin, going down to hell. He was pressed down with an inner compulsion, which made every trip one of soul winning.

VI. THE TEACHING. Verses 24-28

When Paul left Priscilla and Aquila at Ephesus, they did what they did everywhere. They set up a Christian home, where the preachers were always welcome. Many of our modern-day churches were founded in this manner. A Christian family would move to a place where there was no church, they would gather their neighbors into their home, and soon a church would be organized.

There is a certain family, however, which did just the opposite thing. They were active in their church, but the husband was offered a more lucrative position in another place. They did not ask about the Christian influences in this new place—they just went on. When they arrived at their new home they found no Christian church there. But they did nothing about it, and soon God and His church were forgotten. It is true that they made more money, but they allowed their children to drift, and the time came when the children broke their hearts. When a Christian is considering a change, it would be far better to consider the spiritual side than the financial side.

One day a young preacher by the name of Apollos came to Ephesus and was welcomed by Priscilla and Aquila. He was a Jew who had been born in Alexandria. He knew the Old Testament Scriptures and was a very eloquent speaker. But here was the trouble—he did not know the full Gospel. He knew that John the Baptist preached, "Behold the Lamb of God, which taketh away the sin of the world" (John 1:29). But he did not know about the death, the burial and the Resurrection of the Lamb. However, he took all the knowledge he had and used it for the Glory of God. There is a lesson here. We will never know all that we ought to know, but we can use the knowledge which we have for God's glory. If you use what you have God will give you more. The little knowledge which Apollos did have set him on fire for God. We know the whole story of redemption—how zealous we ought to be! He knew only of the water. We know of the blood which saves from all sin. We ought to be on fire for God, telling the Story of redeeming love.

Priscilla and Aquila recognized the deficiency in Apollos' preaching, so they taught him "the way of God more perfectly." These two fine people did not criticize this young man; they sought to help him. Apollos did not resent this help; he welcomed it, for he was a teachable man. May the Lord deliver us from the man who knows it all! Apollos was eager to learn and he became a mighty power for the Gospel. Later on, when he felt led to go to Corinth, the church at Ephesus commended him very highly, and he went down to Corinth to do a great work there, also.

Apollos was such a popular speaker that he almost split the church at Corinth, although he had no wish to do so. Some of the people said, "Oh, what a marvelous preacher Apollos is!"

Others said, "Yes, but he is not as sound in the doctrine as Paul."

Still others said, "Yes, he is fine, but he doesn't make me cry like Simon Peter." They were about to have three factions in the church—an Apollos group, a group which followed Paul, and a group which followed Simon Peter.

Paul rebuked them, saying, "All the preachers are yours. God has given them to you to bless you. But you belong to God and you must act like it." Look at your own pastor. He may lack certain things which other pastors have. On the other hand, he may have certain things which they do not have. So we are to take all the good that we can find in all of them, permitting them to bless our hearts and to lift us up to God.

As we read these chapters in the Book of Acts, we see one

thing about these men which stands out above all others—it is their faithfulness to Christ and to their God-given task. They left all for Him, they suffered all for Him, they gave all for Him. They lived, not for this world, but for the world to come.

David Livingstone was one of the greatest Christians who ever lived. He gave his life away for Christ in Africa. When he died, they brought his body back to England and buried him in Westminster Abbey. The crowds thronged the streets to pay their tribute to him. But one old man stood alone, weeping as if his heart would break. Who was this man? He was a friend of David Livingstone's. They had been reared together, they had played together. When Livingstone decided to go to Africa this friend told him that he was crazy. He said that he was going to stay in London and become rich. He stayed in London, he lived for himself. He was known by very few people, while David Livingstone became the best-known and most greatly loved man of his day. On the day that Livingstone was buried, this man cried out, "I put the emphasis on the wrong world."

I wonder if you are putting the emphasis on the wrong world. Are you living for self and for the things of this world only? How foolish it is to do that! At the end of the way there will be nothing to look back upon but a wasted and misspent life—no hope for the world to come. One should give his life to Jesus, live for Him, put Him first, and every good thing will be added unto him.

CHAPTER NINETEEN

"SPIRITUAL DEMONSTRATION"

Acts 19

IT IS ALWAYS TRUE that when Christ comes into a man's heart, into his inner life, his outer life is also changed. We see a striking demonstration of this in Acts 19. Paul came preaching Christ and multitudes believed on Him. The result was that they threw away their idols, burned their books of superstition, and had their entire lives transformed. It is wonderful to see such evidences of salvation today. "If any man be in Christ, he is a new creature" (II Corinthians 6:17). It is glorious to see sinners saved. It is glorious to see how their lives are changed after they are saved. Yes, when a man comes under Christ's sway his habits change, his speech changes, his companions change, his giving changes, his entire life changes. Paul went into the great city of Ephesus and spent two years there.

I. THE BAPTISM. Verses 1-7

When Paul arrived in Ephesus he found a group of about twelve men who were called disciples. When Paul looked at them he was impressed by the lack of spirituality and power in their lives. They did not look like Christians to him, so he asked them, "Did you receive the Holy Spirit when you believed?"

"We have never even heard of the Holy Spirit," they replied.

"Unto what, then, were you baptized?", Paul asked.

63

They told him that they were baptized unto John's baptism. This answer tells us that they were disciples of John the Baptist, but that they knew nothing of Christ. John had said, "There cometh One after me." They were looking for His coming. They did not know about the great redemption which had been wrought on Calvary, they did not know about the Resurrection and the fact of a living Saviour. A man who does not know Christ in a saving experience does not have any of the fruits of the Spirit in his life. Someone said that Gandhi was a "Christ-like man." No man can be Christ-like who does not have Christ in his heart.

The possession of the Holy Spirit is the normal condition of every Christian. When we are born again, God the Holy Spirit comes to live in our hearts. If we are really saved He is there. We look into many lives today and we see no evidences of the Holy Spirit. This means one of two things. These people either have never been saved, or if they have been saved, the world has crowded out and quenched the Holy Spirit. We must check our own lives and hearts. If we have met the conditions of salvation we have been saved. If there is no spiritual fruit in our lives, we are stifling the Spirit. What are the fruits of the Spirit? We find them in Galatians 5:22-23, "But the fruit of the Spirit is love, joy, peace, long-suffering, gentleness, goodness, faith, meekness, temperance; against such there is no law."

If Paul were to come back into the world today, he would be surprised as he looked into some lives. Again he would say, "Did you receive the Holy Spirit?" If a person's life is worldly, if it is lived all for this earth and little for God, there will be no fruit in the life. If one is unforgiving, unfaithful and prayerless there will be no fruit in his life. We are not to judge, but there are so many barren lives in the churches that one wonders if they know Christ, if they have received the Holy Spirit. The business of a fruit tree is to bear fruit, else it is cut down. The business of a Christian is to bear fruit. What profit is a person to God if he is not bearing fruit?

Paul told these men of the One of whom John spoke, the Lord Jesus Christ. When he did this, they believed, they were baptized, the Holy Spirit came upon them and they acted in the same way the believers did upon the day of Pentecost. This story impresses us again with the great importance of preaching the full Gospel of Christ, and of doing it far and wide. There are many hungry-hearted people, many sincere people, who have a smattering of the truth—they need to be given the full Gospel.

II. THE BOLDNESS. Verses 8-10

We see here again Paul's yearning that his own people might know Christ. He went into the synagogue every Sabbath for three months and of course, he preached Christ boldly. As usual the people rose up against him and fought him and the Gospel. Therefore, Paul drew a line—he did not want to have a quarrel every time he conducted a meeting, so he left the synagogue and went to a school nearby, where he held services. Jesus said, "Neither cast ye your pearls before swine, lest they trample them under their feet. . ." (Matthew 7:6). Paul had the pearl of the Gospel. He offered it to the Jews and they refused it. When they did so he had sense enough to go elsewhere. If a preacher preaches the gospel and the people refuse to hear it, if they will not work with him for the glory of God, he ought to go somewhere else.

We know that Paul was disappointed that he had to make this change, but he was a great believer in the fact that "all things work together for good to them that love God" (Romans 8:28). It worked out in this case. A few Jews heard him in the synagogue, but when he went to the school, this place became the center from which the Gospel went out so that everybody could hear it.

Paul had a hard time. The man who would have been highly

honored everywhere if he had stuck to Judaism was persecuted everywhere because he followed Christ. But he had just one object in his life—to make Christ known. So he said, "This one thing I do, forgetting those things which are behind, and reaching forth unto those things which are before, I press toward the mark for the prize of the high calling of God in Christ Jesus (Philippians 3:13, 14). Then one day he looked back over it all and instead of grieving over his sufferings, he said, "I want you to understand one thing—the things which happened to me have fallen out unto the furtherance of the Gospel."

It would be wonderful today if we could say, "Lord, it doesn't matter what happens to me. I will go with you anywhere and suffer anything if only through me someone will come to know Christ."

A preacher and his friend were going to ride home together at the close of the day. As they started to leave the building to go to the car, a heavy downpour of rain came and they had to wait nearly an hour. Soon they were going down the street in the car, but suddenly there was a big jolt from the rear. Another car had hit them. When they had gotten out of the car, the other man said, "It was all my fault."

The three men sat for a while in the car discussing a settlement. During the conversation the stranger learned that one of these men was a preacher. Then he said, "I am certainly sorry about the accident."

The preacher asked him if he were a Christian.

He answered, "No, but I would like to be."

In a few minutes the preacher led this man to Christ. He knew then why he had been forced to wait in the rain for an hour and why the car had been wrecked. All of us ought to use every opportunity to win others to Christ.

III. THE BLASPHEMY. Verses 11-18

While Paul was in this wicked city, the odds were great against him. He needed a special revelation from heaven to help him fight sin and superstition. So we read that "God wrought special miracles by the hands of Paul." Certain of the people would take a handkerchief which Paul had touched, would lay it upon the body of a sick loved one, and that one would be cured. One who possessed an evil spirit would have one of Paul's aprons placed upon him and the evil spirit would be cast out. Why did Paul have a special power then which men do not have today? In a time of emergency God gives a special power. Paul was propagating the true faith. He was opposed by all the demons of hell. God therefore gave him a special power to convince the people of the truth of the Gospel. Paul was thus able to defeat demons and overcome the power of Satan.

Today men claim that they have power to do these things. Paul never made such claims. Luke said that "God wrought." He was the One who did it. If the people had fancied that there was any virtue in Paul, if they had looked to him instead of God, there would have been no miracle. God simply used Paul as a vessel.

A group of Jews who were there thought that if Paul could perform these tricks, they could do it, too. They heard him use the name of Christ in performing these miracles. "That's the magic formula," they said, "We'll use that name." So they went to some who were possessed of evil spirits, and cried out, "In the Name of Jesus Christ, come out."

The evil spirit exclaimed, "Jesus I know and Paul I know, but who are you? I can whip you." The evil spirit then leaped upon these men, beat them, tore off their clothes, and sent them running out of the house, naked and wounded. They were the most surprised people in all of Ephesus.

There is never any spiritual power in a man who does not know Jesus. A consecrated man can pray for two minutes and power is given to him. A worldly man can pray for two hours, using the same words, and nothing happens. God's promise of salvation is to everyone who comes unto Him in faith.

His promise of blessing and power is only to those who abide in Him. If we who are Christians have demons in our own lives, why not cast them out? We cannot do it in our own strength. We cannot do it without Jesus Christ. We must have Him in our hearts if we want help in overcoming sin.

The success of Paul and the failure of these impostors was soon known all over Ephesus. Fear fell upon the people and the name of Jesus was magnified. Many people believed, confessed their sins, and showed their salvation by their deeds. So we see that God's purpose was realized. The demons were overcome, the word of God was spread abroad, and souls were saved. We understand now why Paul performed these special miracles which seemingly he could not accomplish at other times.

IV. THE BURNING. Verse 19

Many of these converts had been very superstitious. They would write out certain incantations on pieces of paper, pin them on their clothing and carry them around with them. They trusted these things to ward off the evil spirits and to give them good fortune. Today the rabbit's foot in the pocket or the horseshoe over the door are used for the same purpose. When these people came to know Christ, they trusted Him and not the magic books and papers. They brought all these to the market place and burned them. The value of the books was about fifty thousand pieces of silver. Surely we can not doubt the sincerity of their conversion. When a man is willing to give up the valuable things of his old life in order to follow Christ, we know that he has been truly converted.

Imagine this scene. Suppose that one hundred saloon keepers in our city came to church, confessed that they had been living wicked lives and declared that they were determined to get out of the liquor business and to live for Christ. That would be wonderful, but we could not judge whether they were sincere or not. Suppose that one hundred trucks took their liquor down to pour it into the river. Suppose these saloon keepers dismantled their bars and said "We mean business—we have really been converted." Then there would be great excitement in the city and such an occurrence would have a great effect upon the people.

These Ephesian Christians had come to Christ and they were burning their bridges behind them. They were not going back over the bridges into their old sin. When people come to Christ, they ought not to leave any old doors open. They ought to make a clean break with the world. This means leaving the old haunts of sin and breaking off with the old sinful companions. Many a Christian has failed because he did not break with these things when he was converted.

There is an old story of a farmer who came to town once a week, hitched his horse to a hitching post, went into the saloon and became intoxicated. Then one day the farmer was converted. The next time he came to town, a Christian friend watched him and noticed that he hitched his horse to the same post near the saloon. "I am afraid of that," he said. It was not long until the old temptation overcame the farmer. He went back to drinking, just as his friend had feared. When a person comes to Jesus he must change his hitching post! He must not go back into the devil's territory.

As we think of the literature which they burned, we are reminded that we ought to have a burning, also. The newsstands are crowded with vile literature, which is in itself an enemy of Christianity. The children in our homes consume these books and digest them as they do physical food. Physical food makes them physically and mental food makes them mentally and spiritually. We should be careful about the literature which comes into our homes.

V. THE BLESSING. Verses 20-22

In verse 20 we read: "So mightily grew the word of God

and prevailed." These Christians proved their sincerity by their deeds, then the word of God grew and multitudes were saved. Every Christian in the world should show his Christianity. Not by pious talk, not by his profession, not by getting his name on the roll, not by empty form, but by a changed life and a daily loyalty to Christ. The world would then feel the impact of Christianity.

Paul was now having great success in Ephesus and Satan wanted to get him out of town, so he started a quarrel in the church at Corinth. They wrote a letter to Paul, urging him to come down and settle the disturbance. "No," he said, "I must stay at Ephesus." So he sent Timothy and Erastus to Corinth. Satan did not succeed in getting him out of Ephesus, but he did weaken the force of the Lord's work in that place.

VI. THE BRAWL. Verses 23-41

In writing to Corinth Paul said, "I fought with wild beasts at Ephesus." Here is the story of some of his struggles. The temple of Diana was located at Ephesus. It was one of the seven wonders of the ancient world. It was supported by one hundred and twenty magnificent pillars. During the construction of the building any prince counted it a great honor to be allowed to erect one of these pillars. Alexander the Great offered to pay the entire cost of the temple if they would inscribe his name upon it. These offers were refused, but thousands of people contributed to the cost. The greatest painters were proud to have their pictures in the temple and the greatest sculptors vied for the privilege of placing their statues in it. The statue of Diana, which was in the temple, was said to have dropped straight down from heaven. The people worshipped this statue. At certain seasons thousands of worshippers came to Ephesus. This created an opportunity for a very lucrative business. The silversmiths of the city made small images of the goddess or the temple and sold them to the heathens. Then something began to ruin their business. When Paul preached the people turned from idols to Christ. They would have nothing to do with Diana. They quit buying these images and the business of the silversmiths suffered greatly. There are many things a man will pay no attention to, but if his business is hurt, if his money is cut off, he is soon aroused. This was true in Ephesus.

The head of the trade union in the city was a man by the name of Demetrius. He called the silversmiths together, and one by one they told about how their business had fallen off. "This man Paul is to blame for it all," they said. "He says that there are no gods made with hands. Our people are turning away from Diana by the hundreds. If this keeps up no one will believe in Diana, no one will buy our gods, and we will be on charity." These men were too shrewd to let the people know that they were simply interested in filthy lucre. They said this to them, "We must do something about this matter. Our great goddess Diana is being insulted."

The crowd was soon stirred into a frenzy and began to cry out, "Great is Diana!"

The lips of the silversmiths said that also, but their hearts said, "We are losing money—we must kill the Gospel." The Bible says that "the love of money is the root of all evil" (I Timothy 6:10). Here is just another illustration of that truth.

Were these men justified in their fears? They certainly were. Fifty years later Pliny wrote that the Gospel had put all the gods out of business and that their temples were desolate. If the Gospel were given a chance today we could still put the evil works of the world out of business. We are told that fifty-two per cent of the people of America are church members. This makes a majority. If Christ were the King of their lives, they would not only refrain from evil things, but they would take a staunch stand for the right. The liquor business would die, the gambling business would be killed, the desecration of the Lord's Day would cease and America would indeed be a Christian land.

These craftsmen at Ephesus raised such a wild cry that the city was soon in an uproar. A mob was formed which headed for the theatre. This building seated thirty thousand people and probably that many were present on this occasion. On the way to the theatre the mob found two of Paul's friends, snatched them up and rushed into the theatre. We are told that some cried one thing and some another. The majority of them did not know why they had gathered. A mob never thinks, it acts in blind passion. If someone had just said the word, these two Christians would have been torn to pieces. About this time Paul heard what was going on and rushed down to rescue his friends. He was a brave man. He could not bear to leave his friends in danger. He was not afraid of the mob; he was not afraid of death. Faith in God and fellowship with Christ lifts a soul above such fear. When Paul started into the theatre, his prudent friends held him back, saying to him, "You couldn't get a hearing if you went in there. There is no need to throw your life away." So they were able to persuade Paul to leave.

The Jews became alarmed. Since Paul was also a Jew they thought that the authorities might think they were sympathetic with him and might blame them for this trouble. So they put up one of their leaders, Alexander, to tell the Ephesians that the Jews hated Paul as much as they did. Alexander held up his hand for silence, but when they saw that he was a Jew they shouted him down. For two hours the mob cried out "Great is Diana of the Ephesians." During all this time Paul's two friends were standing there in fear of their lives.

When the clamor died out, the town clerk made a speech to the mob. He knew just exactly how to handle them. He said, "*Everybody* knows that the Ephesians worship Diana. These two men have not blasphemed her, neither have they tried to rob the temple. This is not a court of law and you have no right to try these men here. If Demetrius has anything against anybody, he can bring his accusations into the regular court and they will be handled in the right way." Since they were under Roman rule, the town clerk probably lowered his voice as he said, "Our Roman masters are not going to like this violent disturbance. They may call us into question because of it. I advise you to forget the matter, go home, and do nothing rash." The mob then dispersed and the two men were set free. A level head and a brave heart can often turn one thousand rash men back to the right way.

The main thing that we see in this chapter is how the grace of God changes men and gives them courage and strength beyond human possibilities. How did it happen? They put God first in everything and sought His will in all that they did. Oh, that in these modern times we might be filled with the same power and courage that these men had!

A certain college girl wrote home and asked her mother for permission to go to a dance. The mother refused this request. On the night of the dance the girl wrote a letter to her mother, saying: "Dear mother, I was disappointed that I was not able to go to the dance with the others. However, when they were gone, I sat down and comforted myself with the thought that I had rather do my mother's will than anything else on earth."

This mother allowed her pastor to read this letter and he asked her, "Do you love that girl?"

"Love her," she said, "I wish that I could see her now, so that I might put my arms around her and tell her how much I do love her."

It is the same way with our Heavenly Father. If we put His will above everything else in our lives, all of the love in His great heart will flow out to us. Then we can truly say at all times, "His grace is sufficient for my every need."

CHAPTER TWENTY

"SPIRITUAL EXHORTATION"

Acts 20

A dear old preacher had served a certain church for many years. He had won multitudes to Christ, he had baptized many, he had married many. He had seen the children grow into manhood and womanhood. He had buried many of their loved ones. He had wept with them in their sorrows and rejoiced with them in their happiness. Now the day of retirement had come. He was going to move to another city and live with a daughter the rest of his days. On Sunday morning the church was filled with those who came to hear the old pastor's last sermon. That morning as he preached he spoke of many things which had happened during his pastorate. Then as he thought of the future he exhorted them to stay close to God and to be faithful in the good work of the church. At the close of the service everybody in the house came down to the front and shook hands with him. They told him how much he had meant to their lives and the tears were in their eyes as they said good-bye to their pastor. We see this same sort of a scene in Acts 20. The biggest thing in the chapter is Paul's farewell to the Ephesian elders, and his exhortation to them to follow Christ.

I. THE EVANGELIST. Verses 1-5

Paul spent two years in Ephesus. After his trouble with Demetrius and the silversmiths and the mob, he decided to leave the city. He went through Macedonia again, exhorting

74

the Christians there, then he spent three months in Greece. We speak of this trip in a breath, but it was a time of distress for Paul. He met opposition everywhere that he went. We read of this opposition in 1st Corinthians 4:11-13: "Even unto this present hour we both hunger, and thirst, and are naked, and are buffeted, and have no certain dwelling place; And labor, working with our own hands: being reviled, we bless; being persecuted, we suffer it: Being defamed, we intreat: we are made as the filth of the world, and are the off-scouring of all things unto this day."

Today we honor Paul and count him as one of the world's greatest men, but he tells us that in that day they looked upon him as the filth of the world. Today when preachers make a tour around the world, they ride on planes, fine ships and good trains. They stay in the finest hotels and are entertained and honored by the best people. It was not so with Paul—he knew that he would meet trouble everywhere that he went. Surely Paul often remembered what God had said at the time of his conversion, "I will show him how great things he must suffer for my Name's sake."

One day someone must have sympathized with Paul for having such a hard time. Listen to his answer, "I take pleasure in infirmities, in reproaches, in necessities, in persecutions, in distresses for Christ's sake" (II Corinthians 12:10). There is the answer—he did it all for Christ's sake.

II. THE EMBARRASSMENT. Verses 6-12

Paul then went to Troas. He stayed there for several days, planning to leave on Monday morning. They asked him to preach on Sunday night and to help in the observance of the Lord's Supper. All the brethren and sisters came to church. Not often would they have the opportunity of hearing such a great preacher. Paul did not deliver a short essay. He would probably never see them again, he had many things to tell them, so he preached until midnight. I do not know what time they turned the service over to him. It may have been like some of our modern services. I have been invited to preach in certain places and I would be forced to sit and chafe while they went through an hour or more of preliminaries. When the time came for the message everybody would be just about tired out. Maybe that is what happened to Paul. Maybe they felt that they had to put on a big program to impress this prominent guest. Well, it was a hot night. The services were held on the third floor and all the windows were left open to catch a passing breeze. A young fellow, named Eutychus, got the best seat. He sat in one of these open windows. While Paul was preaching this young man's eyes became heavy and he went to sleep. Before long he fell out the window and was killed.

We can see, then, that it is dangerous to fall asleep in church. There is one way to avoid it—go to bed early on Saturday night. Saturday night is Satan's night. It is the time when the world, the flesh and the devil have their highest hours. It is the time when Christians should be at home and in bed so that they can be alert during the Sunday services in God's house. We can desecrate the Lord's Day by spending all our energies on the world Saturday night, and by not being at our best for Christ on Sunday. Sunday afternoon is also a time which we ought to watch. We ought not to spend Sunday afternoon in such a way that we will be ruined for the Sunday night service. It should be a time for rest and not for picture shows, sporting events and the tiresome visitation of friends.

Well, Paul went down and brought Eutychus back to life. He then went back upstairs and continued his sermon.

The story is told of a dear old lady who had insomnia. She consumed all kinds of sleeping pills and medicines but nothing could make her sleep. Finally she said: "There is no use for me to take any more medicine—just take me to my pew in the church—I have slept there for forty years. Probably that will help me." They took her to the church and just as soon as the preacher was well into his sermon she fell asleep.

Some people may never go to sleep in church, physically. But many of them are asleep mentally and spiritually. The word of God is preached, Christ calls for their soul, but they are asleep spiritually. They are dreaming of worldly delights and pleasures. Jesus passes the pew, but they are asleep. Some day they will wake up and will find that they are lost and condemned to hell forever. A Scotch minister preached every Sunday night to a cold, sleepy congregation. One Sunday night after he had done his best he went home in despair, lay down and went to sleep. That night he had a dream. He dreamed that he was in his pulpit, making an appeal for the people to accept Christ. Some of them were asleep, some of them moved about restlessly and some of them were looking at their watches and wishing that he would finish the sermon. Then in his dream he saw the door opening, and a stranger who entered said to him, "Preacher, come with me. Go down to hell and preach to the people there. They will be glad to listen to you." A person can go ahead and pay no attention to the Gospel. He can leave Christ out, but in hell he will wake up and cry out for someone to show him the way of salvation. Alas, it will be too late then.

Too many Christians are asleep, also. They join the church, they are baptized, their names are placed on the roll, but they have gone to sleep so far as any activity for Christ is concerned. A sinful, hungry world waits in darkness, the church of Christ needs help and service. Christ calls, but they sleep on, saying, "Let others fight to win the prize and sail through bloody seas."

They will wake up some day at the Judgment Seat of Christ. The Man with the nail-pierced hands will say, "I gave my life for thee, I saved thee, yet you did nothing for me. I needed you, but you gave your life to other things and my work went undone." What will these listless Christians say in that hour? Oh, as they face Him, they would gladly give everything if they could come back and have another opportunity to serve Him. We may go to sleep, but the devil is always on the job. He comes to every service, he speaks to every heart, he tempts every soul. It behooves us to stay awake. We must not let Satan lull us to sleep.

After all the excitement was over, Paul continued the service and then they observed the Lord's Supper. After that they sat around and talked until daybreak. I am sure that those who were there never forgot that night. It was a joy for them to listen again to the story of Jesus and to hear Paul tell what Christ had done for him and what he had seen Him do for others. The real Christian never gets tired of hearing the old, old story.

> And when, in scenes of glory,
> I sing the new, new song,
> 'Twill be the old, old story
> That I have loved so long.

III. THE ELDERS. Verses 13-35

Paul left Troas and in due time he arrived at Miletus. Miletus was a seaport town thirty miles from Ephesus. Paul then sent a message to Ephesus, asking the Ephesian elders to come down to Miletus for a farewell meeting. These were the men he had led to Christ, the men he had ordained to preach, the men with whom he had labored. He knew that he would never see them again, so the meeting was one of tenderness and sorrow. He made a wonderful speech to these men. It is one of the finest things in literature. In it the apostle simply poured out his heart. This speech was not made in a church, but down by the seaside where they could hear the rippling waves of the sea.

First, Paul talked of his own personal life among them. He said, "You all know my life. It is an open book. You know how I served among you in humility. I didn't covet your money, but I worked with my own hands to make a living."

It is fine when anyone can say, "You know my life and I am willing for you to judge me on that." You cannot judge a man by an hour nor a day, but you must judge him by the entire trend of his life. It takes the hills and the valleys to make up a landscape. It takes the high days and the low to make up a life.

Paul could say, "You watched me for three years; you saw me under all conditions. You know that in my life I tried to exemplify the spirit of Christ."

How many Christians could say, "Look at my life—it is what a Christian life ought to be." Probably most Christians would be forced to say, "Just look at the good days; don't look at the bad." Surely Christians ought to be trying to make everyday a good one, filled with the good things of God.

The Mississippi River in some places flows northward, and in other places eastward, and in other places westward. But the general trend of the river is southward, and it finally wends its way to the Gulf of Mexico. So it is with the life of a real Christian. He often goes the wrong way, but the general trend of his life is toward God. We should seek to grow a little bit more like Him every day.

Paul then told them about the compassion which he had for them. "For three years," he said, "I warned you night and day with tears." The only man who ever wins for Christ is the man of compassion. Jesus wept over Jerusalem; Paul wept over Ephesus. John Knox cried out, "Give me Scotland or I die!" Our religion is too dry eyed today. We need the compassion that sent Jesus to the Cross. Paul had that compassion. When he looked upon men, he sought not to know whether they were rich or poor, but to know if they knew Christ as Saviour. If they did not, he rushed out to do something about it. The Bible tells us that if we warn the lost, even though they die in their sins, we have cleared ourselves. If we do not warn them and they die in their sins, their blood shall be upon our hands. Paul had clean hands—he had done his best. Do we have clean hands? Have we done our best to warn men and to point them to Christ?

Paul spoke of the kind of preaching which he did in Ephesus, saying "I declared unto you the whole counsel of God—I kept back nothing which was profitable to you." The preacher must be a skilled physician and surgeon. He must give the people the medicine which they need, even though it tastes badly. Sometimes he must use the knife, even though it may be painful. All of it must be done in love and all for the benefit of his hearers. Paul now said, "I told everybody, the Jews and the Greeks, that the way to be saved was through repentance toward God and faith toward our Lord Jesus Christ."

The repentance is to be toward God for it is His law which has been broken. The faith must be toward Christ, for He is the object of saving faith. The faithful Bible preacher today says, "If you want to be saved you must repent, you must turn away from your sin and trust the Lord Jesus Christ."

Later, when Paul was in Rome, he wrote to these same Ephesians and gave them the same truth in different words. Ephesians 2:8-9, "For by grace are ye saved through faith; and that not of yourselves: it is the gift of God: Not of works, lest any man should boast."

Paul also said that he not only testified to this truth in the pulpit, but from house to house. That is the pastor's wayside ministry. He is not only to preach to lost sinners in the church, but as he meets them from day to day he is to tell them of the salvation which is in Christ.

A preacher met a young man at the close of an evening service and asked him if he was a Christian. The young man replied, "No, I have heard you preach regularly for several years, but I am not a Christian." The preacher was able to lead him to Christ in a few minutes. In these few minutes of personal work, he did what years of preaching had not done.

Paul mentioned briefly some of the sufferings which he had endured. He said that everywhere he went enemies were lying in wait for him, that they did everything in the world to hurt him and to kill his message. But here is the way Paul felt about it, II Corinthians 6:4-10, "But in all things approving ourselves as the ministers of God, in much patience, in afflictions, in necessities, in distresses, in stripes, in imprisonments, in tumults, in labors, in watchings, in fastings; By pureness, by knowledge, by longsuffering, by kindness, by the Holy Ghost, by love unfeigned, by the word of truth, by the power of God, by the armour of righteousness on the right hand and on the left, by honor and dishonor, by evil report and good report: as deceivers, and yet true; as unknown, and yet well known; as dying, and, behold, we live; as chastened, and not killed; as sorrowful, yet alway rejoicing; as poor, yet making many rich; as having nothing, and yet possessing all things."

Paul gave some wise counsel to the preachers. "The Holy Spirit has put you over the flock," he said, "it is your duty to feed them." What can a preacher feed his people? He can feed them error, he can feed them light foamy food which never touches the vital things of life and which largely leaves Christ out. But if he is wise, he will feed them the Word of God, the Bread of Life.

The pastor is not only to be a warner, he is to be a watcher. As the shepherd watches the flock and keeps the wolves away, so must the Pastor seek to protect his flock from the wolves of this world. Paul mentioned two kinds of wolves, and predicted that they would come in and seek to destroy the sheep. First, he spoke of the wolves which come in from the outside. Today all kinds of outside influences are warring against the church. It is the pastor's duty to warn the flock against these things. It is the Christian's duty to keep away from and out of every connection which does not build up his spiritual life and which does not glorify God. Paul mentioned the enemies which might rise up within the church. That is the deadly kind. When we find in the church those whose beliefs and lives and actions are not conducive to the health of the church, we ought immediately to withdraw from them, if we have not been able to win them to the right way, God's way.

Paul spoke of the grace of giving. He told his audience to "remember the words of the Lord Jesus, how He said, 'it is more blessed to give than to receive.'" We do not find this saying in the Gospels, but Paul rescued it for us and it is one of the finest things ever said about giving. Those who have tried it have proven it to be true. Those who give cheerfully are happier than those who receive. To be a strong, true Christian, to be more like Jesus, one must learn the secret of giving. Jesus had everything. The highest place in heaven was his. The angels sang "Holy, Holy, Holy" around the throne. Jesus was equal with God. Yet one day He gave up all of this and came down to earth for man's sake. He was the richest of the rich, but He became the poorest of the poor. From the moment that He left glory down through the time when He bled His life away on the Cross, even until this minute He has been giving, giving, giving. Some day He will reap the harvest of it all. As He sees the souls come marching home, saved because He gave, He will see of the "travail of his soul, and shall be satisfied" (Isaiah 53:11).

We have an opportunity to be like Jesus. We can give and give and give as long as we live. Then, some day when we stand by His side in glory and watch the souls coming home, we can turn and say, "Lord, I helped you—I gave myself, my money and my service so that these might know about you." He will smile and say, "That is just what I wanted you to do."

Finally Paul told them that he was going to leave them.

"I am going to Jerusalem now. I don't know what will happen to me there, but the Holy Spirit has told me that bonds and afflictions await me wherever I go." If he knew this, why did he not slip into the city, gather a few people around him at night and teach them? Why should he risk his life? Well, that just would not have been like Paul. He had had a great experience, he had a great message to deliver. Everywhere he went something within pressed upon him to publish the good news far and wide. He said, "The love of Christ constrains me." That love constrained him to do his best for Jesus, even though it cost him his life.

Although he knew that hard things awaited him everywhere, Paul did not retreat, but marched straight forward. Listen to his statement in verse 24: "But none of these things move me, neither count I my life dear unto myself, so that I might finish my course with joy, and the ministry which I have received of the Lord Jesus, to testify the gospel of the grace of God." He knew that one day he would come to the end of the way and stand face to face with his Saviour. He wanted to be able to say, "Lord, I never retreated, I never held back. You sent me to preach the glorious Gospel and to witness for You everywhere. I didn't let anything stop me." Oh, I wish that we had his spirit.

IV. THE EMBARKING. Verses 36-38

Paul finished his speech and knelt down upon the beach. With all the elders kneeling around him he offered an earnest prayer for them. When he said, "Amen," all of them came up, put their arms around him and wept as they kissed him good-bye. He had told them that they would never see his face again and their hearts were broken. Soon he boarded his ship. The elders stood on the shore and waved farewell to him as he stood at the rail of the ship. The sound of weeping was heard on the shore as the anchor was weighed and the ship moved out. In a little while the sails were just a white speck on the horizon. With sad hearts the Ephesian elders turned away to their homes and went back to their duties. Never, never would they forget the beloved man who had just left them. I am sure that later on when they met him in heaven Paul took them up to the Saviour and said, "Master, these are the men who carried on the work in Ephesus so nobly after I left them."

We, too, have been left with a great task. Christ's work is our work. He has no hands, no feet, no brains to do his work but our hands, our feet, our brains! Oh, may the Lord shake us out of our lethargy and cause us to become active for Him, so that when we meet Him we will not be ashamed of what we did here with lives He gave us.

Throughout this chapter we see Paul's great concern for the souls of men. He preached, talked, wept, visited, did everything that men might know Jesus.

When Samuel Hadley was superintendent of the Water Street Mission, one of the bowery bums came to the mission on a cold night. This man had been a law partner of one of the men in Lincoln's cabinet. Now he was down and out, brought down by sin. Mr. Hadley had no room for him and had to turn him away. The man came back at one o'clock and again Mr. Hadley had to say, "I am sorry, Colonel, but I can't take you in." The old man, leaning upon his stick, went on down under the Brooklyn Bridge. Hadley could not sleep. At three o'clock in the morning he went out and found the colonel huddled up near one of the piers of the bridge. Mr. Hadley took him home, bathed him with his own hands, and put him in his own bed. The next night at the service the colonel knelt at the altar and cried out, "God be merciful to me a sinner." He arose a new man in Christ Jesus. Before long he was back at his old position, a respected and useful citizen, and an active Christian. That is the task of the church—to rescue the perishing and to lift up the fallen. God help us to be faithful.

Chapter Twenty-One

"SPIRITUAL RESIGNATION"

Acts 21

If there ever was a man who was resigned to God's will, that man was the Apostle Paul. We see this as we follow his life after his conversion. Before he met Jesus on the Damascus Road he was very zealous for Judaism. He gave all of his powers and talents to what he believed. But he became a changed man when he met Jesus. He turned away from the old life and gave all of his fine powers and talents to the service of Christ. He said good-bye to the old life without regret. He counted himself as a man dead to these old things, but alive in Jesus Christ. "I am crucified with Christ," he said, "nevertheless I live; yet not I, but Christ liveth in me: and the life which I now live in the flesh, I live by the faith of the Son of God, who loved me, and gave himself for me" (Galations 2:20).

Again, he said, "For me to live is Christ . . ." (Philippians 1:21). He meant that he wanted so to live that people would feel that Christ was living again in him.

Christ's greatest joy was to do the will of His Heavenly Father. He said, "My meat is to do the will of Him that sent me . . ." (John 4:34). In Gethsemane, Christ stated, "Not my will, but thine, be done." (Luke 22:42).

Paul tried to live the same way. He could say, "It doesn't matter what happens to me, nor where I go—I want to do the will of God." He probably made many mistakes, for the man who never makes mistakes never does anything. Nevertheless, the whole trend of Paul's life was toward the will of God. We will never be what we ought to be nor do all that we ought to do, but God help us to be able to say when we meet Jesus, "Lord, I tried. I did the best I could— I made many mistakes, Lord, but I tried."

Surely then He will answer, "Well done, my child, all your sins and mistakes have been cast into the deepest sea, but I will forever remember that you did your best for me."

As we study Acts 21, as we follow Paul to Jerusalem and imprisonment, we see his resignation to the will of God.

I. THE VOYAGE. Verses 1-3

Paul boarded the ship at Miletus. He had just said farewell to the Ephesian elders. He left them on shore, weeping because he had said that they would see his face no more. As the ship sailed out of the harbor, I can imagine that he pointed upward, as if he were saying to the elders, "I'll see you some day in heaven. I'll see you where the gates are never closed, I'll see you where there are no more sad farewells, I'll see you where there are no tears and troubles and tribulation. I'll see you up there at the feet of Jesus, our blessed Lord, who has redeemed us by His blood." If the song had been written at that time, I am sure that you could have heard these words as the ship moved out: "God be with you till we meet again—'till we meet at Jesus' feet." Then I am sure that Paul went to his cabin, fell upon his knees and thanked God for bringing him to Ephesus and for saving so many of the Ephesians. Then, of course, he asked God to keep these friends in the hollow of His hand forever.

As time hurries by, we never know when we are going to say our last farewell to those whom we love. Many who were with us a year ago are not here today. Many who are here today will not be with us a year from now. But we must remember that in the vocabulary of God there is no such word as "good-bye." Those who love God never part for the last time. Our loved ones are waiting over there for us now, and Jesus is waiting, too. Some day our frail human tents will be folded and we shall enter into the pearly white city—we shall be forever at rest in the presence of our Saviour and with our loved ones who have gone on before.

Paul went on, down to Rhodes. He had seen one of the seven wonders of the world, the Temple of Diana, at Ephesus. The remains of another wonder was in the harbor at Rhodes. The entrance to the harbor is quite narrow, and these people had built a gigantic bronze statue in the shape of a man and had placed this statue with one foot on one side of the harbor and the other foot on the other side of the harbor. The ships sailed into the harbor between the legs of this statue. Before Paul's time an earthquake had broken the legs of the statue and it had fallen to the ground. It was later sold to a Jew for junk and nine hundred camels were required to carry the bronze away. But Paul did not stay in Rhodes. He pressed on toward Tyre.

II. THE VISIT. Verses 4-6

The ship had to be unloaded and reloaded at Tyre. We read that Paul found some disciples there and stayed with them for seven days. Jesus visited Tyre once and it was there that the Syrophenician woman was saved. Under Paul's persecution against the Jerusalem Christians before his conversion, some of them had fled to Tyre and a church was established there. It is wonderful to go to a new place and find kindred spirits there. I guess that today you could go to any place in the world and find a few Christians with whom you could have Christian fellowship.

These disciples were speaking to Paul one day through the Spirit and they told him that he should not go up to Jerusalem. Later in this chapter we find others giving him the same warning. We are not told how Paul received this warning, but he must have felt in his heart that he was doing the right thing, for he said, "Nothing can keep me back." These must have been seven blessed days for the Christians of Tyre. We read nothing about the synagogue, so it is probable that Paul spent his whole time with the believers. Everyday Paul had something new to tell them of Jesus, of his own experience and of what he had seen Jesus do for others. These people knew that they had a great man in their midst, so they laid aside all else and gave him their full time. I am sure that they never forgot this visit.

When the time of parting came there was another scene like the one at Miletus. The men brought their wives and children down to the shore, knelt down and prayed with Paul, and then bade him farewell. Did Paul realize as he made these sad farewells that he was hurrying toward the end of the way? Had God revealed this to him? It seems surely that he had some inkling of it. But he was ready, he was completely in the will of God. If we knew that our time was short, could we say, "I am ready"? We are not ready unless Christ is our Saviour and we are living for Him everyday.

III. THE VERDICT. Verses 7-14

The little company then went to Ptolemais where they spent one day with the Christians in that city. Then they went on to Caesarea and entered the house of Philip, the evangelist. Philip was one of the seven deacons of Jerusalem. Later, when persecution came, he went to Samaria and held a great meeting. God then sent him down to the desert where he baptized the Ethiopian treasurer. Twenty years had gone by and now he is faithfully serving as an evangelist in Caesarea. It had been Paul's persecution which had driven Philip out of Jerusalem. He had not seen Paul since Paul's conversion, but of course, he had heard about him. Now the persecutor visits the home of the man whom he once persecuted, and they have a regular love feast. At the foot of the Cross they had come to love each other. Do you have any difference with anyone? Then bring them and that difference to the foot of the Cross, where in the light of His love every problem can be settled.

Philip was not a great man, but he was a good and faithful man. There was a time when a whole city was moved by his preaching, and another time when a great statesman listened to him. It looked then as if Philip might do as great a work as Paul did. But the years had gone by and we now find him in an obscure corner. He was lost to the outside world, but he was still faithful to Christ. These are the kind of people we need today to do the work of the kingdom. Brilliant people rise and shine and burn out in a little while. God's faithful little people keep on keeping on and God's work survives because of them. They are the kind who are faithful unto death and who will receive a crown of life.

Maybe Philip thought that his work was not noticed, yet here is what happened. Luke came along with Paul and as Philip and Paul sat together during the long evenings Philip told Paul all that had happened right after the Crucifixion and during the early days of the church.

Luke took all of this down and, inspired by the Holy Spirit, wrote the Book of Acts. Philip had been working behind a curtain. Luke lifted that curtain and the whole world came to know the good work which Philip had done.

That same thing is going to happen to us. Some day the curtain will be lifted and every deed will be made manifest. God help us to keep on serving, whether or not anyone sees or commends us. At last we will meet the Master who knows all about it and He will understand and say, "Well done."

We read that Philip had four daughters who prophesied. This is a fulfillment of Joel's prophecy. He said that when the spirit came the "sons and daughters would prophecy." This tells us that women have an active part in the work of

Christ. This has always been true. They were last at the Cross and first at the tomb. They seem to be more interested in the work of the church than the men are—at least they always outnumber the men in the church services. God bless those faithful women who pray, who love the Word of God, who are faithful to the church, and who set an example of Christian living before their husbands and children.

While Paul was in Caesarea the prophet Agabus came down from Judea. He had heard that Paul was determined to go to Jerusalem and he wanted to stop him. He stood up in the company and did a strange thing. He took Paul's girdle, or sash, and with it he tied his own hands and feet. Then he said, "If the owner of this girdle goes to Jerusalem the Jews will bind him in this manner and turn him over to the Gentiles." This thing happened to Jesus at Jerusalem and now Agabus said that it is going to happen to Paul.

Paul's companions and friends then gathered around him and said, "Paul, this is your second warning. You must not go. We cannot afford to lose you. There is a great work yet to be done."

Paul then gave them his verdict. "Are you trying to break my heart?" he asked. "I'm ready to go to Jerusalem and not only to be bound but to die for Jesus." Oh, how this man did love his Saviour!

Has Christ done any less for us than He did for Paul? He saw us bound in the pits of sin, He died in our stead, He shed for us His precious blood. He saved us, He lifted us up, He put us on the road to heaven. He has watched over us and given us every good thing. Why should we give our best to the world and then give Him the fag end of our lives? Why should we crowd our hearts with trivial things and push Him over in a corner? Why should we put any earthly institution above His church? Why should we spend His money for our own needs and use His tithe for our own selfish purposes? Oh, it is only reasonable, it is only right, that

Christ should have the first place in our lives. Paul said here, "I am ready." Can we say that?

When Woodrow Wilson lay dying his personal physician, Admiral Grayson, said to him, "Mr. Wilson, you are dying." He replied, "I am ready." If the death angel came tonight and said, "I have come after you," could we say "I am ready?" We can if Christ is our Saviour. If He is ours we need have no fear. Whatever comes, be it life or death, we can then say, "I am ready for it, for Jesus is mine."

When the others saw that Paul was determined to go to Jerusalem, they quit pleading with him and said, "The Lord's will be done." Paul wanted to go to Jerusalem for two reasons. He had an intense desire to see the Jerusalem Jews saved. They had helped to crucify Christ, but now he wanted them to be saved. Wherever he was, in all of his travels, he was looking back toward Jerusalem and praying that these Jews might believe Christ was the Messiah and accept Him as their Saviour. He stated, "I could wish myself accursed from Christ for their sakes. I am willing to go down to hell for the sake of my kinsmen, if only I could see them saved." The other reason was this. He had taken a large offering for the Jerusalem Christians and he wanted to give this offering to them with his own hands. He wanted to say to them, "Your brethren in the other parts of the world love you and want to help you in your distress."

Was Paul justified in going to Jerusalem? Who was right, Agabus or Paul? We do not know. We do know, however, that the greatest apostle made mistakes. He was taken prisoner in Jerusalem, and he was never free again in his life. Somehow, we can believe, however, that if he did make a mistake, God overruled it all for the best. It is glorious to know that when we do our best, even if we make mistakes, God somehow overrules and makes all things work together for good. However, we are to be sure that we are doing our best.

IV. THE VETERAN. Verses 15-16

Paul and his company now proceeded to Jerusalem. This period of time was between the Passover and the Day of Pentecost. During these feasts a million people came to the city and it was difficult to find a place to stay. God led an old man in Caesarea, who owned a home in Jerusalem, to invite the preachers to stay with him. The name of this man was Mnason. Probably he had been a believer from the beginning of Christianity. The years had gone by and Mnason was no longer a young man. Life had changed for him in many ways, he had lost many early dreams and hopes, but he still held on to a firm faith in Christ.

It is fine to see an old man, below whose feet time is crumbling away, holding firmly to the One who is the same yesterday, today and forever. To have a happy old age, one must live for Jesus all of his days. I am sure that Mnason found Christ's grace sufficient down through the years. He found Him a refuge in time of trouble; He found comfort in Him when his loved ones slipped away; He found Jesus sweeter as the years went by. We ought always to grow, not away from, but toward Christ. Then, when old age creeps upon us, when the step is feeble and the sight is dim, when we are nearing the crossing, there will be a light in our sky, and our faith will be stronger than ever.

V. THE VOW. Verses 17-26

When the company arrived at Jerusalem they were cordially received by the brethren. Paul went before them, gave them the large offering, and told them all that God had done through him in the conversion of the Gentiles. When they heard these things, they rejoiced and glorified God. Yet the next thing which the Jewish Christians said showed that they were a little uneasy about Paul. "Brother Paul, you see many Jewish believers here. They heard that you were teaching the Jews to forsake Moses and his customs. In order to prove that this is false, we are making you a proposition. Four men here have taken a vow. We want you to go in and be one of them. Fellowship with them, and spend some money on them. Then all men will see that you are not forsaking the law of Moses.

Did Paul agree? Yes, he did. He did not believe in mixing customs with Christianity and he had said that the grace of Christ was all that was needed to save men. Yet, he felt that this action on his part would do no harm and that it might enable him to win some of those who were under the law. Again he must have said, "I am become all things to all men, that I might win some." He was willing to do the thing which was distasteful to him if that would help him to gain a hearing for the message of salvation.

Apparently Paul felt that if he had gone before the unbelieving Jews with a reputation that he had forsaken Moses, they would have declared, "We will not listen to this fellow." On the other hand, if they knew that he was a *true* Jew by seeing him observing these Jewish customs, they might say, "He is a good man—we will listen to what he has to tell." So we see why he took the vow with these four men. Was anything good accomplished? Apparently not. Paul mixed Judaism and Christianity and the result was not good. It is the same way today. Some men mix a little of the Bible with some lodge, some ism, some man-made idea, and the result is zero for God. Men need only one thing to save them and help them—that is pure faith in Christ and His saving power, with nothing added and nothing subtracted.

VI. THE VIOLENCE. Verses 27-40

There were many Jews in the city and when they saw Paul in the temple they rushed in, seized him, and cried out, "This man teaches against all holy beliefs. Not only this, but he has polluted the Temple by bringing a Gentile into its sacred precincts." They believed that anyone who brought in an outsider was worthy of death. The Romans did not generally allow the Jews to have the power of death, but the Jews were so jealous of the Temple that the Romans did allow them to go ahead and kill any man found there who was not a Jew. Isn't that some religion? Isn't that prejudice of the lowest type? "If you are not one of us, and you come into our temple, we will kill you." Yet in this enlightened age of 1950, right here in civilized United States, there are certain places of religion where non-members are prohibited from entering.

They never proved that Paul had brought the Gentile into the Temple, but when they saw him on the street with a Gentile, they supposed that if he were willing to be seen with one of them, he would bring them into the Temple. So they dragged Paul out of the Temple, shut the doors behind him and prepared to kill him. In shutting these doors they showed a sorry sense of propriety. It was all right to murder a man, but they must not pollute the Temple. In the case of Jesus it was all right to crucify Him, but it must be done outside of the Holy City. God's house was once a sanctuary. A criminal could rush in and grasp the horns of the altar and be safe until he could have a just trial. Men had forgotten about this, so they pushed Paul out, closed the doors and prepared to kill him. God's house should still be a sanctuary. When the howling winds of the world blow over our souls we should be able to come to God's house and in close communion with Him find peace for our troubled hearts.

The Roman soldiers in Jerusalem spent much time in putting down uprisings among the Jews. When the captain of the guard saw the crowd and heard the uproar and knew that a man was about to be killed, he took a group of soldiers and rushed to the scene of action. The Jews were beating Paul, but when they saw these soldiers they immediately ceased. The captain rescued Paul, put two chains upon him, and then asked, "Who is this man, and what has

he done?" Some cried out one thing and some another, but
Paul was silent. He was thanking God for this deliverance.
The captain did not know all about the case, so he took
Paul into the castle. As they went up the steps Paul looked
out upon that great seething mob of people. He did not
hate them, his heart went out to them. They were lost
and he wanted them to know his Saviour.

So Paul turned courteously to the captain and said,
"May I speak to you, sir?" The captain was surprised. This was
no common ruffian, but a cultured man who could speak
several languages.

"Can you speak Greek?" the captain asked. "Aren't you
the Egyptian who caused trouble here several weeks ago?"
A few weeks before this time an Egyptian had come to Jerusalem, claiming to be the Messiah. A crowd had followed him
and in the disturbance four hundred people were killed.

The captain thought that Paul was this man, but Paul
answered, "I am a Jew. My home town is Tarsus, which is
no mean city. Would you please permit me to speak to
these people?"

The captain knew that there was something fine about
this little man, so he said, "Go ahead." Paul lifted his hands
and the crowd became silent, while he began to speak in the
Hebrew language.

In all these things Paul was the complete master of
himself. He had no fear. He could say, "If God be for us,
who can be against us?" He could look at the mighty mob,
then up to God, and realize that the One who was for him
was far greater than all those who were against him. Elisha
was in trouble once. The King and his great army had come
to make him captive. This did not trouble Elisha at all.
His servant cried out, "Master, what can we do?"

Elisha replied, "We have more with us than we have
against us." Then he prayed, "Lord, open the young man's
eyes." The young man's eyes were opened and he saw all

the mountains around about covered with horses and chariots of fire. They were there to protect God's servants. It is even so with us. If we belong to God as Paul did, if we are serving Him and trying to do the will of God as Paul did, all of God's powers are on our side, and we need have no fear.

When John Wesley lay dying, he gave a glowing testimony, concluding with these words, "Best of all, God is with us." That is certainly best of all! When we receive Christ as Saviour we become the children of God and He will always be with us. He will be with us in life, in death, at the Judgment, and throughout all eternity. Don't you want Him to be with you in that way?

CHAPTER TWENTY-TWO

"SPIRITUAL DECLARATION"

Acts 22

As we finished Acts 21 we saw Paul standing on the steps
of the castle, in custody of the Roman captain. He had been
advised against coming to Jerusalem, but he had come de-
spite these warnings. The Jews had seized him and were
about to put him to death. The Roman officer saved Paul and
was now taking him into the castle. As Paul mounted
the outside steps he looked down upon the great multitude of
Jews and his heart went out to them. He wanted to tell
them about Christ, the Messiah. He asked the captain for permission to speak and this permission was granted. Paul then
held up his hand for silence and as the Jews listened he made
a marvelous speech.

This speech has been called, "Paul's Defense." It was more
than that. It was a declaration of what Christ had done
for him, the chief of sinners.

Some people say, "I can't explain the plan of salvation to
a sinner." Well, the best thing for you to do is just what
Paul did here. You can tell them what you were and what
Christ has done for you. This is the greatest testimony in the
world.

I. The Childhood. Verses 1-3

Paul began his address very respectfully. "Men, brethren
and fathers, hear my defense." He did not count himself as
an outsider, but as a brother. In the crowd he saw many re-

ligious leaders of Israel, so he courteously addressed them as "fathers." He spoke the pure Hebrew tongue and immediately secured their attention. Many of them had just about forgotten the Hebrew language, while some had mixed their Hebrew with other languages. They were pleased to hear him speak in their mother tongue. Paul got off to a good start. He spoke a language which they could understand.

Every preacher would be wise to speak in such a way that the people could understand. He may be tempted to show off his learning, his knowledge of Hebrew and Greek, but the congregation cares nothing for that. Today people want to hear something which reaches down and grips their own lives. The preacher must receive his truth from above, but it must be applied to the hearts of his hearers.

A certain prominent man in England heard the sermon of a great Gospel preacher one Sunday morning. Rushing out of the church, he exclaimed, "That preacher is a fool. He thinks that religion has something to do with practical everyday life." My friends, true religion has everything to do with living. All of the preacher's sermons, therefore, should bring the white heat of God's truth up against the needy hearts of men.

When Paul secured their attention he told them how he had been brought up. "I was born in Tarsus," he said, "but I was brought up in Jerusalem." Tarsus was an important city, a renowned place of education under the Roman Empire. It was also a great commercial center. There as a boy Paul learned to read and write Greek in a masterful style. He also learned the trade of tentmaker. Probably he was in his teens when his family moved to Jerusalem. His parents were strict Hebrews and they wanted their son to know Jewish law. They, therefore, took him to Gamaliel, the most prominent teacher of the day. He was a grandson of the celebrated Hillel and some believe that he was also president of the San-hedrin. Paul was naturally brilliant and he was a very zealous student. He soon became as proficient in the law as Gamaliel himself.

"Like all of you," Paul exlaimed, "I was always zealous towards God." He was simply saying, "Once I was like you." He knew how to gain their attention. He knew that in every mind this question would pop up. "All right, what changed you? What made you what you are today?" This was just what he wanted to tell them. He wanted to tell what Christ had done for him.

II. THE CHAMPION. Verses 4-5

Now Paul told them something that all of them had heard about and many of them had witnessed. "I was the champion for Judaism. I believed there was no other way. But just outside this city a man named Jesus was crucified. Soon the news was spread abroad that he had risen from the dead. A little group of people seemed to believe it, for they went everywhere telling of His Resurrection. They soon had others believing it. When I heard that our own people were following this Way I believed that it was rank heresy, and I took it upon myself to stamp out this new religion. I felt that the way to do this was to kill these people, so I hounded them down everywhere. I went to their homes, dragged them out, cast them into prison and often saw them put to death."

Paul then turned to the High Priest and said, "The High Priest remembers this and so do the older men who are here. You remember when I was given letters unto our leaders in Damascus and when I went down there to find more Christians, that I might bind them and bring them to Jerusalem." How did Paul feel as he told about how he had persecuted Christ and the Christians? A great heaviness surely filled his heart. He wished that these things had never happened.

We too, can also look back and say, "I wish that I had never gone astray. I wish that I had never been so set against the One who loved me and died in my place." But Paul did not linger long on the subject of his past life. They knew all about that, so he hurried on to tell the glorious story of his meeting with the risen Redeemer.

Not one of us is proud of his past sins, but there is one thing for which we can be thankful. We came to Jesus and these sins have been covered by His blood. When we get to heaven He will never bring up the matter of our sins. When God looks upon us, it will be through the blood and in His sight we shall be as white as snow. He has said, "I will put your sins behind my back and remember them against you no more forever. I will cast your sins into the deepest sea. I will remove them as far from you as the East is from the West." Thank God, Jesus does a thorough job when He saves us.

III. THE CONVERSION. Verses 6-13

Paul told about his journey to Damascus. "It was the last day of our trip. I was riding along at noonday, thinking of the delights which awaited me in Damascus, when suddenly a bright light from heaven blazed down upon me." At noontime the Eastern sun was shining in all of its brilliance, but this light was brighter than any sun. Surely it was the light of the face of Jesus. Paul then said, "I fell to the ground and as I fell I heard a voice saying, 'Saul, Saul, why persecutest thou Me?'

Those who were with me saw the light, but they did not understand the voice. I knew that this voice was for me alone. I knew that it came out of heaven. It was not a man's voice, and I tell you that I was greatly frightened. I could not help but cry out, 'Who art thou, Lord?' "

Paul then told them of the answer that came, of how the Voice replied, "I am Jesus of Nazareth, whom thou persecutest." As he spoke this hated name there was a stirring in the crowd. Their anger was mounting and Paul knew that he could not withstand them much longer. "When that answer came," he continued, "I knew that I had been mistaken all along. I came to know that Jesus was not a bad man, but that He was Christ, the Messiah. I knew that He was not in a tomb, but that He was living in heaven with God. I then cried out, 'Lord, what would you have me to do?' He told me to go to Damascus, where I would receive a special revelation. Brethren, I arose to my feet and looked around, but I couldn't see a thing. The vision of the risen Christ had blinded me. They had to lead me into the city of Damascus."

Paul then related how he went into Damascus, where he remained blind for three days. "Finally Ananias came to see me. He was a devout Jew, but a believer in Christ. He called me 'Brother Saul,' and when he did that I received my sight, looked up, and saw Ananias standing before me." This thing that happened to Paul on the Damascus Road was something that he could never forget. He told about it everywhere that he went. The years went by and as he thought about it the light was just as bright as ever and the voice of Christ was just as clear as ever. Do you remember when you were saved? Maybe you went to church and heard a sermon that pricked your heart. You saw yourself a lost sinner. You went home, but you couldn't get the matter off your mind. You could neither rest nor eat. You went back to the church again, you heard another sermon, you felt that God was again knocking at the door of your heart. When the invitation was given you went forward, threw yourself upon His mercy, and surrendered all to Him. When you came out of the church, something had happened to you. The burden of your sin was gone and you were singing, "Oh, happy day that fixed my choice on Thee my Saviour and my God!" My friend, don't ever forget that day. When Satan comes to tempt us, you go back in your memories and rest upon the assurance of that experience. Then in gratitude you should go out to live a little bit better for Him.

IV. THE CHOSEN. Verses 14-21

Paul told why he had been saved, for surely God had a purpose in it all. He said that Ananias told him that God had chosen him to be a witness for Christ. Well, of course, Paul wanted to witness to his own people. He was so intensely patriotic that when he had received the joy of salvation in his own heart, he wanted to share that joy with his own countrymen. But God had other plans. The next time that Paul was in Jerusalem, while he was praying in the Temple, he heard the voice of God, saying, "Get out of Jerusalem quickly. These people will not listen to you."

But, we know, Paul was so zealous for the salvation of the Jews that he argued with God. "Lord, I can't leave the Jews. They know what I have been, they know how I helped to kill Stephen. Now, when they see how I have changed over to the other side, they will know that there is something mighty behind it, and they will listen to me."

God did not argue with Paul. He simply replied, "Get out of Jerusalem—go and preach to the Gentiles."

Yes, God had a purpose in saving Paul. He wanted to send him as a missionary to the Gentiles. Did He not save us for a purpose, also? Yes, He surely did. We are not saved so that we can sit down here, have a good time, do nothing for the Lord, and then come at last to heaven and enjoy all the blessings of eternity. God has a purpose for every life. We must go to Him in prayer and try to find that purpose. A man has a purpose in building a car or constructing a house. Everything that is made is intended for some useful purpose. God has redeemed us. He has a purpose for our lives. He wants to use us. You believe that God calls men to preach. Maybe He is calling you to some service, also. There are some who argue with God as Paul did and who never get around to serving the Lord. Paul found his greatest joy when he quit arguing and followed Christ. So will you.

V. The Condemnation. Verses 22-23

The Jews hated the Gentiles with an intense hatred, so when Paul said, "God sent me to the Gentiles," they saw red. Their blood boiled; they wanted to fight. The very idea of connecting God's name with the Gentiles!

These people went wild, they cried out, they tore their clothes, they took handfuls of dust and threw it into the air. What was their cry? "Let's kill this fellow Paul. He is not fit to live on the face of the earth."

Time after time we see Paul come within an inch of death. Did he court trouble? Did he like to stir up the wrath of the Jews? No, he had just one thing in mind. He saw them as lost sinners and wanted them to know Christ. He never held back the message, even though it meant risking his life.

As a young man Dr. H. A. Ironside worked among the Indians in the West. It was before the days of automobiles, so they rode in large horse-drawn wagons. Dr. Ironside had held a meeting in a certain village one afternoon and at five o'clock he started toward another village where he was to speak that night. As they journeyed toward this other village, they saw that a storm was about to break upon them. The young preacher declared that they would surely get caught in the storm. But the driver said, "I will try to make the Rock before the storm breaks." He whipped up the horses and soon they were in sight of a rock rising up about fifty feet out of the desert. They drove right into a great opening in the rock and in another minute the storm broke in all its fury. The Indians were grateful that they had found a shelter from the storm and began to sing the song, "Rock of Ages, cleft for me."

When Paul looked upon this great company of Jews, he knew that the storm of judgment would soon break over them. His greatest desire was to get them in the cleft of the Rock before the storm came. Oh, that we might feel the same way about those around us who are lost!

VI. The Citizen. Verses 24-30

While the Jews were carrying on this tirade the captain stood in silence. He could not understand their language, he did not yet know the charge against Paul, nor why the Jews were so angry. He decided to examine Paul by scourging, in order that he might get the truth from him. This was a common means used by the Romans, even as today some officials of the law use the third degree to force a confession from a suspect. The command was given and the soldiers began to bind Paul with thongs. Paul then spoke, saying, "Is it lawful for you to scourge a man who is a Roman and uncondemned?"

The officer was shocked by this statement and hastened to the chief captain, saying to him, "You'd better be careful. This man is a Roman citizen."

The captain ran over to Paul and said to him, "Are you a Roman citizen?"

"Yes, I am."

"I am a Roman citizen, also," said the captain, "for I paid a big price for this privilege.'

"But I was freeborn," Paul exclaimed. The Greeks felt that it was a high privilege to be a citizen of Rome, the mistress of the world. They often paid high prices for this privilege.

Perhaps the captain saved his money for a long time, and it was a proud and happy day when he could stand up and say, "I am a Roman citizen. I am a part of the greatest empire the world has ever known." But Paul was born a Roman citizen.

We are citizens of a greater kingdom—the kingdom of God. Our citizenship came to us at a great cost, also. We did not pay the price. Jesus paid it on Calvary. We could weep forever over our sins, we could spend all of our time in the work of the flesh, we could give until it hurts, but we could never purchase one foot of ground in the kingdom. When we come unto Him, we find that He has paid the price for us. All that He has done is put to our account and all of heaven becomes ours.

Well, when the captain learned that Paul was a Roman citizen, he immediately called off the torturers and tried a more orderly way. He called a council of the Jewish leaders to appear with their accusations on the following day. When they came together Paul stood before them and was given a chance to speak again.

Was it an accident that this preacher was a Roman citizen? It certainly was not. Again we see God's purpose at work. Paul's Roman citizenship saved him from death, sent him into a wider ministry and opened up the way for him to go to Rome, the center of the Empire, with the Gospel message.

Paul stood always at some crossroads. One road led to suffering and wanderings and further service; the other road led to suffering and death. But it never seemed to matter to Paul which road he traveled. He just wanted to do God's will. He looked down the road of life and saw a service in which more souls would be saved and this thrilled his heart. He looked down the road that led to death and saw that his death would bring him into the presence of his Saviour. This was the thing that he longed for most of all. So he truly said, "For me to live is Christ, and to die is gain" (Philippians 1:21).

A Wheaton College teacher wrote a fine letter to the faculty and student body. The doctor had told her that she had a cancer and that it was useless to operate. In the letter she said, "If the doctor had been a Christian, he would not have been so hesitant about telling me that I was going to die. He would know that life or death was equally welcome when one lives in the will of God. Please don't give a minute's grief for me. Think of me happily and gaily and just as interested in the school as ever. If you don't see me on the campus next fall I will see you later in the blessed land." The day after commencement this teacher died, but they all knew that she was up there with the Heavenly Father.

Years ago in northern Arizona a missionary doctor from a little mission station found a Navajo woman forsaken in the desert. The Indian medicine man had not been able to heal her, so he told the Indians that she was possessed with an evil spirit, and that she should be taken far away, in order to keep the demons from haunting the village. The Christian doctor wrapped a blanket around her filthy body and took her to the hospital. Upon examination he found that an operation might save her, but that she had just one chance in a hundred. A little group of missionaries prayed while he operated. During the days that followed someone was always at her bedside. Finally, they rejoiced to learn that she was going to get well. The Indian woman said to the nurse, "Why did the doctor do this for me? My own people threw me away and no one wanted me. He is not related to me. Why did he do it?" The nurse told her it was because of "the love of Christ." She had never heard of Christ, so every day one of the missionaries came and talked with her. They had to go all the way back to the creation to make her understand.

The time came when she was well again and when her mind was clear and bright. "You understand the love of Christ, now, don't you," they asked her, "aren't you ready to turn from your old ways and put all your trust in Jesus?"

She was quiet for a minute and then she replied; "If Jesus is anything like the doctor, I can trust Him forever." She had seen Christ magnified in a human life and her heart was won.

Surely many thousands saw this same thing in the life of Paul. My prayer is that someone may see the same spirit in us!

CHAPTER TWENTY-THREE

"SPIRITUAL CONSOLATION"

Acts 23

IN THE GREAT COMMISSION Jesus gave the apostles a command and a promise. The command was, "Go ye therefore, and teach all nations, baptizing them in the name of the Father, and of the Son, and of the Holy Ghost: Teaching them to observe all things whatsoever I have commanded you" (Matthew 28:19, 20). Every time that He tells us to do a thing, He adds a promise of reward, so He said, "Lo, I am with you alway, even unto the end of the world." Paul obeyed this command. He went out to lead men to Christ and Christ surely kept His promise. Several times when Paul was in trouble, the Lord appeared to him and said, "Don't be afraid, Paul, I am with you." We find this happening in Acts 23.

This is the greatest consolation that a servant of Christ can have—not that he is drawing big crowds or taking large offerings or showing great results, but he is consoled most when he feels that Christ is walking by his side. David Livingstone had been in the heart of Africa for sixteen years. When he came home on a furlough, the University of Glasgow bestowed upon him the degree of Doctor of Laws. He stood upon the platform, his face tanned from the African sun and furrowed with the hardships of toil and fever. One arm hung by his side, an arm made helpless by a lion's attack. In his talk he told something of his work in Africa. "I lived in exile, among strangers whose language I did not understand. My life was often in great danger. Shall I tell you what sustained and comforted me? It was this promise, 'Lo, I am with you alway. . .'"

Paul could have given the same testimony. Often his life hung near the brink of death, but somehow the hand of Christ always reached down and brought him out. Paul knew the consolation of Christ's abiding presence.

I. THE COURAGE. Verses 1-5

Paul is now a prisoner. The Roman captain had arrested Paul to save his life. He wanted to know why the Jews accused Paul, so he called a meeting of the Jewish Sanhedrin to gain this information. The Sanhedrin was composed of seventy-one members. They were required to be above thirty years of age, to have a good reputation and to be well versed in Jewish law. These men, zealous for the law, yet lacking the Christian spirit because they lacked Christ, came in, sat down in all their dignity and pulled their robes about them. Then the captain brought Paul in. He was ready to hear both sides. The Romans were great people for law and order and justice, so in an orderly way the captain sought to find out the charges against Paul.

We read that Paul "earnestly" looked upon the council. There was no resentment, no hatred in this look. He was serious and sincere. He hoped that some of them would see the light and come to Christ. He said to them, "You men and I believe in the same God. All of my life I have lived conscientiously before Him, no matter what side I have been on." The high priest who was standing there thought Paul was not good enough to speak about God, so he told one of his assistants to smite Paul in the mouth to prevent him from speaking. Paul's righteous indignation flared up. "God shall smite you, you whited wall. You say that you are judging me according to the Law, but you have commanded that I be smitten contrary to the Law." What did he mean by "whited wall"? You can take a dirty, rotten wall, paint it white, but it will still be dirty and rotten underneath. Paul knew that these priests were just like that. They wore their white robes, but underneath these robes their hearts were still corrupt.

As soon as Paul rebuked the man, someone said to him, "Are you reviling the high priest?"

"I am sorry," said Paul, "I did not know that he was the High Priest, for it is written in the Law that we are to reverence our rulers."

Paul showed his true courage by his quickness to apologize. Many a man has the courage to fight, but he is not man enough to stand up and say, "I was wrong. I apologize." Once I heard a preacher say that he had never apologized to anybody in his life. This means that he never admitted that he was wrong and that someone else was right. A Christian ought to be on the alert. If at any time he says or does a wrong thing, he ought to be quick to apologize.

II. THE CONFLICT. Verses 6-10

Paul now resorted to strategy. We notice that the Sanhedrin was composed of two groups, the Pharisees and the Sadducees. They had some things in common, but differed greatly about many other things. The Pharisees laid great stress on the externals of religion. They claimed to be very pious and they withdrew themselves from the common herd. They believed in immortality, the resurrection, angels and spirits. Paul had once been one of them. The Sadducees were materialists. They sneered at the idea of any resurrection and did not believe in angels and spirits. They had gathered in this common council for a common purpose, yet underneath it all, their hatred and differences were still smouldering. An old Latin proverb advises us to "divide and conquer." Paul decided to divide the council, so he threw in a bomb. "I am a Pharisee and I have been preaching the Resurrection from the dead. For this reason I have been called into question." This was like throwing a piece of meat into a pack of hungry dogs. Immediately their minds were taken off Paul and they went after the question of the Resurrection. The Pharisees said, "We believe in the resurrection."

The Sadducees cried out, "We don't." Their quarrel became so bitter that you could not hear it thunder.

Finally, in spite of their hatred of Paul as a Christian, the Pharisees had to take his side in order to defend their beliefs. "We find no evil in this man," they said. "Maybe an angel spoke to him. Therefore, if we fight him we would be fighting God."

Then the uproar really became uproarious. These men began to fight. They lost all dignity, they pulled hair, they blackened eyes, they tore off the robes of the enemies. Paul was right in the middle of it all and was about to be pulled to pieces, when the captain, who was watching from above, said to his soldiers, "Go down and get that little preacher and bring him up here before they kill him." Again we see how God took care of Paul. Not yet is He through with him, so He had a Roman captain there ready to rescue him.

There is a lesson right here for every church. The Sanhedrin came together for the purpose of condemning Paul. When they began to scrap among themselves, they forgot their purpose and spent all their energy in doing something which would hurt their cause. The church is set for one purpose— to make Christ known. As long as we stay on the main line we will have the blessings of God upon us. But let some trivial issue come in, let someone start a campaign of criticism and faultfinding, and the people will forget the main purpose. The church and Christ's work will then suffer. We must see to it that we are never a party to any of these Satanic schemes.

III. THE COMFORT. Verse 11

That night Paul was pretty blue and discouraged. He was shut up in prison, he could not have fellowship with his brother Christians, he could not preach to the lost, and he had not been able to do anything for the Jews. He was feeling mighty low. God wanted to cheer him up, so in the middle of the night He said to him, "Be of good cheer, Paul. As you have testified of Me in Jerusalem, so must you witness for Me in Rome." Oh, how Paul's heart must have lifted, how he must have sung with joy. Other voices had condemned him, they had called him all sorts of evil names, they had cried out for his blood. The Voice from heaven said, "Cheer up, Paul, I am still on the throne, I am still overruling the affairs of men. I am not going to permit them to kill you, but I will see that you have the opportunity of preaching in Rome." After this, I am sure that Paul went to sleep with a smile on his face, and slept like a baby.

Let a man try to serve God today and he will be surrounded with two groups. There will be one group which will love him and help him in his work; the other group will hate him and seek to hinder his work. They will call him names, lie about him, and do all they can to hurt him. If he is doing the will of God all he needs to do is to go straight on. Then one day, in the midst of it all, he will hear a voice saying, "I am with you, my child."

God was telling Paul here that he was immortal until his work was done. When He gives us a work to do He will watch over us until it is done.

It was even so with Jesus. He was often near death, then you would hear him say, "My time is not yet come" (John 7:6). He went right ahead and before they could slay Him on a cross, there had to come a time when he could say, "I have finished the work which Thou gavest me to do" (John 17:4).

Paul's greatest ambition was to preach the Gospel in Rome. He went always to the great centers, to Antioch, to Philippi, to Thessalonica, to Corinth, to Athens and Ephesus. But now he felt that if he could strike a blow at the heart of the empire, the results might be felt to the ends of the earth. God said, "Paul, your dreams are coming true. I am going to take you to Rome." He did not tell Paul all the hardships which he must endure before he could reach the city of Rome, but even if he had told him, this would not have stopped Paul, for nothing stopped him from going ahead in the service of Christ. In this instance God was rewarding faithful service with an opportunity for greater service. "You have been faithful in Jerusalem, I will give you a bigger task in Rome." God did not say, "You have been faithful, you are all tired out, so I will let you rest," but He did say, "You have been faithful, so I will give you added responsibility and a larger task." If we shine faithfully in our small corners, God will set us in a bigger place.

I can think of many preachers whose lives have been like this. They started out in some small place, but they gave their best powers to the task, they were faithful in every way, and soon their work was making progress. Then it was not long until some big church took note of them and soon they were preaching to thousands of people instead of hundreds. This law runs all through life: "Thou hast been faithful over a few things, I will make thee ruler over many things" (Matthew 25: 21).

As Paul wanted to witness everywhere, so should we. There are two ways in which we can witness, the direct way and the indirect way. Using the direct method, we can speak to those about us, in the home, in business, and in our social set. Using the indirect way we can bring our tithes and offerings into God's house, then missionaries can be sent to the ends of the earth, and when they win souls to Christ, we will have a part and we will receive a reward. Israel had a law that those who stayed at home and carried on the work during the war would share the spoils equally with those who went out to fight. The missionary goes out and the giver stays at home, but both of them want to see souls saved. There will be stars in a crown for the one who goes and for the one who stays. There will be the joy of knowing that both have had a part in God's great redemptive program.

Witnessing for Christ keeps our religion from drying up. If you shut up a flower in the cellar and forget to water it, it will die. If you put a bottle of perfume aside and forget it, it will lose its fragrance. If you shut up your religion in your own heart, and never share it with others, you will soon find that it has lost its zest and its flavor and has become as a dead thing. If you want to grow in grace, if you want your religion to become sweeter every day, if you want it to be a blessing to yourself and to others, you must share your Christianity.

IV. THE CONSPIRACY. Verses 12-22

The next day forty men came together and hatched a plot to kill Paul. These men took an oath that they would neither eat nor drink until they had killed him. This was a dangerous thing for them, for Paul was protected by Roman guards, but they were willing to die themselves if they could just get Paul. They said, "Let's tell the chief priests and elders about it." So they went before the council and told their plan. The religious leaders were delighted. They wanted to see Paul out of the way. They shrank from killing him, but they were not above encouraging these men to do it. They were very religious. They knew it was wrong to murder anyone, but they probably soothed their consciences by saying, "Well, the responsibility will be upon these men and not upon us."

Here was the conspiracy which they entered into. The men said to the council, "Tell the Roman captain that you want to question Paul further. When the captain brings him down, we will rush in and kill him." But God is always awake. He placed Paul's nephew where he could hear about this conspiracy and when he heard it, he rushed to the castle and told Paul all about it. How would you like to hear the news that forty men were simply waiting for an opportunity to kill you? Do you think Paul trembled with fear? No, God had told him that he was going to Rome and all the conspirators in the world could not upset God's plans.

Paul called one of the centurions and said to him, "Take this young man to the chief captain. He has important news for him."

When they stood before the captain, the Centurion said, "Paul, the prisoner, asked me to bring this young man to you. He has something to tell you."

The chief captain had already been greatly impressed by Paul and was glad to do anything for him. He took the boy by the hand, led him aside privately, and said, "Now, tell me all about it." After the boy had told the captain about the plot, he was sent away with the admonition to keep quiet about the entire matter. "Leave the matter with me," said the chief captain, "I will nip this plot in the bud".

This was not the last conspiracy ever made against a preacher. The work in a certain church was growing rapidly. A certain rich man in that church did not like the way the pastor was doing things, so he gathered a few men around him and conspired against the preacher. A meeting was called while the pastor was out of town and could not be there to defend himself. On Sunday when the pastor returned he heard about this meeting and called the church to meet on Wesnesday night in a special business session. The entire matter was brought to light and the little group of disgruntled men was soundly defeated. They soon "felt led" to go to another church. There is nothing meaner nor more unchristian than this. Before entering into such a conspiracy it would be better for us to go out and butt our heads against a wall. There is a way to settle differences, but this is not the way.

In Psalm 37 we read, "The wicked plotteth against the just . . . the Lord shall laugh at him." Here we see wicked men plotting against Paul. Up in the heavens God was laughing. He was working behind the scenes and was going to direct all of these circumstances so as to get Paul to Rome. These forty men were ready to plunge the dagger into Paul's heart, this lad revealed the secret to the Roman officer—they did not know it, but every one of them was a partner with God in getting Paul to Rome. Yes, "God works in mysterious ways His wonders to perform." Often when we think that everything is against us, when we feel that life is not worth living, God is up there in heaven bringing all the circumstances together so that in the end He might be a blessing to us. Oh, if we will just follow Him and trust Him, He will bring us out into the sunlight!

V. THE CONVOY. Verses 23-24

The chief captain now gave these orders to two of his centurions, "I want you to get a convoy ready. Line up two hundred soldiers, seventy horsemen and two hundred spearmen. At nine o'clock tonight you are to take Paul out and transport him safely to governor Felix in Caesarea." Again we are reminded that God is always on the job. "He that keepeth Israel shall neither slumber nor sleep" (Psa. 121:4). Maybe the words in Isaiah 41:10 came into Paul's mind: "Fear thou not; for I am with thee: be not dismayed; for I am thy God: I will strengthen thee; yea I will help thee; yea, I will uphold thee with the right hand of my righteousness."

Did ever a preacher have such an escort? Here are four hundred and seventy Roman soldiers, armed to the teeth, with Paul sitting on a horse in the midst of them. The Romans knew the malice and hatred of the Jews and took these precautions to protect their prisoner. Preachers still need protection today. They need to be surrounded by the prayers of their people, by the love and cooperation of their flock. If your pastor is a true man of God, be jealous for his good name. Give him all the protection he needs, and so help him to do a greater work for the Lord.

VI. THE COMMUNICATION. Verses 25-30

The captain wrote a letter for these men to take to Felix. "This man Paul was taken by the Jews. They were about to kill him, but when I heard that he was a Roman citizen, I rescued him." There is a touch of human nature here. The captain wanted to put himself in a favorable light with the governor. He wanted the governor to know that he was taking care of all Roman citizens, so he said "I rescued him when I heard that he was a Roman citizen." He did not tell the truth. He did not know until after Paul's arrest that he was a Roman citizen. He just wanted to impress Felix. Every man is the hero of his own story.

The captain says in the letter: "I couldn't find this man worthy of death, so when I heard that the Jews were waiting to kill him, I decided to send him to you. I have told his accusers to tell you what they have against him." Paul was on his way to Rome. He would never see Jerusalem again. There was to be trouble all along the way and at the end of the way, he would lose his life. But his ambition was going to be realized, he was going to finish his course with joy. In Philippians 1:23 he said, "I am in a strait betwixt two, having a desire to depart, and to be with Christ; which is far better: nevertheless to abide in the flesh is more needful for you." Soon his work would be ended. He was going to look upon the capitol city of Rome and from that place he would go out into the eternal city of God to live forever with the Saviour whom he loved so dearly.

VII. THE CONFINEMENT. Verses 31-35

Paul soon arrived in Caesarea, the letter and the prisoner were soon delivered to Felix. When Felix read the letter, he said to Paul, "When your accusers come down I will hear thee fully." Turning to the soldiers, he said, "Lock this man up in Herod's judgment hall." So Paul, the chief apostle, God's biggest man of his day, was locked up to wait for a gang of Jewish bigots to come down and accuse him. Paul had many things to endure. He must have had the patience of Job. Often when we are confined, shut-in by sickness or other circumstances, we are prone to grumble. If, however, we submit patiently, all these things will add to our characters and make us stronger Christians. So we leave Paul there, awaiting his trial.

Here is the greatest truth in the chapter. If we stand up for God He will take care of us. Paul never went back on God. When trouble came to him, God was at hand to say, "Here I am, Paul, I will see you through." We all want God to be with us in time of need. Well, He promises His presence to those who live for Him. If we go ahead in our sin and then fall into trouble, we cannot expect God to help us out as long as we are in that sin. But God is long-suffering and very merciful.

A little girl was very sick. Her only hope was a transfusion of blood. Several tests were taken, but they could not find her type. Finally her little brother said, "Try mine." They found that it was the right type and soon the fresh strong blood was flowing from his veins into hers. Later on the boy seemed to be quite pale, and a little bit frightened.

The doctor said to him, "Jimmy, what is the matter?"

"Doctor," said Jimmy, "when do I die?"

"Jimmy," said the doctor, "you're not going to die. And besides, your sister is going to get well." The little fellow was willing to give his blood, even though he thought that it meant his death. We were dying in sin. Jesus came and gave His blood, His very life, for us. Because of that blood we can be saved, if we will but put our trust in the Lord Jesus Christ. Then forever we will have a great Companion to stand by us in life and in death as He stood by the Apostle Paul.

CHAPTER TWENTY-FOUR

"SPIRITUAL PROCRASTINATION"

Acts 24

PAUL, THE APOSTLE, is now Paul the prisoner. He is in Caesarea at this time. The Jews of Jerusalem had sought to kill him, but the Romans had put him under protective arrest. Then forty men made a conspiracy to kill him. When this plot was discovered by the Romans they put Paul under a heavy convoy and brought him to Caesarea to appear before Governor Felix. When he came before Felix he was treated very courteously. Felix said, "I will hear thee fully, when your accusers have come down from Jerusalem." So Paul was kept in prison awaiting the arrival of his accusers.

I. THE DELEGATION Verses 1-9

They had only five days to wait and at that time Ananias, the High Priest, and the elders came down from Jerusalem. They brought with them a hired attorney, Tertullus, who was quite an orator. He was employed to argue their case against Paul. This is the picture: seated on the Judgment seat was Felix, the Roman governor. Over there, alone except for his guards, was the preacher, Paul. Over there, clothed in dignified robes, were the Jewish religious leaders with their attorney, Tertullus. When Felix was seated Tertullus stepped forward and began his speech. His lips were dripping honey as he began. He wanted to gain favor with the governor, so he started out by flattering him on the wonderful record that he had been making in his position. He did some steep lying.

"You brought peace to our country," he said. Yet no man ever stirred up as many rows with the people as Felix did. "You have corrected many evils," he said, but historians tell us that his deeds were infamous and that he ruled in a mean, cruel and profligate manner. "We accept thee with all thankfulness," he said, yet he was never accepted. They hated him worse than they did the devil and never stopped until they forced Rome to have him recalled.

Then Tertullus said, "I don't want to be tedious so I will go ahead and tell you the charges which we have against this man, Paul. Glancing over at Paul in disdain, he accused him of three things. He accused him of sedition, saying that he was stirring up trouble all over the empire. He accused him of heresy, saying that he was teaching things which the Jews did not believe. In other words, he was a Christian. He also accused Paul of profaning the Temple. He did some more tall lying, saying, "We knew that he was guilty, so we arrested him. We were going to give him a fair trial, but Lysias, the chief captain, came along and with great violence took him out of our hands." We remember that they were not going to give Paul a trial at all. They rushed into the Temple, dragged him out, and were about to kill him when Lysias rescued him. There was no trial to it. It was just a mob going about to murder a man.

Now we read a sad note. All the religious leaders said that these things were so. They joined in with the lies of Tertullus. Not one of them had the courage to step up and say, "No, it wasn't exactly that way." Here we go back to an old truth. It is not some form of religion which changes the hearts of men and causes them to do right, it is the presence of hearts were filled with murder and they would gladly kill Paul. Jesus Christ in their hearts. These men had a form of religion, yet they would lie to gain their point. Not only that, but their A religion which does not go down deep enough to change a man's life and his outward actions is a false religion. Christ is the great life changer. "If any man be in Christ, he is a new creature" (II Corinthians 5:17). He not only changes our outward actions, but he changes even our thoughts, imaginations and attitudes.

Any Christian will readily say, "A sinner will drink, steal, lie, or commit adultery, but a Christian must never do these things, for he is a changed person." All of us will agree to this, but let me add somthing else. A sinner will hate others, his heart may be full of malice and envy and unforgiveness, but a Christian cannot have these things in his heart. I know some church members who are far from what they ought to be, even though they talk in very pious language. Their attitudes are mean and little and hateful. "By their fruits ye shall know them" (Matthew 7:20).

What was the purpose of all this lying? They wanted Felix to say, "This is a Jewish matter. Take this man back to Jerusalem and try him under your law." If this had happened Paul would not have lasted two days. The Jews had their assassins ready to kill him.

II. THE DEFENCE. Verses 10-21

The Romans believed in law and justice. Felix heard Tertullus give the Jews' side of the question, but he was not going to condemn Paul until he heard his side. That is a good rule to follow. Too often we hear a man give his side of the story and immediately we rise up and condemn someone before hearing the other side. The wise man gets both sides before making his decision. Paul stood up to make his defence. He was not as imposing as Tertullus, but he was sure of himself, he knew what he was talking about. He knew something else. He knew that God was on his side and that the Holy Spirit would guide him.

Paul began by saying, "I know that you have been a judge of this nation for many years, therefore, I cheerfully make my defense." He did not say what kind of a judge Felix had been, but he was respectful. He was not going to lie. He was simply saying, "In these years you have learned the kind of people these are who accuse me. You also know some of the merits of the Christian religion." Paul continued, "It has just been twelve days since I went up to Jerusalem. It would be easy to get all the facts about my actions. They never found me disputing in the temple or stirring up the people anywhere. They can't prove any of these things." Thus he flatly denied the first charge.

Now he answered the second charge. "I do admit that I am a follower of Christ, but that doesn't mean that I have forsaken God's way. I haven't cast away the God of my fathers. I still believe in the Law and the Prophets and the Resurrection." A real Christian believes in the Old Testament more so than one who rejects the New Testament. In the Old Testament he reads the prophecies concerning the coming of Christ. He believes them and sees them fulfilled in His life, death, burial and Resurrection. Paul was simply saying, "I believe these things as much as you do, but I have gone a little farther." Judaism was the bud and Christianity was the full-blown flower. Judaism was the prophecy and Christianity was the fulfillment. Judaism was the promise— "I am coming," and Christianity was the Presence—"I am here."

Paul never anywhere says that he is perfect, but he does say, "I am trying to live so that I can have a conscience which is clear toward God and man." That is the way all of us ought to live. If we live in that manner the God who knows all would certainly approve.

We ought to live so that no man can point a finger at us and say, "You are a hypocrite—your life doesn't measure up." Each person should look at his own life today. Would God approve of it? What about your home life? Is His Name honored there? What about your business life? Are all deals right in His sight? What about your social life? Can He be taken along? What about your church life? Would he be satisfied with the excuses made? What about your financial life? Is His tithe being brought to His storehouse or being used for yourself? Remember that He must be faced one day. He has a record of all you have done. I hope that you will not be ashamed when you meet Him.

Paul answered the third charge. "You say that I profaned the Temple. Why, I came to Jerusalem to worship at the feast. Neither did I come empty handed, but I brought an offering for my people, a gift from the Gentiles to the Jews. I was in the Temple perfectly quiet and going about my own business when they seized me." Paul now looked around and said, "Where are those men who saw me doing wrong? Why don't they come down and face me? I'll tell you why—they can't prove a thing. These men who are present are acting on hearsay evidence only."

As he came to the close of his speech, Paul said, "I did stand up and declare that I believed in the Resurrection, but surely that is no crime." With these words Paul ended his fine speech of defense. He had answered every charge and his accusers were silent.

III. The Deferment. Verses 22-23

Felix, we are told, knew something about Christianity. He knew that the Christians did not spend their time stirring up trouble. Tertullus' speech did not fool him, so he said, "I will go deeper into this matter when Lysias comes down. In the meantime I will keep Paul here under Roman protection. He can do what he wants to do and his friends will be permitted to visit him."

Can you imagine the disappointment of the Council? They thought surely that they would get to take Paul with them and that soon they would put him out of the way. Now, bitterly disappointed, they filed out of the courtroom with scowls on their faces, and God had delivered Paul again.

Yet, Felix did not declare Paul innocent, nor did he set

him free, although he knew that he ought to have done so. There were two reasons for this. First, he did not want to antagonize these influential Jews. He was a politician and always tried to do the thing which would gain favor for himself. It takes a strong man to say, "This is the right course and I must take it, even if I lose something by it."

The other reason was money. Money enters the picture entirely to often. Felix heard about the big collection which Paul had taken. He thought that if he held Paul prisoner some of his friends might come forth with a bribe in order to secure Paul's liberty. He was read to accept this bribe.

We are told that "money talks." Yes, it talks often in harmful language. For the love of money men and women have sold their honor, their peace of mind, their innocence. But that isn't all. They sell their souls for money, also. Some day in hell that money will talk again. As men brood and suffer that money will come before them and laugh and say, "You loved me, you sought me, you put me before God. You gained me, but you can't use a penny in hell." All the material things which men pile up in this world will not help in the world to come. I would rather be buried in a pauper's grave and rise up to heaven, than to be buried in the world's richest casket and sink down to hell.

IV. THE DOCTRINES. Verses 24-25-a

Felix had married Drusilla. Drusilla was the daughter of Herod, the man who made the great speech and who was smitten to death by the Holy Spirit and who was eaten of worms. She had been married to another man, but Felix wanted her and he enticed her to leave her husband. A divorce followed and she married Felix. In other words, he simply stole another man's wife. Drusilla did not care. She came of a vile family and was glad to become the wife of the governor. One day Felix and Drusilla decided that they wanted to hear Paul preach. They had heard of his power in preaching. They probably had some sort of languid interest in this new religion. The court life was dull and they thought maybe Paul could enliven things. They got more than they bargained for when they sent for Paul to preach to them. Paul the prisoner became Paul the preacher. He did not speak like a Greek philosopher, but like a man on fire for God. The first time that these two men met it was Paul before Felix, now it is Felix before Paul. Paul is the Judge and Felix and Drusilla are the prisoners.

Paul did not flatter Felix and Drusilla, although he knew that they had the authority to put him to death and the power to release him. He did not give a minute's thought to himself. He knew that they were sinful from the crowns of their heads to the soles of their feet. He knew that one day they must face the judgment bar of God, so he jumped right into his sermon. What did he talk about? He did not talk about man's upward progressive march toward perfection. He did not talk about racial prejudice, world peace, or the mystery of the universe. He came right down to where they lived and preached on righteousness, temperance and judgment to come. It was not flattering, but it was right. Paul was not called to be a flatterer—he was called to preach the Gospel.

He talked first of righteousness—God's righteousness, God's holiness, and how far man had fallen from the image of God. He talked about God's hatred for sin and right then he meant the sins of Felix and Drusilla. He wanted them to feel the awfulness of their sin before God. He talked of righteousness to a man and woman who were wholly unrighteous. Righteousness on the human side is rightness of life inside and out. It is the right relationship to God through a divine experience with Christ. It is Christ glorified in every area of human life. It is rightness toward God in all things. Felix and Drusilla miserably lacked this virtue.

Paul spoke next of temperance, which is the "moderate use

of good things and abstinence from all bad things." Paul was here talking about self-control, something which they never exercised. They were both dissipated, uncontrolled sinners. Paul knew about their impure lives and he was courageous enough to say, "Thou art the man, thou art the woman." Surely they thought of their shameful escapades, their adulterous union, the abandoned husband.

Paul's sermon thundered home to them the truth of the seventh commandment. Drusilla squirmed and said to Felix, "I don't like this. Make the fool stop." Felix answered, "I wish that I had never seen him. I would like to stop him, but I can't do it. It seems that the voice of God is speaking through him."

Then Paul spoke of the judgment to come. He could not leave this out. "Pay day is coming," he said, "you can get away with your sin now, but some day you must face God. You can live wicked lives, you can have your good times here, but when you face God and give an account to Him you will be cast into hell. You are the governor, but that will make no difference with God. There is only one way to find forgiveness for your sins—there is only one way to get ready for death and the judgment—you must repent of your sin and turn to God through faith in the Lord Jesus Christ."

Thank God for preachers like Paul! He suited his topic to his audience, he preached what they needed to hear. He used a personal approach, he did not mince words. He said, "Here is your sin and here is what you ought to do about it." Every word was true to the Scripture. He became a watchman on the tower, telling of the conditions which existed, and crying out unto these sinners to do something before judgment came.

V. THE DELAY. Verse 25-b

What was the result of this sermon? What effect did it have upon the preacher's audience? Felix trembled. He had heard great orators, he had heard emperors and kings, but none of them had ever made him tremble as he did under the mighty message of this Gospel preacher. We are not told that Drusilla trembled. She was as deep in sin as Felix, the sermon applied to her just as much as it did to him, but she was not moved. In the same manner two people can sit side by side in a church and listen to the same sermon. One is moved and comes to Christ, the other hardens his heart and refuses Christ. They go out of the building, one on the way to heaven and the other on the way to hell. Yes, Felix trembled. He was greatly moved and deeply convicted. For a moment his whole sinful life flashed before him. He saw himself, not as a great ruler, but as a lost sinner. Out yonder in the future he saw a great white throne, with the Judge of all the earth seated upon it. He knew that this Judge had all power, power enough to punish him eternally for his sins. He trembled as he saw himself, helpless and hopeless, before the throne. Yes, the Holy Spirit revealed all of this to Felix.

What did Felix do—what did he say? Did he say, "Paul, I'll give myself to your Christ—I must be relieved of this burden of sin—I must get rid of this fear?" I wish I could tell you that he did that, but I cannot. Instead he said, "Paul, go thy way for this time. When I have a convenient season I will call for thee." Oh, what a tragic mistake he made! He put off the most important matter in the world and this meant his doom.

Some people today are like that. They have heard the Gospel. They have felt the Holy Spirit piercing their very soul, and have trembled, have wept, have stood first on one foot and then the other. They have known that they ought to confess Christ, but did not come to Him and thus made the greatest mistake of their lives. They say, "I'll accept Christ before I die." But they may not have another chance. They may put it off until it is too late. The Spirit may not come again to knock at the door of their heart, for *God* says, "My Spirit shall not always strive with man" (Genesis 6:3).

Charles Haddon Spurgeon gently rebuked a preacher for not making an appeal to sinners in his morning sermons. The preacher replied, "I didn't intend to preach to sinners this morning. I will preach to them tonight."

Spurgeon answered: "What if some of them go to hell before tonight?" Before night we might be ushered into the presence of God. It is terribly dangerous to put off the matter of salvation.

If Felix had come to Christ it would have meant the giving up of his sins. Drusilla would have to go back to her husband. Felix would be forced to give up his immorality and impurity. He would have lost friends. He would have lost money and he probably would have lost his position as the governor. Oh, but he would have gained *infinitely* more than he lost. His sins would have been forgiven; the peace of God would have entered his soul. Christ would have walked with him daily and his life could have been spent in useful service. At the end of the way he could have gone out to live in heaven with the Lord forever. No matter what we have to give up to come to Christ, it will never compare with what we have gained. On the other hand, "What shall it profit a man, if he shall gain the whole world, and lose his own soul?" (Mark 8:36).

Paul preached to Felix, and Felix said, "Some other day." That day never came, for finally Felix was driven out into exile and, so far as we know, he died without God and without hope. Paul preached to the Philippian jailer; he believed, was baptized, and became a member of the church. For these two thousand years the jailer has been in heaven with Jesus. Felix has been in hell with Satan. That is the difference—which will you choose?

Years ago in a small Indiana town a man made a balloon ascension. The basket in which he ascended was attached to the balloon with three ropes. As the man soared up into the air the people saw him cut one of these ropes. They shouted for him not to cut the second rope, but in a moment they saw him cut that rope. "Don't cut the last rope," they shouted, but in a moment he cut the last rope and came plummeting down to his death. This was his way of suicide. Every time someone turns Christ down he is cutting one of the ropes. Some day without knowing it he will cut the last rope. His last opportunity will be gone and he will go down to death and hell. He should learn a lesson from Felix—not to delay his decision for Christ. There is danger in delay; there is peril in procrastination.

VI. THE DETENTION. Verses 26-27

For two years Paul was kept a prisoner by Felix. When Felix was removed Festus became governor. Paul was still a prisoner. Some historians called these Paul's "idle years." I do not believe it. Paul had certain liberties and I am sure that he used every opportunity to witness, and that he won many to Christ.

Again today you have heard the Gospel—again you have another chance to take a stand for Christ. What are you going to do? Will you go home and laugh and joke and put this matter out of your mind? Will you say: "I have other things to think about now—I will call on God at some more convenient time?" Will you say: "I will hold on to my sin a little longer, some other day I will get ready to meet God?" Listen to what God says: "Today if you hear my voice, harden not your heart . . . Come now and let us reason together, though your sins be as scarlet, they shall be as white as snow . . . I called and you refused." Some day you will face God—you will cry out for mercy, but it will be too late. God will say: "I called and you refused. You sat before the preacher—I touched your heart and you refused to come—you sat up in the balcony—you sat under the balcony. You heard my voice—you felt the impression of my Spirit upon your heart, but you wouldn't come unto me" . . . What does God say next in the Bible? He says: "I will laugh at your calamity." I don't want Him to laugh at me—I want Him to smile and say: "Come in, son, I have been waiting for you. Everything is ready for you."

An old teacher used to say to his pupils: "You should repent the day before you die." "But", they said, "we don't know when we are going to die." "Then", replied the old teacher, "you should repent today." Since you are not sure of one more minute I urge you to come to Christ today. You will never have a better time. You will never, never be sorry that you gave yourself to Christ.

Chapter Twenty-five

"SPIRITUAL EXAMINATION"

Acts 25

In Acts 24 Paul forcibly touched the lives of three people. The first one was Ananias, the High Priest. He came down from Jerusalem to Caesarea and accused Paul of stirring up trouble against the Empire, of teaching heresy in religion and of profaning the temple. He was not able to prove any of these things. The second was Felix, the governor, one of the greatest rascals who ever lived. The third was Drusilla, the wife of Felix. She had been the wife of another man but Felix had stolen her, they had married and they were living a life of sin and debauchery. You will remember that this couple invited Paul to preach before them. He preached on temperance, righteousness, and judgment to come. Felix trembled and said, "Go thy way, Paul, some more convenient season I will call for thee." After this time, the governor called Paul in several times, hoping that he would receive money from him. So far as we know, Felix never had a change of heart, he never found that time when he repented of his sins, and he never trusted Christ.

What became of these three—Ananias, Felix and Drusilla? Ananias, the High Priest, was killed by assassins. Felix, the governor, was driven back to Rome and the last we hear of him he was dying in the mountains, an exile. Drusilla went back to Rome, drifted out near Naples, and in the eruption of Mount Vesuvius she was buried under the lava. Thus ends the career of these three wicked persons who stood before God's man, Paul. They had a chance to be saved, but they rejected their opportunities and went down to death and hell. Oh, we are to be careful how we treat God's message in our hearts! It can mean life or death, heaven or hell. "Today if ye will hear his voice, Harden not your hearts" (Hebrews 3:7, 8).

I. THE ACCUSATION. Verses 1-9

Paul was kept in prison two years by Felix. When Felix was recalled by Rome, he left Paul in prison as a favor to the Jews. Festus then became the governor. History tells us that he was a very conscientious ruler. Three days after he took the oath of office, he went up to Jerusalem to study the entire situation. Although two years had gone by, and although Paul had kept silent all of this time, the Jewish hatred against him was still intense. Just as soon, therefore, as the new governor reached Jerusalem, the High Priest and the chief Jews sought an interview with him, told him all about Paul's so-called crimes and asked the governor to send Paul to Jerusalem for trial. They did not really want Paul to have a trial, they did not really want him brought to Jerusalem. They were lying in wait to kill him.

We see here an example of people who never give up their hatreds. They hugged these hatreds to their hearts, they nursed them and caused them to grow instead of allowing them to die. There are still many people today who have the same attitude. For some reason they begin to dislike someone, they are soon hating them and although the years come and go that hate never dies. It becomes a burden which they must carry around with them. They can never be happy. They are certainly to be pitied.

Leonardo da Vinci was not only a great artist, but he was also a draftsman, engineer and thinker. There came a time when his hatred almost ruined him. Just before he painted the Last Supper he had a quarrel with another painter. Enraged and embittered, he began to paint. One of the first faces that he painted was the face of Judas. He decided to wreak vengeance upon the other artist by painting in his face as the face of Judas. When he had finished painting the face of Judas everybody recognized it as the face of the other artist. Ah, now he had his revenge! He would hand this picture down to shame this man through succeeding generations. Then Leonardo da Vinci set about to paint the picture of Christ, but he could not do it. Some baffling thing held him back, all of his efforts were useless. At length he came to realize that he could not paint the picture of Christ as long as there was hatred in his heart, so he painted out the face of Judas and apologized to the other artist. Then he painted the face of Jesus and the other figures in the picture, which has since become one of the greatest paintings the world has ever seen. Oh, my friend, as long as you have any bad feeling in your heart, you will never show forth Jesus in your life, you will never be happy, you will never be useful! Why not get that burden of bad feeling off your heart? Why not get right with God and man in the matter of your feelings for others?

What answer did Festus give the Jews? "Paul shall be kept at Caesarea. If you have any charges against him, you can come to Caesarea and press your case, according to the law." This was a wise answer on the part of Festus. It was natural for him as a new ruler to wish to gain favor with these people. He could have done this by placing Paul in their power, but his Roman sense of justice caused him to act wisely and well.

Festus spent ten days in Jerusalem, then went back to Caesarea. The Jews were right on the job, they were there ready to accuse Paul. On the next day Festus took his place on the judgment seat and commanded that Paul be brought before him. Now let us get the picture. The governor in his royal robes was sitting in dignity upon the judgment seat. The Jewish leaders, in their priestly robes, were standing in greedy anticipation on one side, while Paul, the little Gospel preacher, in Godly assurance, stood in the prisoner's dock. Festus gave the Jews a chance to speak, and they brought many grievious charges against Paul, but they were not able to prove a single one. Festus recognized the fact that Paul was guilty of nothing which the Roman court looked on as a crime. What was Festus' duty? He should have freed Paul, but he was afraid that he would lose face with the Jews, so he offered Paul a proposition. "Are you willing, if I am present, to go up to Jerusalem and be judged before the Sanhedrin?"

II. THE APPEAL. Verses 10-12

This proposition was unfair to Paul. He was safer at Caesarea than at Jerusalem. Festus previously said that the trial ought to be held in Caesarea, but now he reverses his position. Why? He had come to the place where he wanted to gain favor with the Jews. He was willing to go against his own conscience for personal gain. Today many men are willing to stifle their convictions in order to gain wealth, power or position.

Years ago a very brilliant lawyer lived in the state of Georgia. He was powerful in many ways, but he never gained great riches. Then one day he was offered fifty thousand dollars to represent a rich client in a certain trial. The money would have meant much to him. If he had accepted it he would have been fixed for life. But as badly as he needed the money he declined to take the case. He said that he could not believe in the rightness of the cause he was asked to plead, so he stood up for his convictions, and turned down the money. This took real courage. Festus did not have such courage. He knew that Paul was innocent, but he went against his own convictions to win favor with the Jews.

Paul now gave his answer to Festus. He knew that if he went to Jerusalem it would be the last of him, for the Jews would surely assassinate him. He saw only one way of escape. He must appeal to Caesar as a Roman citizen, then he would be sent to Rome instead of Jerusalem. Today in America if a man is convicted in a lower court, he can appeal to a higher court. He can make these appeals until his case reaches the Supreme Court of the United States. In the Roman Empire a Roman citizen could say to a lower court, "I appeal to Caesar." His trial would stop right there and the Roman officer would be forced to say, "All right, I will send you to the Emperor." So Paul exercised his prerogative as a Roman citizen. "I appeal to Caesar," he said.

Festus replied, "Unto Caesar thou shalt go."

I can imagine the emotions which filled the hearts of the three parties concerned. The Jews went away disappointed. They had hoped to have a chance to kill Paul, now the matter is taken out of their hands. In black hatred and bitter despair they went back to Jerusalem. Festus was relieved. He stood between two fires. On the one side he wanted to be fair and just as a Roman judge; on the other side he wanted to gain the Jews' favor as a petty politician. Now the case is out of his hands and he is relieved that he will not be forced to make a decision. Paul is happy. He wanted to go to Rome and strike a blow for Christ at the center of the great Roman Empire. Now he could go at the expense of the government. One of his fondest dreams was about to come true.

III. The Announcement. Verses 13-21

It was time for Paul to start on his journey to Rome. The case had been taken out of the hands of Festus and out of the hands of the Sanhedrin. It was now Festus' task to send Paul and all the papers on the case to the emperor in Rome. In those days sailing ships did not come along every day, so Paul had to wait. While he was waiting, King Agrippa and his sister, Bernice, came to make a complimentary visit to the new governor. Festus knew Agrippa had great influence, so he decided to lay Paul's case before him. He knew that his own cause would be strengthened if he could get King Agrippa to concur in his decision to send Paul to Rome.

So Festus stated the case to Agrippa. He told how Paul had been confined two years under Felix, how he had found him in prison when he came into office and how the Jews had made their charges against Paul. "Now," says Festus, "I could find Paul guilty of nothing wrong. I would have released him, but he appealed to Caesar, so I commanded that he be taken to Rome." Luke previously gave us the facts, then Festus told the same story. When you lay these two accounts side by side, you see that Festus was very complimentary of himself. Let a man tell his own story and he always makes himself a hero.

In telling the story to King Agrippa, Festus used one sentence which jumps out of the text at us. He said that the Jews disputed about Jesus, who was dead, but that Paul affirmed that Jesus was alive. That is where the big difference comes in. The Christian religion presents a living Redeemer, one who died on a cross, who was buried, who broke the bonds of death and came back to live forevermore. No other religion can make that claim! Who was it that inspired the disciples to go out and give their lives away? Who was it who moved the martyrs to die rather than to renounce Christ? Who was it who saved Paul on the Damascus Road and caused this self-righteous Pharisee to become a flaming evangelist? Who was it who down through the ages changed and transformed lives when all else had failed? Who was it who stood by the bedside of dying saints, causing them to shout for joy as they moved out into another world? Who is it who saves and blesses and helps and comforts you and me as we walk our weary way through a wicked world? Is it a dead man? No, it is a man who conquered death, a man who has all power. It is Jesus, our living Lord.

Paul was right when he claimed that Jesus was alive. He saw his glory in the light which shone down upon him on the Damascus Road. He heard his voice saying: "Why persecutest thou me?" Paul was lifted up into the third heaven and caused to see the glory of the Lord.

He knew that his own life had been changed altogether, he knew that Christ lived in him, he knew that He had changed others as sinful as he was. Paul spoke both from conviction and from knowledge when he cried out, "He lives—Jesus lives. I know that my Redeemer liveth!"

IV. The Appointment. Verses 22-23

When Festus told Agrippa about Paul, Agrippa said, "I would like to hear this man." Festus replied, "I will arrange an appointment for tomorrow." We read that the next day Agrippa and Bernice came in great pomp to the assembly to hear Paul. Look at the scene. The king and his sister were in full regal regalia. Every woman who was allowed to come was eager to see how Bernice was going to be dressed. The Roman cohorts were there, a distinguished body of soldiers who had conquered a hundred countries. The chief men of the city were there. It was a most imposing group.

Then the side door opened and the soldiers came out, leading Paul, the humble servant of Christ, the faithful preacher of the Gospel, God's man of the hour. As Paul faced this group his heart thrilled at the opportunity presented him. He had a great chance to preach the Gospel. Some of these people had never heard a sermon in their lives. They knew nothing of Christ. God managed it so that Paul should stand before the great men of the earth and testify to His grace. In this chapter we do not hear Paul's speech—that comes in Chapter 26. It is one of the greatest messages on record. It convicted a king of his sin.

V. The Assignment. Verses 24-27

Festus introduced Paul. "Here is the man I told you about. The Jews say that he ought not to live, but I have examined him and find in him nothing worthy of death. He has appealed to Caesar so I am going to send him to Rome." The Roman law required that when a man was sent to Caesar all the papers on the case should go along with him. Festus now said, "I have nothing certain to write, King Agrippa. Please examine this man thoroughly and tell me what I should write to Caesar." We will leave the matter there until the next sermon.

One day Paul wrote a letter to the church at Rome. He told of a Christian's suffering, then he almost shouted as he wrote, "We know." Do you get it? "'We know." "We know what?" "We know that all things work together for good to them that love God, to them who are the called according to His purpose" (Romans 8:28). Paul was a living illustration of this great truth. All the forces of hell were against him and it seemed often that he was going down. But God had a great purpose for Paul and He made all these things to work out for Paul's good and God's glory. This is true of us, also. If we belong to Christ, if we seek to follow His purpose in our lives, troubles may come to us, as they did to Paul, but in the end God will make it work out for the best.

A little Chinese Christian woman was afflicted with a dread disease which brought insufferable pain. One day a group of Christian friends went to see her. They sang a few hymns and one of them offered a prayer. When they opened their eyes they saw the tears streaming down the face of the invalid. Soon she said, in the midst of intense pain, "I don't know why, but I do know Him." That is the main thing after all.

When Nansen went on his exploration trip to the North Pole he took a number of recordings with him. On these records his wife had recorded several sweet songs and the prattle of his little baby. In the loneliness of the Arctic midnight he listened to the voices of those whom he loved and he was encouraged and inspired to go on. Oh, when we are rocked upon the waves of life, when the night grows dark and hope grows dim, you and I can listen to a sweeter voice, we can hear Jesus saying, "Whatever comes, be of good cheer, I will be with you to the end of the way!" Thank God for such a Saviour!

Chapter Twenty-six

"SPIRITUAL CONDEMNATION"

Acts 26

As CHAPTER 26 OPENS we find ourselves again in the palace of Governor Festus in Caesarea. King Agrippa and his sister, Bernice, are there paying a visit to the governor. Festus had told the king about his famous prisoner, Paul the Apostle. Paul had been arrested and had been confined for two years. The Jews had sought every way to bring about his death, but the Roman court found him guilty of breaking none of their laws. When Festus proposed to take Paul to Jerusalem for trial before the Sanhedrin, Paul knew that that meant his death. Being a Roman citizen, he appealed to Caesar, the trial was halted, and plans were made to send him to Rome.

When Agrippa heard about Paul's case, he told Festus that he would like to hear the man himself. So on a certain day Agrippa and Bernice came in great pomp to this hearing. An imposing company was present, the Roman military leaders and the great men of the city were there. Festus had Paul brought in, he had him stand before Agrippa, with guards on either side.

"King Agrippa," he said, "here is the man I told you about." Then he went on to tell the story of Paul's trial, the accusations of the Jews and Paul's appeal to Rome. As the chapter closed, the preacher was standing before the king and this imposing company, ready to speak out in defense of his cause. It was a dramatic moment.

I. The Past. Verses 1-11

After Festus finished introducing Paul, Paul was wise enough and polite enough to keep silent. He waited for the king to speak. In a moment Agrippa looked down into the calm face of the apostle and said, "Thou are permitted to speak for thyself." Agrippa did not know that Paul's speech was going to shake him to the depths. When Paul spoke he was more than a man, he was a man possessed, possessed and empowered by the Holy Spirit. This was a great occasion and Paul arose to the greatness of it. He said just exactly the right thing under the circumstances. Some people lose their heads on great occasions, but not so with Paul. He was not afraid. He had not even a touch of stage fright. To other people this man on the throne was a powerful king, to Paul he was just another sinner who needed to know Jesus Christ.

Paul began by speaking directly to the king. Every eye in the room was upon Paul and every ear was listening. "I am happy, King Agrippa, that I can talk to you about the things of which the Jews accuse me. You know all about the Jews and their customs." Festus did not know about these things, but Agrippa did. He knew their laws, their traditions and their fanaticisms. He could, therefore, understand Paul's situation better than Festus. "The Jews know my past life. I lived right there in Jerusalem. I was one of them. They know that I was a strict Pharisee. All down through the ages the Jews have had a hope of a coming Messiah. We all believed it, we learned it at our mothers' knees. Then one day a man by the name of Jesus came along. He claimed to be the Messiah and did many marvelous works, but we put Him to death, for we felt that we were right in doing this. However, His followers said that He had risen from the grave and that we were wrong. This attitude filled me with anger. I persecuted these Christians and even went into strange cities to find them and to punish them." This was Paul's past. He loved Jesus now with his whole heart, but surely that heart must have ached as he remembered how he had persecuted Jesus and His followers.

I'm sure that all Christians look back upon the days before their conversion and think of how they hurt the heart of Christ. We wish that we had come to Christ sooner than we did. But is it not glorious to know that all of this is covered by the blood—that God has forgotten all about it? We could go down to the seashore and make deep tracks in the sand. Soon a mighty tide will come rolling in— when it goes out no sign of the track is left. Our sins were many and deep, but when we come to Jesus they are covered by His blood, and there is no record left in heaven against us.

In relating the past Paul told of his faith in the Resurrection. He believed that Jesus had conquered death, that He was living. He preached this belief everywhere. This was the thing which incensed the Jews. If they accepted His Resurrection, then Christ must be the Messiah. They were willing to die before they would believe that this poor Peasant was the Messiah. But He did arise—He is alive. Go into the graveyards of the world and we will read these words upon the tombstones, "Here lies So-and-So." But when we come to the grave of Jesus, we see written across it in letters of living flame, "He is not here: for He is risen . . ." (Matthew 28:6). He came back to earth—men saw Him and touched Him. Through the inspiration which they received they had the power to go out and witness for Him, to shake the world for Him, and to die for His sake.

But that is not all. Listen to Him, "Because I live, ye shall live also" (John 14:19). Christ's Resurrection is a guarantee that we shall live again. Our steps may lead down into the grave, but He has built some steps going up and out on the other side. We have a living Lord. If we put our trust in Him, someday we shall follow Him up in the sunlit pathway which leads to glory. And "so shall we ever be with the Lord" (I Thessalonians 4:17).

He lives, He lives, Christ Jesus lives today!
He walks with me and talks with me
Along life's narrow way.
He lives, He lives, salvation to impart!
You ask me how I know He lives?
He lives within my heart.

II. THE PREPARATION. Verses 12-18

Paul quickly passed on from what he had been to the thing which had happened to him, the thing which changed him for time and eternity. He forgot that he was talking to an earthly king and remembered only the King of kings. His face lighted up with a heavenly radiance, as he said, "Oh, King, at midday I saw a light from heaven, brighter than the light of the sun. I heard a voice which I knew was the voice of Jesus. I was saved that day and sent forth to preach the Gospel to the Gentiles."

In the olden days people believed that you could wake a sleepwalker simply by calling his name. Well, here was Paul, asleep in sin, dead in sin. Jesus waked him when He called out, "Saul, Saul!" He not only waked him, but He changed him. The hater of Christ became the lover of the Lord, the persecutor became the preacher, the sinner became the saint.

We may never have the experience which Paul had, but He calls us by name as surely as He called Paul. The Gospel is meant for us. If we are lost, God calls us. We must not pass that call over to someone else, it was meant for us—"thou art the man." He is saying to us, "My child, give me thine heart. Leave your sin and come and taste the good things I have for you. Do not delay, now is the hour."

Let us go back to the words which Jesus spoke to Paul on the Damascus Road. "Saul, Saul, why persecutest thou Me?" This was a reasonable question. Why should Paul persecute Christ? Had the Lord ever said a word against him? Had he ever hurt him, had he ever grieved him? Surely there was nothing in Jesus' character to cause this persecution, for He was pure and holy. He went about doing good, He raised the dead, He healed the lepers and fed the hungry. This same question could be asked of you. Why do you persecute Him? Why do you turn your backs on Him? Why do you sin against Him? Why do you leave Him out of your lives? Why do you disobey His commands? Why do you rob Him of tithes and offerings? Why do you give your energy to the world, when His church needs you so badly? He has done nothing but good for you all the days of your lives. He gives you every breath that you draw. He has saved and blessed you. Why do you persecute Him? Why do you crucify Him afresh? Why do you not use your lives for Him?

This meeting which Paul had with Jesus on the Damascus Road and his subsequent visions prepared him for his ministry. He went forth to do a great work because he had met the risen Christ, and surrendered to Him. No man is ready to go forth and bless the world until he has met Jesus.

III. The Preacher. Verses 19-23

After Paul told of his conversion and call he burst forth in a great declaration, "Oh, King Agrippa, I was not disobedient to the heavenly vision!" He went on to tell what he had done, how he had turned away from the old life and had preached Christ in many countries. He told about how the Jews had caught him and had sought to kill him. "But," he says, "they haven't stopped me. I am still witnessing to the grace of God. I am telling every one about the Christ who died, who arose again, who saved me and can save them." What a preacher Paul was! Nothing could stop him from telling the old, old story.

What was the secret of Paul's life? Here it is: He had a vision from heaven. Instead of turning his back upon that vision, he followed the gleam and did exactly what Christ had told him to do. Many a man has the vision, he hears the voice, but he turns again to the world and fails to do what God would have him do. When Dr. A. J. Gordon made the last speech of his life, he spoke to the young Baptists of Boston. In his speech he said, "Never say 'no' to God."

Another great preacher, when asked the secret of his success, said, "I never said 'no' to God."

We ought to say "no" to many things. We ought to say it to the devil when he tempts us, to sinners when they seek to lead us astray, to all the allurements of the world, to the temptation to be at ease in Zion. But we should never say "no" to God. When He calls on us to give Him our best He promises His best in return, but many of us answer "No." He calls us to be faithful to His church and we answer "No." He calls us to love one another, and we answer "No." He calls us to tithe and promises a rich reward, but we answer "No," and use God's money for ourselves. He calls on us to take up a cross and serve Him, but we answer "No," because we want to take it easy. Oh, He never says "No" to us—He supplies every need! If we are wise we will never say "No" to God.

While attending a young peoples' convention in Athens, Georgia, I felt the call of God to preach the Gospel. I went back home to Atlanta and everyone discouraged me. I had gone through only two years of high school, I was married and had one child. But God gave me the strength to say this, "God has called me to preach, and I must preach." I would talk to someone about the matter and they would discourage me. But always, as I walked away from them, I had to say to myself, "God called me to preach and I must preach." I shudder to think what might have happened if I had not obeyed Him.

It is futile and foolish to spend one's life in opposition to God's will. We cannot expect joy and happiness and power when we go up against God. God says, "Do this." We say, "I will not." We are going up against a force a billion times stronger than ourselves and we will surely fail. That is like a rabbit running in front of a locomotive, expecting to stop it. That is like a rowboat trying to stop an ocean liner, like a sparrow trying to stop a B-29 airplane, like an ant trying to halt an atomic bomb. God's will is always best. If we are wise we will always try to follow that will. We read in the Book, "He that doeth the will of God abideth forever" (I John 2:17).

IV. THE PRESUMPTION. Verses 24-25

As Paul concluded his speech to Agrippa, Festus cried out, "Paul, you are beside yourself, you are crazy, too much learning has made you mad. You have been talking about a vision and a voice from heaven. You have been talking about a Man who rose from the dead and ascended into heaven. You are insane." That is the way the hard, practical man thinks about Christianity. It is not madness to be in earnest about money or power or pleasure, but it is foolish to be earnest about Christ and salvation and eternal life. Here are those two men—Paul and Festus. Which is the saner, the one who thought that the only thing worth living for was to get all that he could out of the governorship, or the one who counted all things but trash if he might win Christ?

One man looked up to heaven and said, "I see nothing up there—I will get all I can down here." The other looked up and saw Jesus. He bowed before Him in a lifetime of service and received in his heart the hope of everlasting life. Which, I say, was the saner?

Festus said, "You are crazy," but Paul replied, "I am not mad, most noble Festus, but I speak the words of truth and soberness." Paul knew what he was talking about. He had had an experience that nothing in the world could shake. If we, too, have met this wonderful Christ, if we have received Him into our hearts, the whole world may jeer at us, but we can say with Paul, "I know whom I have believed . . ." (II Timothy 1:12). We know from what Festus said that Paul was a brilliantly educated man, and Jesus had captured that bright mind and all of its powers were being used for God's glory. I see men in the church today who have many talents and I would to God that they would give all these talents to the Lord. What mighty things they would be able to do for Him!

V. THE PERSUASION. Verses 26-29

Paul then said, "King Agrippa, you know about these things of which I speak. The crucifixion of Christ did not happen in a dark corner. It took place in broad daylight before ten thousand witnesses!" Suddenly Paul whirled upon the king and cried out, "King Agrippa, do you believe the prophets? I know that you believe them." It was a moment of great tenseness and emotion.

Agrippa replied, "Paul, almost thou persuadest me to be a Christian." Certain Bible scholars say that Agrippa spoke those words in ridicule and sarcasm.

I cannot agree with them, especially when I hear Paul's passionate reply. "I would to God that not only you, but that all in this room were Christians." Surely Paul would not have spoken that way if Agrippa had been joking. Paul wanted to see those people saved. His heart overflowed in a yearning for their salvation. The greatest thing that he could wish for them was that they might know Christ.

Agrippa was the king—he had great possessions, he had been highly honored. Yet, if on that occasion he had stepped down and said, "Paul, I believe all that you have said, I take your Christ as mine," he would have received infinitely more than he ever could have received from any position on this earth. His sins would have been forgiven, his name would have been written by the hand of God in the Lamb's Book of Life, he would have become a child of God, he would have gained a daily Companion and a Friend in the hour of death. His feet would have been planted on the pathway which led to the city of Glory. Poor old Agrippa—the greatest mistake he ever made was when he turned Jesus down!

Years ago a woman in Glasgow, Scotland, rented an empty store building. In this building she started a Sunday-school class of rough boys and carried on the work for many years. She won those boys to Christ and sent them out to live good lives. When she died her boys came back to the funeral. Some of them were the most important men in the country. They bought a tombstone for her grave and under her name they had these words inscribed: "All that she ever told us about Jesus is true."

If Agrippa had accepted Christ that day, later on he would have met Paul in heaven and he could have said, "Thank you, Paul, all that you told me about Jesus was true." Do not turn Jesus down, do not be just "almost persuaded," come to Him and find that the half has never yet been told. Jesus is more wonderful than anyone can ever describe.

The tragedy of Agrippa was the tragedy of "the almost". He almost repented of his sin, he almost accepted Christ, he almost became a child of God, he almost entered the kingdom of heaven. He missed heaven and glory because he was simply "almost persuaded." John Bunyan said, "There is a way to hell from the gate of heaven." Agrippa took that way. He was in sight of heaven. He could almost hear the heavenly choir singing out its welcome to him. He took a step forward toward Christ, then he turned back into his sin and chose the way of death.

Alas, Agrippa is not the only one who has done that! Today men hear the Gospel message, they feel the call of Christ, they feel the urge toward God and heaven, they almost take the step which means eternal life. Then they turn the Lord down, go back toward the old life, and walk again on the pathway which leads to hell. I plead with you not to do that thing. If you feel the slightest impression toward Christ, come and fall in His arms. He will gladly receive you, for He says, "Him that cometh to me, I will in no wise cast out" (John 6:37).

VI. The Purpose. Verses 30-32

Just as soon as Paul said, "I would to God that all of you were Christians," the king stopped the proceedings, rose up from his throne and left the room. The Gospel arrow had pierced his heart. A wounded deer will leave the herd and go aside to some thicket. This is what Agrippa did. He ran off to get away from the impression made by Paul's sermon. Agrippa and Bernice and Festus had a conference. "This man is not worthy of death or bonds," they agreed. They saw something different, something wonderful in Paul. They knew that he had been in touch with the Infinite. "We could free him, but he has appealed to Caesar and we must send him to Rome."

Thus we see man's purpose working into God's purpose. It was God's purpose for Paul to go to Rome. In Chapter 23 God appeared to Paul and said, "Paul, be of good cheer, you must bear witness unto Me also at Rome." The purpose is working out.

Agrippa and Bernice and Festus are now in their eternal home. The fires which burn hottest about them are the fires of memory. They look back and remember that marvelous day in Caesarea when the great preacher stood before them and tried to entice them across the line of salvation. They were not far from the kingdom that day, but they would not come in. Down through the eternal ages they cry out in anguish, "Oh, if we had only done that day what we knew we should have done!"

Shakespeare says:

There is a tide in the affairs of men,
Which, taken at the flood, leads on to fortune;
Omitted, all the voyage of their life
Is bound in shallows and miseries.

The tide for three people rose that day. If they had taken

it at its crest, their lives would have ended in salvation, but they let it pass and their lives became bound in the shallows of time and the miseries of eternity. It is so with men.

A soldier was coming home from the Civil War. Four years had he been away from home, four years had he been separated from his family, four years of war and bloodshed and suffering. He came to the river which separated him from his home on the hill on the other side. Oh, how eager he was to get home and to clasp his loved ones to his bosom! He got into a boat and rowed into the stream. He did not know it, but the boat was leaking. When he arrived in the middle of the stream, at its deepest point, the boat sank, and since he was not able to swim he went down to a watery grave. He was almost home, but he lost his life. One can get almost home spiritually and then lose his soul forever.

Do not delay, do not postpone, do not say, "I am almost persuaded." Come all the way to Jesus today.

CHAPTER TWENTY-SEVEN

"SPIRITUAL CONSTERNATION"

Acts 27

Paul's greatest human ambition was to visit Rome, the capitol and center of the great Roman Empire, where he might strike a blow for Jesus. He knew that if he could get the Christian religion firmly established in Rome the effect of it would be felt to the ends of the empire. God had promised Paul that he would have this privilege of witnessing in Rome, but for some time it seemed that Paul's dream would not come true. The Jews sought to kill him, yet one day when they were about to beat him to death a Roman officer stepped in and saved him. They kept Paul in prison for two years, but finally as a Roman citizen he made his appeal to Caesar, the tide was turned, and plans were made to send him to Rome. As Chapter 27 opens we find that Paul was still in custody, and that he was awaiting a ship to take him to Rome.

I. THE WARNING. Verses 1-12

In those days there were no passenger ships such as we have today. Even the emperors, when no galley ships were available, took passage upon cargo vessels. They had no compasses and no charts. Paul sailed in three ships on the way to Rome. First, being placed in charge of a Roman centurion, he boarded a ship going to Asia Minor. When they came to the city of Sidon the centurion courteously permitted Paul to go ashore in order that he might visit his friends in that city. The centurion did not send a guard with him—he trusted him. He had been with him just a few days, but he had come to know that Paul was different.

Is it not a fine thing when other people see that we are different, because we have been with Jesus? A Christian ought to be different. In character and life he ought to stand out from the crowd. If people can know us from day to day and not see something different about us, surely we are not living as a Christian should. A man in our city was putting insulation in the house of one of our church members. He accidentally knocked off some of the plaster, littering up one of the rooms pretty badly. He then brought the lady of the house in and showed her the damage which had been done. She calmly told him that it was all right, and that she was sure he could not help it. "Are you a Christian?" he asked.

"Yes, why?"

"I knew you must be," he replied, "nine out of ten women would have 'raised cain' about it. You are different —you must be a Christian." Is it not fine when our actions and our words make someone else feel that we are akin to Jesus?

Well, next day Paul sailed to the city of Myra. There the centurion found a ship sailing to Italy, so he engaged passage for himself and his prisoners. This ship was from Alexandria and was loaded with wheat. Rome depended upon the Valley of the Nile for its bread and a steady line of commerce stretched across the Mediterranean between Egypt and Italy. They sailed out into the Mediterranean and soon reached the island of Crete. They stopped at a place called The Fair Havens and spent some time there. Soon the season was upon them when it was dangerous to sail across the open sea. Paul, never backward at any time, stepped up to the centurion and master of the ship and warned them that it would be dangerous to sail at this time. "Sirs," he said, "I perceive that this voyage will bring much harm, not only to the ship, but to our lives." How did Paul know this? Was he an experienced sailor?

No, in some way God must have put this into his mind, for there is simply no other explanation for it.

However, the owner of the ship paid no attention to Paul's warning. After all, Paul was just another Jew, a prisoner of Rome, a person of no consequence! Ah, the centurion learned better than that before the voyage was over. Winter was now coming on and since Fair Havens had very poor accomodations for travelers, the ones in charge decided to put out to sea, to anchor at Phenice and to stay there for the winter. Paul must have been disappointed, but he knew that "all things work together for good to them that love God" so he just trusted God and kept quiet.

II. THE WINDS. Verses 13-14

On a certain day the warm south wind began to blow softly. The captain laughed at Paul's warning and set out on his way with a gay heart. When he had gone a little distance, he realized his mistake. The wind changed and was soon beating upon them in all the fury of a tempest.

This voyage can be likened to the voyage of life. We start out in high hope, with the soft south winds blowing all about us, but when we have gone just a short way, we run into storms which we can never weather in our own strength.

"Ah," say some, "I am young and strong. I will get along all right."

Oh, let me say, that vigor and health can all be lost in a day.

"But," say these people, "I have money, I will get along."

Yes, but those riches can take wings and fly away.

"But," they say, "I have friends and loved ones, they will help me." You can have them one day and they will be gone the next.

What I want to say is that amid the storms of life we need something stronger than a human arm. We need a chart, a compass, a pilot. Jesus is all of these. When the storms of

life beat about us, we can cling to Him and never go down. So
we should put all of our faith in Him; then when the winds
beat upon us, we can hear Him say, "Be not afraid, I am with
you. I am the Master of ocean and sky, I will bear you up."
Every true Christian has had this experience. Troubles came,
but they looked up to the Lord and felt courage and strength
entering their souls. Then they have gone ahead, brave as
a lion, knowing that the One who is with us is greater than all
those who are against us.

III. THE WORRIES. Verses 15-20

We are told that when the north wind, called Eurocly-
don, blew upon them, they could not sail into the wind so
they had to run before it. It was easier to have a wind at
their backs than to have to face it and fight it. Soon they ran
under the shelter of a small island called Clauda. This
knocked off the wind and gave them a breathing spell. All
of them pitched in, went to work, and tried to strengthen the
ship for the rest of the journey. They soon saw that if they
waited any longer they would be dashed upon the quick-
sand. So they set sail, but as they started out the wind
pounded upon them again and they were driven furiously
before it.

The next day the storm was still raging. Those on board
were afraid that the ship would go down at any minute.
Suddenly the captain gave orders to lighten the ship and all
those on board began to haul up the bags of grain and throw
them into the sea. Wheat is a valuable commodity, but there
comes a time when human life is worth more than material
possessions. The third day was worse than ever. They tore the
sails down and threw them into the sea. The ship was now a
helpless thing in the hands of the storm, with everybody
waiting for the end. It does not say here that all of these
people prayed to their various gods, but I am sure that they
did. Men always cry out for help when they get in deep

trouble. When the sun is shining they may say that they do not believe in God, but when they get in a hole, they call upon Him. Then, as soon as the trouble has passed away, they say good-bye to God. They have no time for God when the skies are clear, but let the storms come and they fall upon their knees.

Paul and his companions drifted for days. No sun appeared by day and no stars by night. There were two hundred and seventy-six people on board—two hundred and seventy-five of them were filled with despair. We read that they gave up all hope of being saved.

There are some people who will say, "I have given up all hope of being saved. I have gone on too long—I have sinned too deeply, it is too late, there is no hope for me." Oh, it is never too late! "As long as the lamp holds out to burn, the vilest sinner may return."

Jesus says, "Him that cometh to me I will in no wise cast out" (John 6:37). Christ can save unto the uttermost all who come unto Him by faith. I could tell of many who have gone into the depths of sin, who have lived for years without a Saviour. But I have seen Jesus reach down, lift them up and redeem them. He can do the same for you, no matter what your condition.

IV. THE WORD. Verses 21-26

Yes, hope had died out for two hundred and seventy-five people on this ship, but one man was there for whom the lamp of hope still burned brightly. The sun and the stars were hidden, but Paul looked up and saw a brighter Light. His sky was clear, his mind was at ease. He stood up now to revive the hope of the hopeless travelers. He had established himself among them as an unusual man, so they listened to him. In the hour of crisis men are always ready to listen to the man whom they believe has been in touch with God. The wind was still howling, the waves were still pounding the ship, the sky was still black and there was no help in sight, but when Paul spoke all of this was changed. A ray of hope fell upon the wild waves and across the helpless ship. First, Paul told them that they should have taken his advice and not have put to sea at this season. He was not saying "I told you so"; he referred to his former advice in order to induce them to listen to him now. He wanted them to say, "He was right the other time—we will listen to him this time."

Hear him now, "Be of good courage, we are going to lose the ship, but not one single life will be lost." This was a wonderful piece of news. How did Paul know? On what did he base his hope? He did not say, Be of good cheer, we have a fine pilot and he will bring us through." He did not say, "Our vessel is seaworthy." He did not say, "The storm is dying down." No, he based his hope on his faith in God. "I was praying in a secluded corner of the ship when one of God's angels came to me. You know, I belong to God and serve Him. This angel brought me a message from God. He told me not to be afraid, that He was going to take me and all of you safely to Rome." What a message! What hope he must have brought to those people! "Let the winds blow, and the storms beat. God will bring us through. Hallelujah!"

God says the same thing to us. "If you put your trust in Me, nothing on earth can crush you. I will hold you up, I will see you safely through, I will take you home at last." Many things in the world are against the child of God. These things beat against him like the waves against Gibralter, but the Christian will stand and soon he will learn to say with Paul, "I am persuaded that neither death, nor life, nor angels, nor principalities, nor powers, nor things present, nor things to come, nor height, nor depth, nor any other creature shall be able to separate us from the love of God, which is in Christ Jesus our Lord" (Romans 8:38, 39).

Note Pauls words, "I belong to God—I serve God." "I belong to God"—that is the inner life. "I serve God"—that is the outer life. It is true that God created all men, but they do not belong to His family until they come to Him by faith in Christ. "As many as received him, to them gave He power to become the Sons of God . . ." (John 1:12). God does not count anyone as belonging to Him until that one feels his dependence, leaves all else, and trusts in him. Four things can possess life—sin, self, Satan or the Saviour. The first three must be deposed. Christ must reign if we are to belong to God and mean anything to the world. There are two centers of life—God and self. Life revolves around one or the other. Are we always thinking of self? Or are we thinking of God and trying to please Him. Paul said, "I belong to God."

Now, if he belonged to God, God could use Him, so he said, "I serve God." God possessed his inner life, so his outer life was full of service. Why is it that today men do not serve God? Why are they not faithful to Him? It is because they are not right on the inside. Get them right on the inside and you will not have to worry about their service to Him. If all church members were right in their hearts, if they let God rule those hearts, we would never be forced to worry about church attendance, about service, about gifts. The secret of Paul's great life of service and the secret of all other good men of God is that first of all they got right with God in their hearts, they gave Him first place, and a wonderful life of service naturally followed.

Notice that Paul was not ashamed of his relationship to God. He stood up before them all and said, "I am a Christian —I am serving God." This confession must have made a tremendous effect upon those men. Paul would not dare to have made this confession if he had not been living a good, consistent life before them every day. If we live for the world, the flesh and the devil all the week, our Sunday display of religion will be of no effect.

Did they believe what Paul said to be true? They must

have, for from then on he was the master of the situation and they carried out his every suggestion. I know this. Paul certainly did believe. Listen to his cry, "I believe God. I believe that it shall happen even as He said." The storm was still beating, there was no land in sight. But Paul did not see the storm; he saw God. He knew that God was stronger than all the waves which beat against the ship. He knew that God would keep His word.

Do we believe God? When He tells us to come unto Him that He might save us, we believe it. We put our trust in Him, for we are willing for Him to save us from death and hell. Yet most of us stop right there.

Do we believe His other promises? He tells us that He will answer our prayers, that if we ask, we shall receive. But we do not believe that promise, for we do not pray as we should. He tells us that He will give us wisdom if we ask for it. Do we believe that? No, we rely on our own resources. He tells us that He will bless our lives if we put them in His care. Do we believe that? No, we risk our own puny human schemes. He tells us to put Him first and that He will give us all that we need. Do we believe that? No, we say, "I must look after myself and if there is anything left over, God can have it." Oh, I wish that we could all cry from the depths of our souls, "I believe God—I will never doubt. I'll turn my life over to Him and let Him run it, for He can do a better job than I can." Why not let God be the Senior Partner in that business, that profession, that farm? Why not believe the promises in His word? Why not give Him first place in all of our living, giving, working, playing, in every area of life?

So Paul, the great man of faith, stood upon God's promises. He told this crowd that God was going to take a hand and save them all. He even told them that they would be cast upon a certain island. We see that the angel even took care of the smallest details in giving the message to Paul. Victory always comes when a man believes God. It came to Paul and will come to us.

Dr. Clovis Chappell says that when he was a young man he went to serve a church which was split wide-open by internal strife. He decided that something must be done, so he planned a revival meeting. He sent for a man to help him. This man was not a preacher, but a farmer, a man great in prayer. Day after day the man prayed, and Chappell preached, but nothing happened. One church member said, "There's no use to go on, you can't do anything with this situation. We've tried everything and nothing does any good."

The praying farmer said, "You would not say that if you knew my Lord as I know Him." The last night came and still there was no movement toward God. The members were still hating one another. But the praying farmer said to the preacher, "You speak what God tells you to say and He will do the rest." At the close of the meeting a revolution took place. The church members confessed their sins, made up their differences, and souls were saved. The church and community were never the same again. Why? Because of the prayers and faith of one man who believed God. Paul said, "I believe God." Do you?

V. THE WISHING. Verses 27-29

On the fourteenth night the ship was still being driven up and down on the sea. They wondered why it did not go down. The sails were gone, nobody was running the ship, it was just drifting before the storm. If we could have seen it, we would have noticed a Great Hand under the ship, keeping it from going down. That hand was God's hand—it was His purpose to carry the ship safely in. Suddenly a cry rang out, "Breakers ahead!" The sailors knew that they were near land. They sounded the depth and found it to be twenty fathoms, and then fifteen fathoms.

The captain was afraid that the ship would be dashed to

pieces on the rocks, so he gave the order, "Anchors astern!" Four anchors were cast out of the back of the boat. If they had been cast in front the storm would have swung the boat around and brought it closer to the rocks. The ship stopped right there and everybody waited and wished for the day. When our loved one is sick and the doctor tells us that the crisis will come in the night we patiently sit by the bedside and wish for the day. So these people sat in the ship, waiting, praying and wishing for the day to come.

We notice that they cast out four anchors to keep them from drifting. The soul needs anchors, also, to keep it from drifting. Here are some of the anchors—the Bible, prayer, the Cross, church relationship, fellowship with other Christians, and the blessed hope of the Lord's return. We need to tie up to these great anchors of the soul. Then we will not drift with the tides of life and our ship will never be wrecked on the rocks.

VI. THE WAITING. Verses 30-41

About this time the sailors decided that they had better save themselves. They did not care for the prisoners and the passengers, they simply wanted to save their own lives. They lowered a boat and were about to get in it, when Paul said, "Unless you stay in the ship you will not be saved." Paul had become the master of the situation. When he said this thing, the men turned back, cut the ropes that held the boat and let it fall into the sea. Just about daybreak Paul said, "For fourteen days you have been so worried that you haven't eaten anything. I advise you to eat something now. It will strengthen you. I promise you that not a hair of your head will be hurt." He then took food and said, "Let's give thanks to God." He lifted his voice to heaven, thanked God that He had brought them safely through, and was going to take them safely to the land. When he finished all of them ate their food and we read that they were all of good cheer. Paul was the cause of it all. He changed their despair to hope, all because he believed God. He did not hesitate to witness for Him and to tell them that God's power was greater than the storm. In every crisis we need men to call our attention to God, to tell us that He lives, He loves, and will take care of us.

When the day dawned and they looked toward the land, they saw a small inlet. They felt that they could run the ship into this inlet and be safe. In order to save time they did not take the anchors on board, but cut the anchor ropes with axes. This loosed the ship and, driven by the wind and current, the ship leaped toward the shore. At first it seemed that they would make a safe harbor, but some distance from the shore the ship ran aground. The fore part of the ship stuck fast, but the hind part was beaten by the waves and was soon breaking into pieces.

VII. THE WONDER. Verses 42-44

In time of common peril, some men become heroes, and some beasts. The soldiers forgot all about what Paul had done and planned to kill him and all the prisoners, lest they should swim out and escape. However, God said that all of them would arrive safely on land and that Paul would go to Rome, so He moved upon the centurion to prevent this murder. He gave orders that everyone should throw themselves into the sea and try to get to land. The prisoners were loosed and everybody leaped into the sea. Some were on boards, some were on pieces of the mast and some were swimming desperately. Soon a great number of dripping figures were climbing out of the water—two hundred and seventy-six of them. They were all there, they were all safe, just as Paul said they would be. They landed upon an island.

The great lesson in this chapter is how God works behind the scenes to care for His people and to carry out His own great divine purpose. It was not the skill of the sailors which saved the ship and the two hundred and seventy-six people aboard. Under ordinary circumstances, all of them would have been lost. It was the power and might of a great God which did it. Here is comfort and help for us. The centuries have gone by, but the same great God still looks after His children. In devastating difficulties, in trials and in troubles, the child of God has a Father to bring him out safely. If Christ is our Saviour, then God will be our Father, He will take us into His family and care for us in every time of need.

A number of years ago a ship met with disaster on the shores of the Isle of Wight. In the confusion a young woman was swept overboard. She found a piece of wreckage and clung to it, but soon she was drifting down the channel and out to sea. A few hours later the captain of another vessel saw an object floating in the distance. He sent some sailors in a boat to investigate. Before they reached their object, they heard a woman's voice lifted in song:

> Jesus, lover of my soul, let me to Thy bosom fly,
> While the nearer waters roll, while the tempest still
>   is high!
> Hide me, O my Saviour, hide,
> Till the storm of life is past;
> Safe into the haven guide,
> O, receive my soul at last!

On that piece of wreckage, drifting out to sea, the woman had peace in her heart. She had peace there because she had Jesus there, she had flown to Him and hidden herself in Him.

My friend, life may be very bright and sunny now. But some day troubles will come, the waves will roll over your head. Some day the judgment fires will burn. You are going to need a Saviour then, so I plead with you to turn your back upon sin and the world today. Come and put your trust in Him. Then He will bear you up, carry you safely through and land you upon the shores of glory where you will be at home in Heaven forevermore.

Chapter Twenty-Eight

"SPIRITUAL TRANSLATION"

Acts 28

As Chapter 28 opens Paul and his fellow travelers stood on the shore of a little island. Their clothes were wet, they were shivering in the coldness of the dawn. They had been on a Roman ship for many days, a storm had driven them westward over the Mediterranean Sea, and now in the early morning hour their ship had been grounded. As the wild waves tore the ship to pieces the passengers, two hundred and seventy-six in number, jumped, into the sea and made their way safely to land. God had promised through Paul that everyone on the ship would be saved, but that the ship would be lost. This promise was kept, as are all the promises of God. The ship was gone, but the two hundred and seventy-six people were safe on the little island. This little island was called Melita; today it is called Malta. During World War II it was the most heavily bombed spot on earth.

Where is Paul going? Why is he on this ill-fated ship? He was on the way to Rome to preach the Gospel there. He did not know it, but he was going to lose his life in Rome for Christ. But this did not bother him. He was ready to live or die for Jesus. He was a prisoner of Rome. One day the Jews, who hated Paul and all that he stood for, were about to kill him. The Romans rescued him by arresting him, he had been a prisoner for over two years, he had finally made an appeal to Caesar and now he was on his way to Rome, under protection of the Roman Centurion.

162

I. The Treatment. Verses 1-2

Here we see these men huddled on shore, wet, cold, weary, anxious. They wondered what kind of a reception they would have at the hands of the islanders who were even then being attracted to the beach. The first question asked of the islanders was this, "Where are we?" Some of those who could speak Greek told them that they were upon the Island of Melita. As a whole these people could not speak Greek, so they were called Barbarians. To the Greeks there were only two groups of people in the world, the Greeks and the Barbarians. These people were not Greeks, so they must be Barbarians. No, they could not speak Greek, but they could speak the language of kindness and mercy. Their hearts went out to the shivering passengers. They built a big fire, received them kindly and did everything they could to comfort them.

These people were heathens, but they were human. We can learn a lesson right here. Christians ought always to be kind to others, especially the unfortunate. Our first duty to others is to tell them of our Saviour, and we can often gain a good approach to them by some deed of kindness.

Charles Bradlaugh, the celebrated English infidel, once made a scathing attack on Christianity before a group of working men. He dared anyone to answer him. A plain man had the courage to stand up and say, "In this town there is a Christian missionary. I have often driven him from my door. But some months ago I lost my job, and my wife was sick. I soon became ill, also, but none of my infidel friends came to help me. This Christian missionary came and provided everything which we needed. His wife came and nursed us and cooked for us. If it had not been for them, my wife and I would not be living today. When we were well enough, we asked them why they had done this, and they told us that it was for the love of Christ. I say that a religion which makes a man do all that for another man who has hated and cursed him is a good thing. From now on I am going to be a Christian." Yes, if we were more kind and more helpful, people would see that there really is something to our religion and they would want it for themselves.

II. THE TESTING. Verses 3-9

Paul was always a helpful man, so he busied himself picking up sticks and throwing them upon the fire. He found the warmth and comfort which he needed in helping others. He was one of the greatest men who ever lived, yet he was not above common labor; with it he blessed others and was blessed in return. Well, as he placed the wood on the fire, a viper came out and fastened its fangs in his hand. This was the month of November. The serpent had evidently curled itself up for its winter's nap, but when it was roused by the heat, it struck Paul's hand, fixed its fangs in the flesh and hung on. The natives knew that this viper was poisonous, so they immediately said, "This man is a murderer. He has escaped the sea, but justice is pursuing him and now he will die from the viper's bite." They were heathens, but they had the conscience to know the difference between right and wrong. They felt that if this man was a murderer he deserved punishment.

We often hear the question, "If a man has never heard of Christ, will he be lost?" Does not this instance show that even if a man does not know about Christ, God has given him some light and he must answer for it? The natives did not know Jesus, but they had enough light to know that sin ought to be punished. John 1:9 tells us that Christ lighteth every man who cometh into the world. So we see that a man in some faraway island, even though he has not heard about Christ, receives some light and must answer for it. It is our duty to see that he knows how to follow the light. We must show him Jesus Christ, the Light of the world. That is where missions come in.

The natives said, "Calamity has come to this man. He must be a bad man."

They were mistaken, and we often make the same mistake. We see someone suffering and we say. "God sent this suffering because of evil." This may not be the case at all. Some of the greatest Christians have been the greatest sufferers.

Here is the irony of it. When we prosper and when blessings flow into our lives, no one comes around to say, "God is pleased with you." But when we suffer, they are quick to pronounce judgment, saying, "You are paying for your sins." People like to tell us that we are getting just what we deserve. The Bible does not promise a Christian that he will have immunity from trouble.

The doctor can give you an injection and say, "You are now immune from a certain disease." But when you are saved, no injection in the world can keep you from having trouble. On the contrary, we are told that these things are the common lot of Christians. John 16:33—"In this world ye shall have tribulation: but be of good cheer! I have overcome the world." God does not promise to keep us out of trouble, but He does promise to be with us while we are in it.

God often permits trouble to come to us because trouble gives us our greatest opportunity to prove to unbelievers that He is omnipotent. God did not keep the Hebrew children out of the fire, but He kept the fire out of them. He did not keep Daniel out of the lions' den, but He kept the lions from hurting Daniel. He did not keep Lazarus from dying, but He delivered him from death. He did not keep Peter from going to jail, but He brought him out by His power. He did not keep Jesus from the Cross, but He raised Him from the dead. In each case He allowed the suffering to come, then He showed His mighty power in deliverance. Remember, then, when we suffer, that God is mighty to deliver.

What did Paul do? He shook the viper off into the fire and was not harmed a bit. The natives expected him to become swollen and to fall down dead. When they had looked a great while and nothing happened, they changed their minds. "He is a god." It does not take much to change public opinion. When the viper landed on him, they said, "He is a murderer." When he shook off the viper they said, "He is a god."

In this old life there are certain vipers which threaten us. With God's help we need to shake them off. Maybe it's the business men's viper, the viper of dishonesty. They are often tempted to take a short cut to fortune. They do a small thing which is not honest, but which does not seem to amount to much, and they feel all right. These things grow and grow, leading to the embezzler's cell or the suicide's grave. God does not settle His accounts at the end of every week, but He does make a final settlement. The viper of dishonesty must be shaken off before it is too late.

It may be the viper of worldliness. You have worldly and social ambitions, so you put God up on a shelf and seek the things of this world. One day you will find that it is all vanity, that you have failed because you allowed the world to come in between you and God. There is the viper of ungoverned temper. You nurse that viper and it grows stronger every day. It hurts you, it hurts everybody around you, it hurts your influence for Christ. Throw that viper off and ask God to help you keep sweet. There is the viper of malice and hatred. There is someone whom you do not like, so you carry that hatred in your heart until it cankers your soul. Nothing harms like a bad attitude toward others. You can never be happy as long as you have such an attitude. That is one burden I don't want to bear. Remember this— if you don't love everybody, you are not living like Jesus. There is the viper of self-indulgence. Lust fills your heart, liquor fascinates you, your only thought is to indulge the body and satisfy the flesh. "The wages of sin is death." Shake off that viper and be a pure man for God.

But you say, "My viper is too strong. I have nursed it until it is my master. I can't shake it off." But Christ can set you free. You will fail in your own strength, but if you go to Him in time of temptation, if you ask His help, if you depend upon Him wholly, you will win the battle.

Since Paul is the hero of this story, we do not read about the other people who were on the ship. We presume, however, that they found lodging on the island of Melita. Paul must have been highly respected, for he and his companions lived in the governor's palace. It is always good to have Godly men around us. The chief man, Publius, soon learned that lesson. His father was quite ill, so Paul went in to the sick room, prayed for the man, laid his hands on him and healed him. Paul's reputation spread and soon sick people from all over the island came to Paul and were healed. When Paul was tested, they found out that he was indeed a man of God.

III. THE TRAVELING. Verses 10-15

Paul and his companions spent three months on this island. The record does not tell us about Paul's evangelistic work, but I am sure that he was busy winning souls. He was not concerned simply with healing bodies. Every time he touched a sick man he told him of Christ's power to save. During that time we read that he was "honored with many honors." When the time came for them to leave they were loaded down with many presents. This shows us that in three months' time Paul and his companions had won the hearts of these people. Paul did it because he was an unselfish Christian, living for others and for Jesus. People sometimes wonder where we stand. We cover our religion with a bushel and our lips are dumb about Jesus. But nobody ever had to wonder about Paul. He lived every day in such a way that they knew he was different. He never lost an opportunity to witness for his Lord.

Paul now entered another ship, one which had wintered in the island. The winter was now over and it was safe to sail. They sailed to Syracuse, then to Rhegium and finally landed at Puteoli. Here the three Christians, Paul, Luke and Aristarchus, were delighted to find a band of Christians. After being out to sea with unbelievers for such a long time, it was a joy for them to find a group who loved the same Christ whom they adored. They stayed in Puteoli seven days, during which time Paul thrilled them with the story of his own conversion and life, and the marvelous way in which God had delivered them from the storm.

Someday life's little voyage will be over for us. All of the storms will be weathered and God will bring us safely to the port of heaven. There we will meet our loved ones who have gone on before; there we will meet our Saviour. What a reunion that will be! No more pain, no more tears, no more death, no more sorrow, but joy and peace forever and ever. We shall spend eternity, not boasting of our own deeds, but praising God and singing the praise of the Lamb whose blood saved us from our sin.

Some years ago one of my deacons, who was agent for the express company, took me with him to the railroad station at dawn. I watched him as he released a coop of carrier pigeons. They were one thousand miles from their home loft. They flew straight up into the air, circled around two or three times, then headed directly toward their home, a thousand miles away. The next day the deacon received a telegram saying that everyone of the pigeons had arrived safely at home.

We believe in Christ, he is our Saviour, but we are bound down by the cares of this world. Some day God is going to release our souls, we will leave the old body down here in the grave, but our soul will soar up to be with God. We will be in heaven in the twinkling of an eye, and the angels can flash back to earth the glad message "Home at last." It may be that Christ will return in the air before we die. So much the better, for then we will not experience death, but when He breaks through the blue we will be caught up to meet Him in the air, and "so shall we ever be with the Lord" (I Thessalonians 4:17). These are the two roads to heaven. One goes through death, the other through the Rapture. We can never travel either of these roads unless Jesus is our Saviour.

After this week at Puteoli the company set out to march to Rome, one hundred and forty miles distant. The Christians in Rome heard that they were coming and sent two parties out to meet them. One went forty miles to the Appii forum, the other went thirty miles to the Three Taverns. We read that when Paul met them, "he thanked God and took courage." Surely this was a touching meeting. For many years Paul had been hungering to see these brethren. In a letter he had poured out his heart to them. Now he was getting old, he had been through many hardships, he was conscious that he was nearing the end of life. We can well understand that the sight of these brethren cheered and blessed the heart of the aged apostle. Probably some of his old friends were in this group, Priscilla, Aquila, and others. As Paul looked upon these Christians, he knew that the kingdom was advancing in the world's capitol and he rejoiced at the thought of it. He was going now to stand before Caesar. He did not know what the outcome would be, but he forgot it all in the joy of seeing Christ's friends in a foreign land.

IV. THE TESTIMONY. Verses 16-24

Paul and his companions soon arrived in the city of Rome, where Paul was given an unusual privilege. He was allowed to live by himself with a Roman guard in attendance. During his imprisonment, he was chained to different guards. He won many of them to Christ, and soon there was a large group of "saints in Caesar's household." After all of Paul's grueling experiences, you would think that he would want to rest. But in three days he called all the chief Jews together for a talk. He could not go to the synagogue, so the synagogue came to him. The fact that they came showed that they realized his importance. He was facing trial and he wanted to see how they felt about the matter, but deep down in his heart he was hoping to win some of them to Christ.

"I will tell you why I am here as a prisoner," Paul said to the Jews. "The Jews of Jerusalem accused me of teaching things contrary to our customs. I assure you that I am not guilty. Down through the years Israel has been looking for the Messiah. I believe that He has come, and because I dared to say so I am bound with this chain."

These Jews were too cunning to make a direct statement, so they said, "We haven't received any official papers from Jerusalem against you. We have heard of your Christianity and we would like to hear more of it. We know, however, that this sect is spoken against everywhere." Paul therefore appointed a day to go over the matter with them. When they came to see Paul, he opened the Scriptures and all day long sought to convince them from the Bible that Christ was the Son of God and the Saviour of the world. They had many bitter disputes, but Paul always pointed to the Scriptures, held his ground, and won out. We read that " some believed, and some believed not." Paul was happy over the results. These were his first converts in the city of Rome.

V. THE TURNING. Verses 25-29

After Paul's day of teaching and persuading concerning Jesus, the Jews prepared to depart. As they were leaving, Paul said, "Just one more word. Isaiah prophesied well concerning you. The Holy Spirit spoke through Him, saying that your ears and eyes would be closed to the truth, and that you would not be converted and saved, because your hearts were not open

to receive God's truth. Now this salvation will be offered to
the Gentiles and they will receive it." These are the last
recorded words of Paul. God dealt patiently with the Jews for
hundreds of years. Now He turned from them. The Jew had
shut himself out, and the Gospel was passed over to the Gentiles. It is seldom now that we see a Jew coming to Christ.

Men are still following the same course taken by these Jews.
Jesus and salvation are offered to them, but they close their
eyes and ears, go on in sin, and the end of their lives is
tragic doom for eternity.

Several years ago the submarine Squalus dove to the bottom
of the Atlantic Ocean in two hundred and forty feet of
water. The sailors soon discovered that the submarine was
helpless. They could not bring it to the top. They sent
up a chemical substance which made a red smudge upon
the water, and later sent up a buoy. They were hoping that some
ship would see their plight and come to their rescue. They
realized that their help must come from above. Soon the
submarine Sculpin set out in search of the Squalus. They
found the red smudge and the buoy and knew that the other
submarine was on the bottom of the sea at that point. Before
they could get their rescue work going, twenty-four hours
had passed by. Then they sent down a giant ten-ton diving
bell, took out a few men, and brought them safely to the
top. They kept this up until all thirty-three of the men on
the Squalus were saved. Not one sailor refused to be rescued.
All of them gladly accepted the way of salvation.

My lost friend, you are on the bottom, the waters of sin
are covering you. You need help and that help must
come from above. Jesus says, "Accept Me, I will bring you
out. I will rescue you from sin, I will save you if you will
only trust Me." Oh, how tragic it is when men refuse His
way of salvation, when they pass up the only way they have
to be saved. The Jews turned away that day when Paul

preached, and as they did so they sounded their own death knell for time and for eternity.

VI. THE TRIUMPH. Verses 30-31

After this time we find that Paul stayed two years in his own house in Rome. Thousands of people came to see him and he won many of them to Christ. He had perfect freedom to preach the Gospel. It seems that the letters written to Lysias and Festus had influenced the Roman government in his favor. If you had asked anyone in Rome the question, "Who is the greatest man in the city?", they would have answered, "The Emperor." Ah, how wrong they would have been. This poor Jewish prisoner, with God's power behind him, was far greater than any man in the city. His influence upon the world has been greater than all the emperors who ever lived.

The Book of Acts ends rather abruptly. Some scholars say that Luke intended to write another book, telling about Paul's further work and death, but that Luke met his death before this book was written. It seems that after two years Paul was set free, made another journey, and was brought back to Rome, not as an honorable prisoner, but as a felon. Tradition tells us that Paul suffered martyrdom under Nero.

Nero was one of the meanest men who ever lived. He had Rome burned and blamed it on the Christians. He had them killed in every conceivable way. He laid off new streets and instead of putting statues along the way, he put up iron pillars and chained Christians to each pillar. He would then pour oil and tar over these Christians and set them afire, while he rode up and down the street in the light of these burning martyrs. It is thought, however, that Nero had Paul beheaded.

Just before his martyrdom, Paul wrote a letter to Timothy. "I am now ready to be offered," he said. "The time of my departure is at hand. He added, "I have fought a good fight, I have finished my course, I have kept the faith: henceforth there is laid up for me a crown of righteousness, which the Lord, the righteous judge, shall give me at that day: and not to me only, but to all them that love His appearing" (II Timothy 4:7, 8). As Paul was led out to the slaughter we see a great block of wood, a surly soldier, a shining axe. But Paul sees a crown of glory and a beloved Saviour awaiting him. As his head is placed upon the block, we hear him say: "Lord Jesus, receive my spirit." The axe is lifted, the blade flashes in the sunlight and comes down with mighty power. Paul's head rolls off the block, but his soul soars to the heights of Heaven. Now Paul, it is as you said, you are "absent from the body but present with the Lord. For me to live is Christ and to die is gain. For we know if our earthly house of this tabernacle were dissolved, we have a building of God, an house not made with hands, eternal in the heavens." Good-bye Paul, we will meet you there some day when life's battles have all been fought and when the mists of earth have rolled away.

Paul was one of the greatest men who ever lived, not because of his learning, his brilliance, his oratory, his works, but because Jesus absolutely filled his life. He took possession of every thought Paul had, He guided every deed. But if Paul could have written his own epitaph, I am sure that he would have placed these simple words on his tomb: "Paul, a servant of the Lord Jesus Christ." We shall not look upon his like again, but may God help us to have more of his spirit.

What a meeting Paul and Jesus must have had in heaven! Paul had met Jesus on the Damascus Road, he had had other visions of Him. He kept the face of the Lord in mind and a hope of seeing Him again in his heart. When Paul got to heaven, I am sure that all the choirs sang and all the saints rejoiced. Many of those whom Paul had led to Christ were waiting at the gate to thank him. But the greatest moment was when he looked into the face of Jesus and laid his hand in the nail-pierced hands. I can hear Jesus saying, "You did a good job, Paul. I have been watching over you. I know how you gave up all for My sake, how you stood up for me, how you suffered for Me. But that is all over now, Paul. Enter thou into the joy of thy Lord. No more tears, Paul, no more trials, no more beatings, no more shipwrecks, no more hardships. You are home at last, Paul, and I am glad to have you here."

Then I hear Paul saying, "It was worth it all, Lord, just to see Your face and to hear Your voice. I could go through it all ten thousand times and never repay You for what You have done for me. Thank You for coming into the world, for dying on the Cross, for saving my soul, for keeping me and bringing me home to heaven. I don't know how long eternity will last, but I know that I will never have time enough to thank you for all You have done. Worthy is the Lamb that was slain to receive power, and riches, and wisdom, and strength, and honor, and glory, and blessing" (Revelation 5:12).

Oh, friend some day the end is coming for you and me. It may be soon. We have not done all that Paul did for Jesus, but if we have trusted Him as our Saviour, at the end of the way we will be received into heaven and given all the joys that Paul has. Don't you want that? Don't you want your sins washed away? Don't you want the best Friend that a man ever had to be your Friend? Don't you want to go home to heaven at last? All these will be yours if you will repent of your sins, trust Christ, and confess Him as your Saviour.

My latest sun is sinking fast,
My race is nearly run;
My strongest trials now are past,
My triumph is begun.

I know I'm nearing the holy ranks
Of friends and kindred dear,
For I brush the dews on Jordan's banks,
The crossing must be near.

I've almost gained my heavenly home,
My spirit loudly sings;
Thy holy ones, behold, they come!
I hear the noise of wings.

O bear my longing heart to Him,
Who bled and died for me;
Whose blood now cleanses from all sin,
And gives me victory.

O come, angel band,
Come and around me stand;
O bear me away on your snowy wings
To my immortal home.
O bear me away on your snowy wings,
To my immortal home.

Printed in the United States of America